Palgrave Macmillan Studies in Banking and Financial Institutions

Series Editor: **Professor Philip Molyneux**

The Palgrave Macmillan Studies in Banking and Financial Institutions are international in orientation and include studies of banking within particular countries or regions, and studies of particular themes such as Corporate Banking, Risk Management, Mergers and Acquisitions, etc. The books' focus is on research and practice, and they include up-to-date and innovative studies on contemporary topics in banking that will have global impact and influence.

Titles include

Steffen E. Andersen
THE EVOLUTION OF NORDIC FINANCE

Seth Apati
THE NIGERIAN BANKING SECTOR REFORMS
Power and Politics

Dimitris N. Chorafas
BASEL III, THE DEVIL AND GLOBAL BANKING

Dimitris N. Chorafas
SOVEREIGN DEBT CRISIS
The New Normal and the Newly Poor

Stefano Cosma and Elisabetta Gualandri (*editors*)
THE ITALIAN BANKING SYSTEM
Impact of the Crisis and Future Perspectives

Violaine Cousin
BANKING IN CHINA

Peter Falush and Robert L. Carter OBE
THE BRITISH INSURANCE INDUSTRY SINCE 1900
The Era of Transformation

José Manuel Pastor Monsálvez and Juan Fernández de Guevara Radoselovics (*editors*)
MODERN BANK BEHAVIOUR

Juan Fernández de Guevara Radoselovics and José Manuel Pastor Monsálvez (*editors*)
CRISIS, RISK AND STABILITY IN FINANCIAL MARKETS

Franco Fiordelisi and Ornella Ricci (*editors*)
BANCASSURANCE IN EUROPE
Past, Present and Future

Franco Fiordelisi, Philip Molyneux and Daniele Previati (*editors*)
NEW ISSUES IN FINANCIAL AND CREDIT MARKETS

Franco Fiordelisi, Philip Molyneux and Daniele Previati (*editors*)
NEW ISSUES IN FINANCIAL INSTITUTIONS MANAGEMENT

Kim Hawtrey
AFFORDABLE HOUSING FINANCE

Jill M. Hendrickson
REGULATION AND INSTABILITY IN U.S. COMMERCIAL BANKING
A History of Crises

Paola Leone and Gianfranco A. Vento (*editors*)
CREDIT GUARANTEE INSTITUTIONS AND SME FINANCE

Caterina Lucarelli and Gianni Brighetti (*editors*)
RISK TOLERANCE IN FINANCIAL DECISION MAKING

Roman Matousek (*editor*)
MONEY, BANKING AND FINANCIAL MARKETS IN CENTRAL AND EASTERN EUROPE
20 Years of Transition

Philip Molyneux (*editor*)
BANK PERFORMANCE, RISK AND FIRM FINANCING

Philip Molyneux (*editor*)
BANK STRATEGY, GOVERNANCE AND RATINGS

Imad A. Moosa
THE MYTH OF TOO BIG TO FAIL

Simon Mouatt and Carl Adams (*editors*)
CORPORATE AND SOCIAL TRANSFORMATION OF MONEY AND BANKING
Breaking the Serfdom

Victor Murinde (*editor*)
BANK REGULATORY REFORMS IN AFRICA

Anders Ögren (*editor*)
THE SWEDISH FINANCIAL REVOLUTION

Özlem Olgu
EUROPEAN BANKING
Enlargement, Structural Changes and Recent Developments

Fotios Pasiouras
GREEK BANKING
From the Pre-Euro Reforms to the Financial Crisis and Beyond

Daniela Pîrvu
CORPORATE INCOME TAX HARMONIZATION IN THE EUROPEAN UNION

Ramkishen S. Rajan
EMERGING ASIA
Essays on Crises, Capital Flows, FDI and Exchange Rate

Allesandro Roselli
FINANCIAL STRUCTURES AND REGULATION: A COMPARISON OF CRISES IN THE UK, USA AND ITALY

Yasushi Suzuki
JAPAN'S FINANCIAL SLUMP
Collapse of the Monitoring System under Institutional and Transition Failures

Ruth Wandhöfer
EU PAYMENTS INTEGRATION
The Tale of SEPA, PSD and Other Milestones along the Road

The full list of titles available is on the website:
www.palgrave.com/finance/sbfi.asp

Palgrave Macmillan Studies in Banking and Financial Institutions

Series Standing Order ISBN 978–1–4039–4872–4

You can receive future titles in this series as they are published by placing a standing order. Please contact your bookseller or, in case of difficulty, write to us at the address below with your name and address, the title of the series and the ISBN quoted above.

Customer Services Department, Macmillan Distribution Ltd, Houndmills, Basingstoke, Hampshire RG21 6XS, England

---

Modern Bank Behaviour

Edited by

José Manuel Pastor Monsálvez and
Juan Fernández de Guevara Radoselovics
Universitat de València, Spain

palgrave
macmillan

First published 2013 by
PALGRAVE MACMILLAN

Palgrave Macmillan in the UK is an imprint of Macmillan Publishers Limited, registered in England, company number 785998, of Houndmills, Basingstoke, Hampshire RG21 6XS.

Palgrave Macmillan in the US is a division of St Martin's Press LLC, 175 Fifth Avenue, New York, NY 10010.

Palgrave Macmillan is the global academic imprint of the above companies and has companies and representatives throughout the world.

Palgrave® and Macmillan® are registered trademarks in the United States, the United Kingdom, Europe and other countries

ISBN: 978–1–137–00185–6

This book is printed on paper suitable for recycling and made from fully managed and sustained forest sources. Logging, pulping and manufacturing processes are expected to conform to the environmental regulations of the country of origin.

A catalogue record for this book is available from the British Library.

A catalog record for this book is available from the Library of Congress.

10 9 8 7 6 5 4 3 2 1
22 21 20 19 18 17 16 15 14 13

Printed and bound in Great Britain by
CPI Antony Rowe, Chippenham and Eastbourne

Contents

Figures

Tables

Contributors

Stefano d'Addona is Associate Professor in Economics at the School of Political Sciences at the University of Roma Tre, Italy. He obtained his PhD from Baruch College (CUNY, USA), where he was awarded the Oscar Lasdon Award for the best dissertation in the area of finance. His work covers the areas of intersection between macroeconomics and finance, including aggregate behaviour and asset pricing, financial risk measurement and asset pricing in open economies. His contributions have been published in several international journals, including *The Journal of Financial and Quantitative Analysis, Macroeconomic Dynamics, The International Journal of Theoretical and Applied Finance,* and *Applied Economics*.

John K. Ashton is Senior Lecturer in Banking at Bangor University, UK, and previously worked at the ESRC Centre for Competition Policy at the University of East Anglia, and at Leeds University and Bournemouth University. He has written extensively on topics including retail financial services, competition policy and the interface of regulation and business, the economics of the water and energy industries, market definition, and the financing of small firms.

Cristina Bernini is Assistant Professor in Economic Statistics at the Department of Statistical Sciences, University of Bologna, Italy, where she obtained her PhD in Statistical Methodology for Scientific Research in 1996. She has taken part in numerous national and international projects, and has acted as a referee for several national and international statistical and tourism journals. She is member of CLADAG and the Italian Statistical Society. She has served as the assistant editor of *Almatourism – Journal of Tourism, Culture and Territorial Development*, and is involved in the High School of Tourism Sciences (Rimini, University of Bologna). Her main research interests include tourism modelling, applied econometric and longitudinal studies in economics, and policy evaluation.

Antonio Carlo Francesco Della Bina is Assistant Professor of Corporate Finance at University of Bologna and adjunct professor at University of Perugia, Italy. He holds a PhD in Banking and Finance from the University of Bologna and was a visiting scholar at the Haas School of Business (University of California, Berkeley, USA). His research examines securities analysis, market efficiency, capital structure and international finance. He has published several articles in Italian and international academic journals, and has also presented his work at international conferences (Financial Management Association, World Finance Conference, Multinational Finance Conference).

Roberto Bottiglia is Full Professor in Banking and Finance and Director of the Business Administration Department at the University of Verona, Italy, where he teaches Bank Management. He graduated in Business Administration from the Bocconi University of Milan. Research topics include agricultural credit, financial marketing, IT in banking, the structure of financial systems and banking strategies, and the crisis of the major banking groups in Europe and the USA.

Paola Brighi is Professor of Banking and Finance in the Faculty of Economics at the University of Bologna, Italy. She obtained her MA from the University of Louvain-la-Neuve and PhD from the University of Ancona. She has been a visiting scholar at the University of Wisconsin. She has published articles in journals and contributed chapters to books. She has also presented her works at many international conferences (Financial Management Association, European Financial Management Association, International Finance and Banking Society etc.). Her research interests relate to banking structure, relationship lending, bank geographic diversification, efficiency, cooperative banks, and SME finance.

Santiago Carbó-Valverde is Professor of Economics and Finance at the Bangor Business School, UK. He was formerly Professor of Economics at the University of Granada, Spain. He is a researcher at the Spanish Savings Banks Foundation (FUNCAS). He is also Research Professor at the Instituto Valenciano de Invetigaciones Económicas (Ivie). He obtained his PhD at the University of Wales, Bangor, UK. He was formerly consultant at the Federal Reserve Bank of Chicago. He has been (and in some cases is) consultant for public and private financial institutions such as the European Central Bank. He has published more than 200 papers on financial system in journals such as *European Economic Review*, *Journal of Money, Credit and Banking*, *Review of Finance*, *Journal of International Money and Finance* or the *Journal of Banking and Finance*. He has participated in conferences and international forums, including the G-20.

Barbara Casu is Reader in Banking at Cass Business School, City University, London, UK. She is Associate Editor for the *European Journal of Finance*, as well as acting as a referee for a number of leading banking and economics journals. In addition, she is Associate Senior Fellow at the Centre for European Policy Studies in Brussels (Financial Institutions and Prudential Policy Unit). Her research interests focus on the areas of bank efficiency and productivity change; the implication of the Single European Market for financial services on bank structure, competition and performance; bank privatization, and mergers and acquisitions; and bank stock performance. Her research has been presented at international conferences and published in leading journals, including the *Review of Economics and Statistics, the Journal of Banking and Finance* and the *Journal of Business, Finance and Accounting.*

Laura Chiaramonte holds a PhD in Business Administration from the University of Verona, Italy. Her research interests include hedge fund strategies, the evolution of financial systems, the drivers and effects of bank acquisitions, domestic and cross-border banking consolidation in Europe, the causes and consequences of the subprime crisis, the role of bank CDS in the recent financial crisis, and the new liquidity rules for banks (Basel III).

Juan Fernández de Guevara Radoselovics is Assistant Professor at the University of Valencia and Associate Researcher at Instituto Valenciano de Investigaciones Económicas (IVIE). He graduated in Economics in 1995 and received his PhD in 2005. Between 1997 and 2008 he was a member of the technical staff at IVIE. His research interests include financial economics, banking, productivity and social capital. He has jointly published more than five books and several articles in Spanish in international journals such as *Journal of Banking and Finance, Regional Studies, Journal of International Money and Finance, The Manchester School, Revista de Economía Aplicada,* and *Revista de Economía Financiera,* among others. He has collaborated in more than 20 research projects for firms and institutions. He has also been associate researcher on several projects of the Spanish National R+D+I Plan.

Juan Cándido Gómez-Gallego is Assistant Professor in Financial Economics at the Catholic University of Murcia, Spain, where he is a member of the research group 'Stochastic models of economics variables' E0B1-03, at the University of Murcia. He has presented his work at numerous international conferences. He has contributed chapters in books and has published papers in journals. His research is focused on the evaluation of economic efficiency in the financial sector.

Juan Gómez-García is Full Professor in Statistics for Economics at the University of Murcia, Spain. He acquired his PhD in Mathematics at the University of Murcia. He is the main researcher of the research group

'Stochastic models of economics variables' E0B1–03, at the University of Murcia, and also an assessor and advisor of ANECA (La Agencia Nacional de Evaluación de la Calidad y Acreditación), and a founding member of the journal *Investigaciones Regionales*. He has published more than 30 papers and presented his work at over 30 international conferences. He is the author of several chapters of books about financing and efficiency in the Spanish university system. He has been main researcher in five research projects with national financing. His research is focused on the evaluation of economic efficiency in public and private sectors.

Gimede Gigante is Researcher of Banking and Finance at the Finance Department of Bocconi University, Milan, Italy. He was a visiting researcher at the Department of Finance at Columbia Business School, NYC, USA, in 2010–2011, and a research fellow at University of Rome Tre, Italy, 2009–2011. He acquired his PhD at the University of Rome in 2009.

Robert S. Hudson is Professor of Economics at the University of Newcastle, UK, a fellow of the Institute of Actuaries and a chartered mathematician. Robert is also the author of a book on stock market investment, over 40 refereed articles in leading international journals and a wide range of other publications, and has presented at many universities and international conferences. Before entering the academic world he provided actuarial consulting services to a large number of companies of all sizes, has extensive business experience in financial services, and has subsequently directed research projects for a number of 'Blue Chip' commercial sponsors. His main research interests are financial markets, the financial services industry – particularly pensions and insurance – and the financial behaviour of individuals.

Caterina Lucarelli is Associate Professor of Economics of Financial Institutions at the Faculty of Economics, Università Politecnica delle Marche, Italy, where she teaches banking, stock markets and international banking. Her research interests are focused on market microstructure, stock exchanges, financial risk tolerance and wealth management. She has coordinated many research projects at both the national and international level and has published several contributions in national and international peer-reviewed journals and books.

Simona Maggi is Strategic Analyst at AIPB (Associazione Italiana Private Banking). She has played a managerial function at the international level within organizational processes and commercial networks. Since 2006 she has been responsible for external relations and for the design of AIPB's main research projects involving both universities and other centres of research. As Head of AIPB's Press and Communication working group, she coordinates strategy and communication.

José Manuel Mansilla-Fernández is working on his PhD on Banking and Corporate Finance. His main research topic is bank market power, monetary policy, investment, trade credit and exports. He has published in *Cuadernos de Información Económica* and *Perspectivas del Sistema Financiero*. He has also presented at Wolpertinger 2011, XIX Finance Forum, SAE Forum 2011, and the 10th Annual International Industrial Organization Conference held at George Mason University (Arlington, VA, USA).

José Manuel Pastor Monsálvez is an associate professor at the University of de Valencia, Spain, where he received his PhD in 1996. He specializes in banking and regional economics. He has received scholarships from several institutions – Valencian Regional Government, Caja de Madrid Foundation, and FIES (Fundo de Financiamento Estudantil) – and was a visiting researcher in the Finance Department at Florida State University, USA (1996–1997), and an external consultant for the World Bank. He is co-author of 18 books and has published 41 articles in national and international academic journals, including *Annals of Regional Science, Applied Economic Letters, Applied Economics, Applied Financial Economics, Economics Letters, European Journal of Operational Research, International Journal of Transport Economics, International Review of Applied Economics, Institutions and Money, Investigaciones Económicas, Journal of International Financial Markets, Journal of Productivity Analysis, Journal of Transport and Statistics, Manchester School, Regional Studies, Revista Española de Economía,* and *Transportation*. He conducts research on various competitive projects, as well as projects with private firms and public administration.

Concepción Pérez-Cárceles is Assistant Professor of Statistics at the Catholic University of Murcia, Spain, where she is a member of the research group 'Stochastic models of economics variables' E0B1–03. Her research focuses on the estimation and analysis of efficiency in financial institutions and on the evaluation of quality in universities. She has presented her work at several international conferences. She has contributed two book chapters and published papers in journals.

Daniele Angelo Previati is Full Professor of Financial Institution Management at the Faculty of Economics Federico Caffè, Third University of

Rome, Italy. He is also Head of the Department of Business and Law at the same university, and SDA Bocconi Professor of Banking and Insurance.

Ming Qi is a PhD candidate at University of Granada, Spain. His research interests focus on commercial bank management and non-cash payment instruments. In recent years, Ming Qi has been involved in various empirical studies on banking sector, housing price volatility and payment system of emerging markets. During September to November 2011, he was a visiting scholar at Hohenheim University in Stuttgart, Germany. He was supported by the Marsden Foundation to pursue research at Massey University, New Zealand. He was also awarded grants, by the Spanish Economic Association (SAEe) and Bertil Danielsson Foundation, for the presentation of papers at several international conferences.

Francisco Rodríguez-Fernández obtained his PhD in Economics at the University of Granada, Spain. He is Professor of Economics at the same university. He completed his postgraduate studies at the Universities of Modena and Bologna, Italy. In addition, he is currently a researcher at the Spanish Savings Banks Foundation (FUNCAS), and has participated in competitive research projects funded by the Spanish Government, the Regional Government of Andalucía (Junta de Andalucía), and the European Commission. He has published over 50 papers in national and international journals on banking and financial systems, competition, and economic growth, among others, including *European Economic Review, Review of Finance, Journal of Money, Credit and Banking, Journal of Financial Services Research, Regional Studies, European Urban and Regional Studies, Journal of Economics and Business, Journal of International Financial Markets, Institutions and Money, Journal of Banking and Finance, Moneda y Crédito, Revista de Economía Aplicada,* and *Papeles de Economía Española.*

Ngoc Vo is a senior associate in the Financial Service Advisory Team at PricewaterhouseCoopers (PwC), Ho Chi Minh City, Vietnam, specializing in banking performance improvement. She has helped to establish an asset liabilities management and fund transfer pricing framework for a local joint-stock commercial bank. Prior to joining PwC, she had over four years' experience in various fields of corporate banking working for two foreign banks: as Corporate Credit Analyst for VID Public Bank Joint Venture, and as Officer of Business Promotion Division for Mizuho Corporate Bank, both in Ho Chi Minh City. She has managed a portfolio of multinational corporate clients across different industries, including providing cash management, payment solutions and financial instruments to hedge interest rate and foreign exchange rate volatilities, and also providing legal advice relating to clients' business operations. Ngoc holds an MA in Banking and Finance (Bangor University, UK), a BA in Corporate Finance (Ho Chi Minh City University of Economics) and a BA in English Linguistics and Literature (Ho Chi Minh City University of Social Sciences and Humanities). Her MA thesis offers an assessment of the performance of banking firms in South East Asia and Latin America, in the light of financial liberalization, financial crises, and financial sector reforms.

Jonathan Williams is Professor of Banking and Finance at Bangor Business School, UK. He lectures in Banking and Development, and International Banking, at graduate level, and is the Director of Graduate Studies Research at Bangor Business School. His research focuses on financial deregulation and its impact on the banking sector. Currently, he is researching foreign bank entry and competition; bank resolution and financial stability; and diversification, governance and bank distress. His most recent papers include studies of the bank privatization process, risk decomposition in the insurance sector, and how to treat cross-firm heterogeneity in bank efficiency scores. Williams has published on regional banking and the liberalization and restructuring of banks in emerging markets. He is known for his early work on European savings banks with works on management behaviour, bank efficiency, technical change and productivity, and economies of scale. He is a contributor to major banking sector studies commissioned by the European Commission, UK Treasury, and the Spanish Savings Banks Foundation amongst others. His more recent work on emerging markets banking sectors includes studies of bank restructuring, privatization, foreign bank entry, governance and mergers and acquisitions. He writes extensively on Latin American and South East Asian banking sectors.

Introduction

José Manuel Pastor Monsálvez and Juan Fernández de Guevara Radoselovics

This text presents an updated insight into key facts impacting on financial institutions after the financial crisis, and highlights areas of major policy and academic interest. The book includes a selection of papers on this issue which were presented at the past European Association of University Teachers of Banking and Finance Conference (otherwise known as the Wolpertinger Conference) held at the Universitat de València, Spain, in September 2011. From a range of perspectives and approaches the chapters analyse a number of topics related to banking and the financial markets, such as payment protection insurance, intellectual capital, cost efficiency and its relation with bank branch distance and size, bank restructuring and bank stability, credit and liquidity risk, and business models for the wealth management industry among others.

Chapter 1, by John K. Ashton (Bangor University) and Robert S. Hudson (Newcastle University), examines the causes and consequences of the mis-selling of payment protection insurance, the subsequent prohibition of joint sales, and the effects of this event on the UK financial services industry. They provide empirical evidence to justify the regulatory judgement made, and they explain the nature of the regulatory judgement and the outcome of this judgement for the firms involved. They state that this is a very large market which has had a variety of problems, particularly in the sales of this financial service. They also observe that the costs of this judgement for the financial firms which sold this insurance product are very large and will clearly run into many billions of pounds. The authors conclude that despite the apparently clear-cut nature of these conclusions, this outcome has clearly not helped any of the key participants involved in this mis-selling episode; since many thousands of customers have been mis-sold a financial product, some firms have had to pay huge amounts in both fines and customer redress, and regulators have been obliged to divert a lot of resources to this market at a time when the need for financial regulation in many areas has been high.

The financial crisis significantly affected the entire banking industry. It has been largely attributed to the excessive growth of mortgage lending and the property market boom. Although the crisis began with the US subprime mortgage meltdown, other countries (especially Ireland and Spain) have also experienced similar problems. At an empirical level, bank lending has been found to be strongly correlated to property prices in an international context. Over the past decade, both the mortgage market and the real estate sector have experienced dramatic growth. **Chapter 2**, by Santiago Carbó-Valverde (Bangor Business School), Francisco Rodríguez-Fernández (University of Granada and the Spanish Savings Banks Foundation) and Ming Qi (University of Granada), analyses the interrelation between bank mortgage loans and property prices in China. In addition, they test the actual effects of monetary policies and the sociodemographic change. By using bank-level data, they disentangle the factors determining the growth of mortgage credit and house prices in China, to find evidence of a significant and positive relationship between house prices and mortgage loans; rising property prices stimulate the demand for mortgage loans. Credit expansion also contributes to soaring property prices. They demonstrate the positive impact that urbanization has on the growth of mortgage lending. The chapter also states that regarding monetary policy, the required reserve ratio is effective in controlling the mortgage credit boom; meanwhile interest rates play an active role in controlling house prices. These findings have important policy implications. The authors conclude that with the explosively growing mortgage market in China there is still room for improvement in the financial system related to housing. In particular, they advocate the introduction of a diversified repayment pattern to meet the demand of households with steady incomes or otherwise, and the creation of a residential mortgage loan insurance and a mortgage-backed security market.

As a consequence of the international financial crisis, some governments have designed restructuring processes in order to improve bank stability. These strategies normally include injecting liquidity and/or capital, sanitizing bank balance sheets, and consolidating troubled banks with healthier banks through an M&A process. These are often accompanied by legal reforms to strengthen the competitive environment of the banking systems, such as removal of restrictions on foreign banks or privatizations. **Chapter 3**, by Ngoc Vo (PricewaterhouseCoopers) and Jonathan Williams (University of Bangor), is devoted to analysing whether the restructuring of the banking sector, usually targeted at distressed banks, increases bank stability. The authors consider whether or not the bank restructuring processes adopted in the largest Latin American economies (Argentina, Brazil and Mexico) resolve the regional banking crises of the mid-1990s, and they conclude that the existing legal structures to resolve troubled banks were minimal and were insufficient to deal with the problems facing central banks. On the other hand, legislative reforms allowed central banks to use the good bank/bad bank model of resolution in which assets and liabilities are transferred between banks. The removal of restrictions on foreign bank entry and foreign bank acquisition of local banks became a tool to recapitalize the banking sector, and privatization allowed gains in efficiency.

The empirical evidence is not sufficient to determine whether there is a preferred resolution strategy, because the results vary across the three countries analysed. Nevertheless, the authors also present cross-country evidence that, as in the literature, shows how the privatized banks were significantly more unstable prior to the privatization processes. Regarding the effects of foreign acquisition, the authors conclude that it improved bank stability in the immediate post-resolution sub-period in Mexico, and weakened bank stability during the more economically stable period in Argentina and Brazil.

The financial crisis has also affected the patters of firm financing behaviour. **Chapter 4**, by Santiago Carbó-Valverde (Bangor Business School), José Manuel Mansilla-Fernández and Francisco Rodríguez-Fernández (University of Granada and Spanish Savings Banks Foundation), focuses closely on the analysis of the effects of changes in monetary policy interest rates on the price of trade credit and financing behaviour of firms in Spain. Trade credit is one of the most important financial sources for Spanish firms, and this study reveals that the pattern of trade credit changed significantly in Spain after the financial crisis. It is observed in particular that although trade credit became more expensive, the volume of trade credit decreased after the financial crisis. Authors find that trade credit showed an even more abrupt change than did bank financing. Finally, the existence of both a 'competition effect' (that is, changes in monetary policy leading to convergence in the price established by firms within the same industrial sector) and a 'complementarity effect' between trade credit and bank financing is found in a period of rising interest rates.

The financial crisis also increased the liquidity risk both intensively and rapidly, affecting the stability of individual banks as well as the entire financial system. **Chapter 5**, by Laura Chiaramonte (University of Verona), Barbara Casu (Cass Business School) and Roberto Bottiglia (University of Verona), emphasizes the need to pay more attention to liquidity risk and its connections with other banking risks. The authors affirm that Basel I and II managed liquidity risk with non-harmonized procedures based on strict rules which were nevertheless demonstrated to be inadequate in the face of the degree of market complexity. In order to solve this problem, the regulators (mainly the Basel Committee on Banking Supervision, but also the European Commission and the Committee of European Banking Supervisors) developed a series of normative measures to regulate liquidity risk: the Liquidity Coverage Ratio (a short-term rule), intended to enhance resilience to potential liquidity disruptions over a 30-day horizon; and a longer-term structural rule, named the Net Stable Funding Ratio (NSFR). The authors focus only on the NSFR, investigating its value on a sample of top-tier international banks in the pre-crisis period, during the crisis and in the post-crisis period, in order to identify which banks fulfil the new structural liquidity risk measures. Their results show the existence of a negative relationship between bank size (in terms of total assets) and the NSFR value, while highlighting that the banks with structural liquidity furthest from the minimum requirements are those that would probably be included in the systemic risk list drawn up by the Group of Governors and Head of Supervision; these banks tend to be bank holding and holding companies, or commercial banks. On the other hand, the banks with their liquidity structures in line with the new NSFR liquidity requirements are the cooperative banks, saving banks, or real estate and mortgage banks, operating on a smaller geographical scale, and also smaller in terms of total assets.

The financial crisis affected not only solvency but also bank efficiency. The next two chapters analyse some aspects relating to bank efficiency in the Italian and Spanish banking systems respectively. **Chapter 6**, by Cristina Bernini and Paola Brighi from the University of Bologna, analyses the cost efficiency of the Italian banking system and concretely to what extent the bank business model affects bank efficiency. The authors assert that in recent decades banks have become large and centralized with a more hierarchical organizational structure. Also, while technological innovations such as credit scoring have made the evaluation of SMEs easier, consolidation processes have made the financial institutions larger and their interactions with SMEs more complex. The effects of both these factors on bank efficiency depend on how good a substitute hard information about borrower quality is for soft information; for example, evidence supports that the distance between bank and borrower is very important. Relationship lending becomes easier if the bank is part of the local community and loan officers can personally interact with their borrowers, so the shorter the distance between the borrower and the bank, the stronger the relationship between the two, making the process of credit evaluation easier. This chapter also analyses the effects of the distance between local branches of a bank and its headquarters on cost efficiency. Their results confirm that distance is important and its is clear that bank groups with a local organizational structure are more efficient than banks that are large and far apart. As expected, the recent crisis generated a general reduction in cost efficiency; however, minor and mutual banks, and banks located in the centre and the north of the country, seemed to react better to the financial crisis. The results also suggest that, besides distance, other features such as size and income diversification influence the banking structure organization and affect geographical cost efficiency distribution.

Similarly **Chapter 7**, by Concepción Pérez-Cárceles and Juan Cándido Gómez-Gallego (both of the Catholic University of Murcia) and Juan Gómez-García (University of Murcia) analyses cost efficiency. Concretely, they use the stochastic frontier approach in order to analyse cost efficiency in Spanish savings banks. Unlike most of the previous studies, this technique is used to estimate the total cost function as well as the financial cost function. In addition, several accounting and financial ratios are included in order to establish whether or not the beginning of the financial instability situation influenced cost efficiency. The main conclusion is that the recent financial instability reduced the financial cost efficiency of Spanish savings banks and therefore their total cost efficiency. The authors identify some of the causes of the reduction in cost efficiency and conclude that the increase in competitive pressure as a result of globalization and economic integration and the mergers process will reduce market power and force the Spanish savings banks to devise a strategy to reduce the levels of inefficiency.

'Intellectual capital' is a broad-based term considered synonymous with a bank's intangible assets. The success of companies has traditionally been based on their efficient use of physical capital; however nowadays it is intellectual capital, rather than physical capital, which is much more relevant, thus becoming a competitive advantage for a bank. This change raises several questions about the possible impact on related disclosure practices by banks. **Chapter 8**, by Gimede Gigante (Bocconi University) and Daniele Angelo Previati (University of Rome 3), investigates some factors which have not previously been presented in the literature, regarding intellectual capital performance in the Spanish, Portuguese and Greek banking sectors. The study makes several contributions. First, it examines an emerging area of accounting disclosures that is being demanded by stakeholders but has yet to be investigated to any substantial extent. Second, prior research has provided evidence of the relationship between the performance of a firm in terms of economic, environmental and social matters with disclosure levels related to the same themes, but no evidence about the link between the level of disclosure on intellectual capital and the actual intellectual capital performance of a firm. In addition, their study assesses the relationship between other key organizational-level control factors and the level of disclosure of intellectual capital. The results indicate that, contrary to previous research, organizational size and physical capital financial performance are not associated with the amount of intellectual capital information disclosed by publicly listed companies. The authors assert that the lack of such an association could be due, among other reasons to (a) the small size of the sample and (b) the fact that the companies used from FTSE-100 have similar size , and that did not enable the potential impact of organizational size to be fully realized. The authors conclude by pointing out some drawbacks of the study and areas of future research.

Chapter 9, by Paola Brighi (University of Bologna), Stefano d'Addona (University of Rome 3) and Antonio Carlo Francesco Della Bina (University of Bologna) empirically tests a multi-factor model on the Italian stock market through a GMM test of their three-factor model augmented by a momentum effect. They use stock market data from 1986 to 2010. Their results show that the expected return anomalies persist over the time horizon analysed, and are mainly connected to size and value characteristics; the momentum anomaly, however, plays only a marginal role. More specifically, they find that the size premium is confirmed for a domestic Italian investor. The GMM test of the three-factor specification appears to support the Fama and French model applied to the Italian stock market. Concretely, for the case of the Italian stock market in 9 out of 16 portfolios, the null hypothesis that the over-identifying restrictions are satisfied cannot be rejected, but meanwhile there is very weak evidence of a momentum effect.

Finally **Chapter 10**, by Caterina Lucarelli (Università Politecnica delle Marche) and Simona Maggi (Associazione Italiana Private Banking), proposes a theoretical framework which sets alternative business models in the wealth management industry that they test using experimental data. Their map of business models arises when wealth managers potentially create a mix of business process standardization/customization with 'make or buy' choices, after carrying out an external and internal strategic analysis. As far as demand is concerned, the amount of wealth under management is integrated with a new criterion, one of clustering customers according to their propensity to take risks and their willingness to diversify their investments. In addition, internal conditions in the wealth management organization are covered. Information on operational demand and supply derived from a unique dataset of Italian wealth managers covering almost 90% of the national industry, allows the reliability of the theoretical layout to be tested and the positioning of a relevant sample of Italian wealth managers to be shown. The operational data supports the concept that the business models map can be a reliable instrument both to describe and to guide the strategic positioning of wealth managers. Theoretical business models corresponding to direct customization may unambiguously be undertaken by three different clusters of Italian wealth managers.

José Manuel Pastor Monsálvez and Juan Fernández de Guevara Radoselovics thank Philip Molyneux, the Palgrave Macmillan Studies in Banking and Financial Institutions Series Editor, for the opportunity to coordinate this book. We are also grateful for the help from Ivie's editing department, especially Susana Sabater, the collaboration from Palgrave Macmillan staff (Beverley Copland and Lisa von Fircks) and of two of the senior members of the Wolpertinger Club (Francisco Pérez and Javier Quesada). Our research into banking was carried out within the framework of the Spanish Ministry of Education and Science support through research programs ECO2011–23248 (José Manuel Pastor Monsálvez) and SEJ2010–17333/ECON (Juan Fernández de Guevara Radoselovics).

1
The Mis-selling of Payments Protection Insurance in Mortgage and Unsecured Lending Markets

John K. Ashton and Robert S. Hudson

1.1 Introduction

In January 2009, the UK competition law judgement body, the Competition Commission (hereafter CC), stated that the joint sale of credit or payment protection insurance (hereafter PPI) with lending, including unsecured, mortgage and credit card borrowing, was to be prohibited after 2010. This judgement also required that single premium insurance policies should not be employed in this market, demanded that greater customer information provision be provided, and required PPI to be unbundled from other financial services when sold. Although these measures were legally challenged in October 2009 by Barclays plc on the grounds that prohibiting the sale of credit insurance reduced customer convenience, they were largely upheld in a provisional decision by the Competition Appeal Tribunal, published in May 2010 (CC, 2010).

Concurrent with this legal debate was a major growth in the number of customer complaints as to their dealings in PPI markets and principally as to whether this insurance service had been sold inappropriately to them, and also whether a premium refund could be sought if they had paid a single premium and then repaid the debt to which it related. Many, yet not all, banks rejected many of these complaints, which were then forwarded to the UK financial services arbitration service, the independent Financial Ombudsman Service. This body accepted that the vast majority (over 80 per cent) of these complaints were valid. Further, following the rejection of the legal appeal by Barclays plc on the CC judgement, the Financial Services Authority (FSA) started a process of redress for customers mis-sold PPI with lending (FSA, 2010). This process involved firms settling the substantial backlog of PPI complaints and claims for customer redress for mis-selling.

This examination outlines the form, scope and function of PPI markets, the criticisms of these markets which led to the regulatory intervention, whether or not this major regulatory step was justified, and the outcome of this judgement for the financial services industry.

Assessment of these legal and regulatory judgements of the UK PPI market is important for many reasons, relating to both the scale and profitability of these markets for the financial services industry and the consumer distress apparent in the mis-selling of this financial service. First of all, mis-selling has historically been very expensive for firms in terms of customer redress, with past cases of mis-selling costing UK financial firms nearly £15bn, of which £3bn was paid in customer redress for mortgage endowments mis-selling, £11.8bn was paid in customer redress for pension mis-selling and £195m was paid in customer redress for split capital investment trust mis-selling (see FSA, 2011). This area of activity has also occupied financial regulators, and prior to the financial crisis heavily influenced press coverage of financial regulatory matters. Not least, financial mis-selling also adversely affects customers who when faced by mis-selling are exposed to substantial personal financial risks and can lose confidence in otherwise highly beneficial financial services such as saving and investment. Indeed the role of PPI in encouraging the rise in over-indebtedness is repeatedly identified by the UK government (e.g. Department for Business, Enterprise and Regulatory Reform, 2007; hereafter BERR). In the light of these characteristics of financial services mis-selling, it is perhaps surprising that to date so little has been recorded within the academic literatures on this issue.

To add to the, albeit limited, academic coverage of financial mis-selling and PPI, this chapter examines the foundations and implications of the CC's judgement of PPI and the subsequent process of customer redress of PPI mis-selling led by the FSA. This examination is undertaken by means of a range of approaches. After a review of the academic literatures, we first undertake a thematic review of wider regulatory or 'grey' literatures examining PPI sales in the UK, USA and Europe, and secondly assess regulatory principles breached in the final notices issued and fines imposed by the FSA in cases of PPI mis-selling before this prohibition was imposed. The third form of assessment examines the key assumption underlying claims that the PPI market was anticompetitive; that a cross-subsidy developed between PPI and the loans these insurance services protected. The two largest PPI markets in the UK – PPI sales with unsecured lending and mortgage finance – are examined in this assessment using two different data sources. Lastly, the consequences for the firms involved in this PPI mis-selling episode are considered, with particular emphasis placed on the levels of fines imposed by the FSA and the levels of customer redress expected to be paid by firms. In conclusion, we summarize these results and suggest areas for future research.

1.2 The UK market for PPI

PPI provides varying combinations of accident, sickness and unemployment insurance, and is used to protect the loan payments of policyholders in the event of them losing their income. PPI provides cover in the case of a borrower having an unexpected fall in income, and is designed to pay off the debt as repayments if the policyholder is adversely affected by accident, sickness or unemployment. This financial service is perhaps unusual in that it provides cover to both the borrower, who will not default on their debt after an unexpected event, and also the lender which is assured their lending will be repaid if this policy pays out.

The UK PPI market is substantial; in 2006 it is estimated that 20 million PPI policies were in operation in the UK (Office of Fair Trading, hereafter OFT, 2006). Unsecured lending PPI plans accounted for 45 per cent of the overall UK credit insurance market, and were valued at £2,013m in 2006 (CC, 2007), and mortgage payment protection insurance for first and second charge mortgages accounted for 24.9 per cent of the PPI market, valued at £1,099m in 2006. This sector also expanded rapidly, with annual growth rates of 15 to 20 per cent for the period 2000–2005 (OFT, 2006), and currently is experiencing a decline (CC, 2008). For example the take-up of mortgage PPI on all new mortgage contracts fell from a high point of 24 per cent in 2003 to 18 per cent in 2007. A further feature of the PPI markets is the very high proportion of policies that have been provided at point of sale with the loan contract (for example, estimates for mortgage PPI vary from 88 per cent (Ford et al., 2004) to 95 per cent (OFT, 2006).

While most forms of PPI have emerged as private sector solutions to the costs of loan default, in the area of mortgage provision this insurance also acts as a complement to the system of state income support (Department for Environment, Transport and the Regions, 2000). As a buoyant owner-occupied housing market contributes to a successful economy (Department of Environment, Transport and the Regions, 2000) this form of insurance has been encouraged by successive governments. Indeed this use of PPI has been observed internationally (see Ross and Tootell, 2004). The requirement for wider provision of high quality mortgage PPI has also increased substantially in the last decades. Since the

1970s, UK home ownership has become more diverse in socio-economic terms, with the proportion of borrowers from lower-income households, unskilled workers and older people rising (Ford et al., 2004); this movement was supported by a range of UK government policies including the right to buy (Ford and England, 2000). These changes occurred concurrently with the re-regulation of the UK mortgage market, leading to a major growth in the variety and range of mortgages, often with non-standard features (Scanlon et al., 2008). While these shifts have had positive outcomes, such as reducing the number of households which could not access credit, and reducing discriminatory practices such as not lending to single persons and women, this change has reduced the quality of UK mortgage lending overall (Stephens and Quilgars, 2008). These changes, in combination with variable or short-term fixed rate mortgage contracts being the norm in the market, resulted in UK mortgagors facing more uncertainty than mortgagors in most other nations (Miles, 2005) hence needing additional financial protection – such as that provided by PPI.

The market for mortgage PPI developed partly in response to changes in government support for mortgagors. Since 1948 the UK government has supported mortgagors claiming unemployment benefits via arrangements variously named national assistance, supplementary benefit, income support and jobseekers allowance (Ford and Quilgars, 2001). Prior to 1987, mortgagors in receipt of these subsistence benefits would receive payment of their full mortgage interest payments (Ford and England, 2000), and historically mortgage lenders collaborated with this system and exercised forbearance by not initiating home repossession from recipients of this state welfare, an agreement given semi-legal status in 1991 (Ford and Quilgars, 2001). This welfare safety net was curtailed in 1987 and 1995, more recently extended in 2009 but further reduced in 2010, when the level of interest supported was limited to the Bank of England lending rate.

1.3 Criticisms of PPI markets

1.3.1 The regulatory journey to PPI mis-selling

Despite the scale, utility and public policy importance of PPI, this form of insurance has been the focus of repeated regulatory scrutiny internationally, and surrounded by persistent allegations of poor value and inappropriate sales. Initially the provision of PPI faced strong criticism (e.g. Department for Environment, Transport and the Regions, 2000), and investigation and subsequent legislation by UK central government (BERR, 2007). This legislation considered the modernization of the UK consumer credit law and the role of PPI in credit decisions, within both a white paper (DTI, 2003)[1] which detailed the perceived high cost and low quality of cover offered by PPI, and the subsequent Consumer Credit Act (2006). Of greater pertinence to this discussion, PPI was also repeatedly investigated by three UK regulators concerned with consumer protection, competition policy and financial services markets (see OFT, 2006; CC, 2007, 2008; FSA, 2007a). These investigations followed concerns raised initially by consumer bodies such as the Citizens Advice Bureau (CAB) which reflected an increasing frustration with industry practice in the sale of PPI (CAB, 2005) and growing numbers of consumers using the Financial Ombudsman Service after their claims of PPI mis-selling had been rejected by the banks concerned.

The FSA examined PPI issues repeatedly from 2005, using thematic reviews of the PPI market in both supervisory investigations into and mystery shopping studies on (FSA, 2005, 2006, 2007a) firms sampled from the wide range of companies distributing PPI, including retailers, car dealerships, brokers, banks and building societies. Problems were particularly identified in firms which do not undertake financial services as their main line of business, especially car dealerships which sell PPI alongside car finance. General concerns which have persisted throughout these visits include limited information given to consumers, a lack of awareness of product exemptions, and a failure to indicate the voluntary nature of PPI. Indeed whilst pressured selling has been rare, firms often present the acceptance of both the loan and PPI as the norm and expect an explicit rejection of PPI by the customer (FSA, 2007b).

Following this FSA activity and a super-complaint[2] by the CAB, PPI provision was examined by the UK competition law enforcement and consumer protection agency, the OFT (2006). This report indicated that significant concerns existed as to the sale of the PPI, and subsequently the provision of PPI was referred to the competition law investigative and judgement body, the CC. This investigation, in turn, led to the prohibition of the joint sales of PPI that we considered in the introduction to this chapter. A detailed legal discussion of the PPI case is provided by Grey (2011).

It is also important to recognize that concerns with mis-selling PPI are not restricted to the UK, and that these criticisms have been mirrored in other nations. In the USA, the 'packing' of credit insurance within credit services such as home and consumer loans (Federal Trade Commission, 2001; hereafter FTC) has been criticized, even involving Senate hearings in the 1970s. This regulatory attention focused on home and consumer loans, and raised concerns including the mis-selling of PPI, misleading advertising, including insurance within a credit agreement without explanation, and not fully revealing insurance costs within total loan costs (FTC, 2001). Recent FTC cases have resulted in large fines for banks and finance companies which have packed PPI with consumer loans in a manner against the interests of the consumer. Indeed, 8 per cent of all consumer complaints received by the Federal Reserve concern additional fees and charges, including PPI. This form of financial services provision is therefore one of the most persistent sources of consumer complaints for US financial regulators (Federal Reserve Board, 2007).

Lastly the cost of PPI has also been raised at a European level (European Commission, 2005) in relation to wider aims of harmonization of consumer protection. EU credit market concerns include the removal of barriers to the provision of information on credit decision making, on the form of interest rate setting and on distinct debt collection practices (DTI, 2003). In particular a Europe-wide approach for calculating the total cost of credit for consumers, including add-on costs, is important (European Commission, 2005).

1.3.2 The academic assessment of PPI markets

Distinct from this body of regulatory evidence, a small yet valuable academic literature has also emerged which has also presented a broadly critical perspective on the sale of PPI, considering the determinants of PPI take-up, and the perceptions of and satisfaction with these products.

The take-up of PPI has been investigated using both formal models and surveys. Using a survey, Pryce and Keoghan (2002) indicated that the premium price has a limited influence on PPI purchase decisions. In contrast, environmental factors and particularly past experience of unemployment are the strong determinants of mortgage PPI take-up. Further UK survey evidence indicates that mortgage PPI is very expensive, is limited in coverage and has regressive elements (Burchardt and Hill, 1998). Modelling this situation Pryce (2001) indicated the decision to take out PPI for mortgages is rational. More recently (De Meza et al., 2007) indicate that the approach adopted by PPI salespersons can influence purchase decisions. This study, while identifying the PPI market as fertile ground for coercive sales, did not empirically test for the presence of such sales. As indicated in the text, survey evidence for the UK and the USA, and repeated FSA investigations, reported as final notices of regulatory action, all indicate that assumptive sales rather than coercive sales is the dominant sales method in this market.

US academic assessments have focused on the method of sale of PPI, with sales approaches and involuntary tying arrangements a primary concern. This emphasis arises from the widespread use of PPI and the associated high profitability of this product. Survey evidence has indicated that most customers do not appreciate any obvious coercion, yet feel obliged to purchase PPI (Polden, 1983). Durkin (2002) indicates that cross-selling lends itself to coercive sales, and PPI sales have focused on older and lower socio-economic groups – groups particularly prone to coercion (Barron and Staten, 1995). Other US contributions have emphasized the limited competitiveness of mortgage PPI markets, overpriced policies (Allen and Chan, 1998) and requirements to re-examine the legal treatment of PPI (Spahr and Escolas, 1986).

Lastly, the academic literature examining mortgage PPI has considered the perceived quality and historically low take-up of these mortgage PPI policies. Past assessment of the perceived quality of mortgage PPI has assessed whether policyholders have avoided problems such as mortgage default. Ford and Quilgars (2001), using a postal survey, reported that 20 per cent of those in receipt of mortgage PPI developed arrears. Also using a postal survey, Ford and England (2000) reported that a third of mortgage PPI policy holders developed mortgage arrears compared to half of the recipients of income support for mortgage interest. Further, these studies also indicate considerable mortgagor confusion as to what mortgage payment protection insurance actually covers, and how this differs from other forms of insurance. Diaz-Serrano (2005) comments that mortgagors with unstable work histories and ill-health problems are precluded from many policies, reducing the coverage available to average mortgagees. Lastly, Ford et al. (2004) reports that the propensity to take-up mortgage PPI is closely related to the level of savings held by a household and the age of the mortgagor.

1.3.3 The regulatory causes of the PPI mis-selling episode

In summary, the preceding regulatory and academic investigations reviewed have indicated poor value of PPI, limited competition in credit insurance markets, unhelpful sales techniques, and limited public comprehension of PPI. Within a more detailed review of the regulatory and academic literature, we draw out the primary concerns which have been linked to these wider themes. In this assessment, two bodies of regulatory, or 'grey', literatures are examined. Initially the large number of UK and some US regulatory reports are considered. From this assessment, the most frequently raised issues or themes are identified. These themes include: poor value of products, consumer inertia and sales techniques, poor provision of information and the adverse use of market segmentation. The results of this assessment are reported in Table 1.1.

Secondly the final notices, the record of disciplinary actions undertaken against firms for a breach of financial regulations judged by the FSA, are reviewed. The UK system of regulation follows a principles approach where firms are expected to follow certain regulatory principles when operating in financial services markets. This review of 23 cases concerning PPI mis-selling emphasizes which of these regulatory principles are breached in these cases to more clearly indicate the causes of this mis-selling episode. We may conclude that breaches of Principle 3 predominate, involving the failure of management systems. Such matters have included not forwarding all information to the customer to make a full decision, and systematic failures in the monitoring of staff selling PPI. A large proportion of cases also display breaches of Principles 6, 7 and 9, relating to customer interests, communications with clients and relationships of trust with customers respectively. These regulatory breaches relate to a diversity of issues in practice; for example, these cases include adding the cost of single premium PPI plus interest to the quotation for the loan without the customer asking for it, or not informing customers of the characteristics of the PPI, often due to inadequate staff training and competence. The distribution of these regulatory breaches by regulatory principle is displayed in Figure 1.1.

1.4 Was the regulation decision to prohibit PPI and loan joint sales justified?

1.4.1 Incentives within PPI markets

Central to the judgement prohibiting the joint sale of PPI with lending was the assumption that PPI was used to cross-subsidize credit. This outcome can arise when PPI is sold with credit jointly rather than independently. There are incentives for firms jointly distributing PPI policies to offer higher quality policies than firms independently distributing these policies. PPI is developed to provide lending repayments in the event of a policyholder suffering a fall in income due to unemployment, critical illness or accident. In the event of a successful claim, both the policyholder and the firm providing a loan with PPI are beneficiaries of these payouts. The PPI policyholder benefits from a payout as payments are made, will not default on the lending and will not face the repossession of their home. The loan provider jointly distributing PPI will also benefit from better coverage and quality, as they are guaranteed

Table 1.1 A thematic assessment of PPI (payment protection insurance) mis-selling concerns

Issue	Evidence raised in the Grey Literature
Poor value of PPI	All the UK regulatory investigations (OFT, 2006; FSA 2005, 2006, 2007a, 2007b, 2007c; CC 2007, 2008; DTI, 2003; CAB, 2005) emphasized the poor coverage of PPI and the potentially adverse techniques used to sell these products. Specifically the OFT (2006) reported consumers receive poor value due to the very low proportion of premium income paid out in claims. The claims ratio for unsecured loan PPI is 18%; a level far lower than other forms of insurance, such as car insurance (84% over the same period; CC, 2008). Low pay out ratios' for PPI are also recorded in the USA where the FTC (2001) reported most lenders and insurers retain more than 40% of premiums. The commissions paid to PPI distributors are also very high averaging 59% (OFT, 2006) over the 2000–2005 period. The actual insurance cover offered by PPI is often limited (OFT, 2006; CC, 2007, 2008; FSA, 2006; CAB, 2005; DTI, 2003). Claims are generally payable in the event of a decline in, or loss of income, and are usually paid for monthly intervals for a period not exceeding 12 months. Loss of income resulting from factors under the control of the insured party such as relationship breakdown, or voluntary unemployment is generally excluded from these policies. Further claiming loss of income due to illness may be problematic with claims in respect of pre-existing conditions generally being invalid. These factors make PPI a very profitable area of operation.
Consumer inertia and sales techniques	The UK regulatory investigations all indicated customers do not actively search for PPI due to customer inertia. Customers report they perceive PPI to be a relatively unimportant element of the credit decision and often purchase this insurance product from lenders (OFT, 2006). In many of these credit decisions customers focus on the loan interest rate, shopping around for the lowest rate and purchase PPI to assist their credit application (OFT, 2006). Mystery shopping experiments (FSA, 2005, 2007b) report while most customers are not pressurized, a third are unaware of the PPI costs and are not provided with a clear statement of price (FSA, 2007b). The point of sale advantage leads to 80% of all PPI being sold in combination with banking credit services (OFT, 2006). This situation provides difficulties for other providers to access customers leading to a low level of competition for PPI (CC, 2008).

(*Continued*)

Table 1.1 Continued

Information provision concerns	Information provision problems are exaggerated when PPI suppliers are reluctant to inform customers as to the true cost of their product. Information availability also differs between PPI suppliers. This problem is compounded as PPI often lacks upfront advertising information. Alternatively a limited number of suppliers have emphasized the relatively low costs of their PPI as a key marketing tool when advertising unsecured lending services (CC, 2008). Indeed amending the current complex UK advertising regulation for financial services to assist consumers' comprehension within credit decisions is a recognized policy priority (DTI, 2003). Widespread evidence also exists that many firms selling PPI provided no written materials and often only use an oral script emphasizing the products' benefits (FSA, 2007c). As insurance policy characteristics vary in the scope of cover, policy comparison is difficult to undertake. US evidence (Lacko and Pappalardo, 2007) similarly identifies that a substantial proportion of mortgage customers have difficulties in determining whether credit deals actually includes additional fees for PPI and other 'extra' product features.
The adverse use of market segmentation in payment protection insurance (PPI) markets	The focused sale of PPI to lower socio-economic groups and younger persons (CC, 2007); groups with reported low financial literacy (FSA, 2005) is observed and is linked with low levels of consumer comprehension compound the competitive concerns in this market. Indeed the OFT (2006) indicates '*...evidence suggests that how consumers purchase their PPI, their understanding of the product and the quality of information available to them hinders competition*' (my emphasis). The DTI (2003) further indicates over half of all customers fail to comprehend the terms in credit agreements and 77% find the advertising language difficult to comprehend. This decision-making process is also complicated by setting a single premium. Over 93% of UK PPI for unsecured lending uses a single premium for the duration paid at the start of the loan period (CC, 2008). These practices, also identified in the USA (FTC, 2001) make it difficult for customers to learn through repeated purchase experience.

continued repayments. Therefore a firm distributing PPI jointly with mortgage lending will benefit from a policy with more inclusive coverage and higher payouts in the case of a successful claim. Conversely, an independent supplier of PPI is not a recipient in the case of a successful claim payout and so has no incentives to offer a higher quality PPI policy.

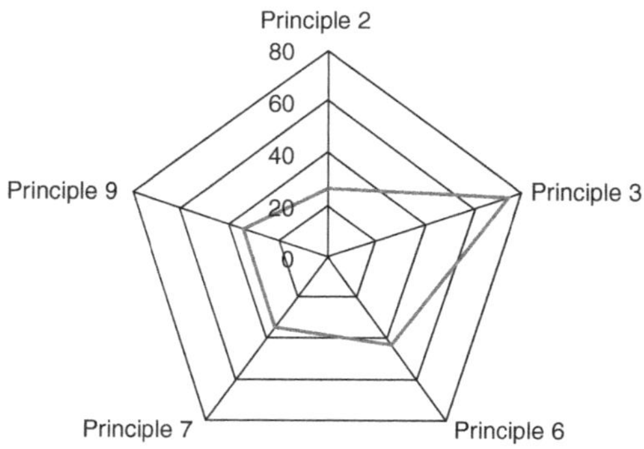

Principle 2	Skill, care and diligence	A firm must conduct its business with due skill, care and diligence.
Principle 3	Management and control	A firm must take reasonable care to organize and control its affairs responsibly and effectively, with adequate risk management systems.
Principle 6	Customers' interests	A firm must pay due regard to the interests of its customers and treat them fairly.
Principle 7	Communications with clients	A firm must pay due regard to the information needs of its clients, and communicate information to them in a way which is clear, fair and not misleading.
Principle 9	Customers: relationships of trust	A firm must take reasonable care to ensure the suitability of its advice and discretionary decisions for any customer who is entitled to rely upon its judgment.

Figure 1.1 The distribution of breaches of regulatory principles for PPI related final notices
Notes:

These issues of joint and independent sales are also compounded by the origination and sale of PPI as block policies, with identical policies designed for particular lenders or brokers and offering similar levels of cover and costs. Only a limited amount of this business is sold at an individual level where the policy is written for an individual's circumstances and concerns. As block policy origination aims to provide profitable policies for a wide range of customers, restrictive clauses are included to exclude individuals with different economic and individual risks and minimize adverse selection. As different people have distinct probabilities of suffering from certain illnesses, incurring accidents and becoming unemployed, insurance firms use a range of sorting devices to separate risk groups for these outcomes (Borenstein, 1989) and, when block polices are sold, to exclude many higher-risk customers. As incentives exist for low-risk customers to distinguish themselves and gain a lower premium, this discrimination will persist. These moral hazards can be even more acute for unemployment insurance, often included in PPI, as the individual can influence the prospect of finding new employment and the probability of losing their job (Chiu and Karni, 1998). Attempts to amend these quality problems have included the use of benchmark products and regulation of mortgage PPI sales through the mortgage code, a voluntary code adopted by many UK mortgage lenders between 1997 and 2004 (Ford and Quilgars, 2001).

These forms of code have not been adopted for other PPI markets. Indeed there are major differences between PPI markets. The OFT (2006) reported that the mortgage PPI market has a large number of both joint and independent suppliers and good compliance with regulations, and that relative to users of other forms of PPI, customers who take out MPPI (mortgage payment protection insurance) are more likely to shop around for this insurance service. The CC (2009) further reported that unlike unsecured lending and credit card PPI, a relationship, albeit a weak one, between the premium price and policy quality does exist for MPPI.

1.4.2 PPI data

To determine if the cross-subsidies from PPI to loans occur and whether or not the basis for the CC judgement on joint sales of PPI with credit is sound, we examine whether any differences exist in terms of PPI premiums and quality due to the method of distribution. To achieve this we employ two sources of data; one from the FSA and the other from a private financial data provider, Moneyfacts plc. We also examine both unsecured personal loan PPI as this is the most common form of borrowing in the UK (BERR, 2007) and mortgage PPI due to its distinct public policy importance.

Initially, cross-sectional data from the FSA comparison website on PPI in both unsecured and mortgage PPI markets is considered.

- For unsecured lending, we took 101 PPI policies provided by 35 financial services firms that issue PPI either separately as a distinct product or jointly with a loan offering. This information was accessed in October 2008 and provides information for a policy for £5000 borrowed over three years by a 40-year-old employed male working 40 hours per week. Included in this data are the common features of a PPI for £5000 borrowed over three years provided both by firms that issue PPI as a stand-alone product, and by firms that sell PPI jointly with loans.

- The FSA data was also provided by the FSA comparison website on PPI for 281 mortgage PPI policies provided by 67 financial services firms that issued PPI either independently or jointly with a mortgage loan. This information was accessed in August 2010 and provides information for providing a MPPI policy for monthly mortgage payments of £500, £1,000, £1,500, and £2,000 borrowed by a 20-, 40- and 60-year-old employed person working 40 hours per week (data for £500 borrowed by a 20-year-old was unavailable).

The quality of PPI depends fundamentally on the terms and conditions under which benefits are payable. Both these cross-sectional datasets allow assessment of the cost and quality differences between the PPI policies provided jointly by lenders and independently. In both cases a high proportion of the products considered are designed for independent rather joint distribution.

PPI data is also provided by Moneyfacts plc, and represents the cost of a £5000 unsecured loan repaid over a 36-month period, with and without PPI. A single loan size of £5000 is employed to remove variation in fixed costs due to the size of the loan made. The data is recorded monthly for 10 years, from 1 January 1998 to 31 December 2007 for 84 banks offering 208 joint credit and PPI products. This data represents the vast majority of UK joint PPI and unsecured personal lending products provided over the sample period.

1.4.3 Assessment of cross-subsidies and differences in costs attributable to the form of PPI distribution whether independently or jointly with loan sales

Tables 1.2 to 1.4 give evidence on the levels of cross-subsidies, and the cost differences relating to PPI policies distributed independently and those sold jointly with loans of various types. Table 1.2 indicates that substantial differences exist between mortgage PPI policies which are offered separately and jointly. Panels A and B consider the premium levels and quality of the policies respectively. Table 1.3 considers the cross-section of unsecured lending PPI policies. Table 1.4 considers the distribution of unsecured loan and PPI costs over time.

Of the mortgage PPI policy data provided in Table 1.2, Panel A shows that premium costs rise with the level of cover. Clearly the age of mortgage PPI policyholders influences the premium costs for policies sold independently; younger applicants pay less for mortgage PPI policies, probably reflecting a lower chance of them suffering illness. It is surprising that this age effect is not observed for the jointly sold policies.

Table 1.2 Mortgage PPI premium costs and policy characteristics

Panel A: Cost of monthly mortgage PPI cover								
Average monthly MPPI cost £'s		Independent distribution (252 policies)		Joint distribution (20 policies)		Total (272 policies)		T test
Full time employee/Age		Mean	Std dev.	Mean	Std dev.	Mean	Std dev.	
£2000 cover	20 years	99.98	36.00	117.33	24.13	101.26	35.52	−2.12*
	40 years	106.98	31.51	117.24	24.79	107.70	33.16	−1.39
	60 years	127.45	50.86	116.83	24.20	126.67	31.16	0.92
£1500 cover	20 years	66.48	29.87	84.51	17.95	67.99	29.47	−3.25**
	40 years	73.53	25.23	84.34	18.25	74.41	24.89	−2.26*
	60 years	102.83	40.08	84.31	18.80	101.28	39.07	2.50*
£1000 cover	20 years	44.13	19.89	55.70	12.55	45.15	19.62	−3.13**
	40 years	49.02	16.75	55.54	12.54	49.53	16.53	−2.08*
	60 years	68.59	26.60	55.50	12.67	67.44	25.94	2.75*
£500 cover	20 years	–	–			–	–	
	40 years	22.13	9.98	28.38	6.20	22.59	9.88	−3.21**
	60 years	34.35	13.27	27.81	6.43	33.80	12.95	2.71**

(Continued)

Table 1.2 Continued

Panel B: Mortgage PPI policy characteristics and restrictions
281 MPPI policies provided by 67 financial services firms

Employed full time	Independent	Joint	Total
Maximum number of monthly mortgage payments	15.19	12.44	14.96
Waiting period accident and sickness days before payments made (days)	79.17	47.49	76.63
Waiting period unemployment before payments made	77.43	47.49	75.04
Percentage of policies with back to day one cover	39.8	33.6	39.2
Period for which pre-existing conditions excluded	16.92	13.98	16.71
Percentage of policies that exclude pre-existing conditions	1.62	10.4	2.38
Percentage of polices which are portable and can be moved to different mortgages	93.8	33.2	88.9
Percentage of policies with additional benefits	74.1	54.7	72.5
Coverage of backache (%)	99.6	99.0	99.6
Restricted coverage of backache (%)	12.0	87.9	18.1
Coverage of stress (%)	100.0	100.0	100.0
Restricted coverage of stress (%)	7.0	84.2	13.3
Number of observations	3394	298	3692

Notes: Denotes statistically significant at 1%, ** denotes statistically significant at 5%, * denotes 10% significance

Table 1.3 Unsecured Lending PPI premium costs and policy characteristics

Unsecured lending: 35 firms offering 101 policies, October 2008			
Unsecured loan PPI for £5000 borrowed over 3 years		Average	Std dev.
Total cost over term (joint distribution includes the cost of the loan)	Independently Jointly	£189.69 £932.85	£93.54 £180.75
Maximum number of monthly payments for accident and sickness	Independently Jointly	15.46 17.40	10.10 11.70
Maximum number of monthly payments for unemployment	Independently Jointly	11.15 11.20	2.64 3.34
Waiting period (days) before payment of accident and sickness payments	Independently Jointly	82.37 15.00	66.54 11.39
Waiting period (days) before payment of unemployment payments	Independently Jointly	57.01 28.50	53.53 17.04
Pre-existing conditions – number of months before the policy enacted medical information required	Independently Jointly	23.15 14.80	3.09 11.22
Proportion of policies with certain restrictions		Independently	Jointly
	Backache	0.96	0.33
	Stress	0.97	0.33

This may possibly reflect a lower emphasis placed by firms on this effect, as mortgages are generally less likely to be taken out by older people, and there may also be a lower risk of the firm suffering from adverse selection, as these applicants will already have undergone some underwriting during the process of being granted the mortgage. At ages 20 and 40, the cost of policies sold independently tends to be lower (often at statistically significantly levels) than that of those sold jointly.

The quality of mortgage PPI policies is reported in Panel B of Table 1.2. Neither set of jointly or independently distributed policies provides a dominant set of benefits. It can, however, be seen that the quality of benefits provided does to some extent reflect the priorities of the institution that sold it. The policies sold jointly provide on average a higher maximum number of monthly mortgage payments, and independently sold policies have substantially longer waiting periods. Little difference is observed between jointly and independently distributed MPPI policies for provision of cover going to back to day one of the initial claim and for the period for which pre-existing conditions are excluded.

Table 1.4 Comparison of rankings of the relative costs of insurance and credit for unsecured loans

Financial firm	Total cost loan	Total cost of PPI*	Diff. ranks loan and PPI costs	Financial firm	Total cost loan	Total cost of PPI*	Diff. ranks loan and PPI costs
Capital One Bank	6361.272	1291.232	−1	Post Office	5555.896	832.0696	−21
Britannia	5980.149	1153.776	−10	First National Bank	6299.413	831.4435	27
Bank of Scotland	5892.855	1125.752	−19	Royal Bank of Scotland	5811.05	831.3462	2
The Funding Corporation	5685.475	1089.985	−36	Halifax	6014.371	823.7695	22
HBOS	5887.154	1066.579	−18	MBNA	5924.687	821.71	17
British Gas	5547.684	1043.646	−46	National Australia Bank	5903.651	816.0777	13
Discover	5671.26	1042.8	−35	Marks and Spencer	5884.233	807.3009	11
General Electric	5554.055	1032.778	−43	Allied Irish Banks	5823.921	800.394	9
CVC Capital Partners	5736.96	1022.04	−23	Morgan Stanley	5690.995	793.6794	−1
Airdrie Savings Bank	6050.16	1017.36	3	Sainsbury's	5660.688	792.9011	−7
Lloyds/TSB	5924.043	1015.794	−6	Abbey National	5685.787	771.4027	0
Arbuthnot Banking Group	6509.52	1006.974	11	Liverpool Victoria	5705.804	715.6513	6

Colonial	6106.818	968.4318	8	Peoples Bank of Connecticut	5910.48	712.44	21
AA	5691.257	957.5881	−23	Woolwich	5931.796	709.1604	27
Cooperative Bank	5695.347	927.2155	−21	Alliance and Leicester Bank	5635.333	690.316	−4
Barclays	6008.917	925.4956	5	Phone a Loan.Ltd	5919.912	677.376	25
Paragon Group	6037.78	905.5405	8	Leeds & Holbeck	5559.708	667.1077	−4
Lloyds TSB	5942.63	894.2744	4	TESCO	5663.4	649.08	2
HSBC	5923.948	889.7669	1	Northern Rock	5599.835	629.1859	−1
Natwest	6059.268	888.3216	14	Rheinisch-Westfälisches Elektrizitätswerk AG	5649.12	615.6	2
HFC Bank	6043.374	870.1989	14	Nationwide BS	5709.658	597.3163	16
Citigroup	5821.292	868.1262	−5	Bank of Ireland	5755.864	591.6096	20
Danske bank	5539.242	867.7849	−29	American Express	5673.22	589.7867	10
Standard Chartered Bank	5951.52	848.2186	12	Newcastle BS	5671.26	585.9	9
Norwich and Peterborough	5750.34	843.81	−5	Saffron Walden BS	5501.52	550.8	−1
Prudential	5827.166	839.2728	1	Skipton Building Society	5501.52	550.8	−1
Royal Bank of Scotland	6208.92	833.4	24	Coventry BS	5696.693	511.4175	20

Independently sold policies are far more likely to be portable than jointly sold policies. This potentially reflects the relatively greater desire of firms distributing MPPI policies jointly to retain mortgagors. Independently sold policies are also more likely to offer additional benefits and are much less likely to place restrictions on claims due to backache and stress.

Table 1.3 considers unsecured lending PPI cost and some policy quality differences for policies distributed jointly or independently. The cost differences are substantial; the cost of a PPI policy for a £5000 unsecured loan repaid over three years is less than a quarter of the cost when it is offered separately rather than jointly with a loan. This extreme difference between policies sold jointly and independently may be misleading when the characteristics of individual policies are considered.

While all these PPI policies indicate that (for £5000 over three years) they offer the same level of cover, their policy characteristics vary considerably, as indicated by the difference in the average values of the various characteristics between independently and jointly sold policies, and the substantial standard deviations of these values indicating differences between companies. The maximum number of monthly payments for accident and sickness and unemployment indicate that the policies will not cover the costs of the loan repayment indefinitely. On average, payments for less than a year are provided for cases of unemployment, and less than 18 months for an accident- or sickness-related case. There are, however, not particularly big differences between independently and jointly sold policies in terms of the maximum number of payments they provide. The delays in payments (waiting periods) written into these policies mean that in some cases payments are not actually forwarded until six months have ensued after a claim. Independently sold policies tend to have substantially longer waiting periods, probably indicating the greater risk that they might experience adverse selection.

Another test of the cross-subsidy hypothesis can be made by comparing the rankings of the relative costs of insurance and credit for unsecured loans, as shown in Table 1.4. If there are no cross-subsidies, the firms with the highest insurance costs should also have the highest loan costs. In other words the rankings of the firms, whether sorted by insurance cost or alternatively by total loan cost, should not be significantly different. The non-parametric rank sum test to consider the hypothesis that companies with the highest insurance costs also have above average loan costs is rejected at the 1 per cent level (test statistic –2.7106). Thus we have strong evidence of cross-subsidy between PPI and loans with firms with high insurance costs having relatively low loan costs.

Overall we may conclude that when independently and jointly sold policies are compared, differences in unsecured loan and mortgage PPI premiums and policy quality do appear to exist. Those polices which are independently distributed tend to have lower costs, with this cost difference being very large in the case of policies linked to unsecured loans. Policies distributed in different ways do, however, provide different benefits which to some extent reflect the particular objective functions of the distributing companies. Given this, it is not self-evident that the cheaper costs associated with independently distributed policies necessarily represent better value for all consumers. Hedonic analysis does, however, strongly indicate that for mortgage PPI, after adjusting for different levels of benefits, independently sold policies are significantly cheaper. (Ashton and Hudson, 2011b). Moreover, we do see strong evidence of cross-subsidies in the unsecured loan market, with firms with high insurance costs having relatively low loan costs. These results of these various analyses are broadly supportive of the actions of the CC. Further discussion of the analysis of these datasets is provided in Ashton and Hudson, 2011a, 2011b).

1.5 The consequences of the PPI decision for firms

The costs to the UK financial services industry from both the judgement to limit PPI joint sales and also the following process of customer redress have been very high. Both substantial fines – of, in some cases, up to £7million – and potential claims for customer redress from this 'mis-selling' incident are expected to be significant for the industry.

Prior to the CC judgement, a number of firms were served final notices, resulting in fines and in some cases public censure. Fines were imposed by the FSA in 21 of the 23 cases which were viewed to involve PPI mis-selling. Of these cases, three involved individuals that held regulated roles within the firms concerned, and on them an average fine of £24,500 was imposed. The remaining 20 cases affected firms, and involved fines of £12,619,700 in total shared between 18 of the firms, while 2 received a public censure for their behaviour. Between 2006 and 2008, 16 firms have been publicly censured or fined between £14,000 and £7m. These fines increased dramatically, from 2006 when there were three cases resulting in £725,000 in total fines to 2008, when there were eight cases leading to over £9m in fines. These punishments varied from lower fines for retailers and car dealerships to heavy fines for banks. These

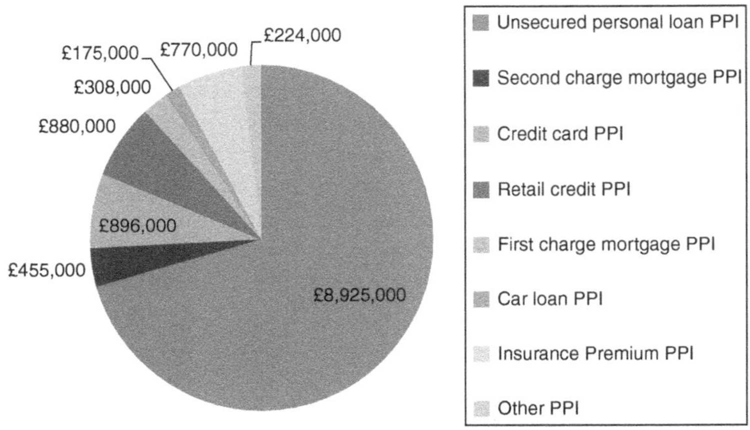

Figure 1.2 The level of fines imposed by type of PPI
Source: FSA.

fines were imposed on a wide range of different areas, as reported in Figure 1.2.

A further cost of the regulatory judgement is the redress firms have had to make to customers where PPI has been, or perceived to have been, mis-sold. These costs are still unclear in their entirety, yet can be estimated from both the provisions that many banks have issued in their accounts to pay for this additional extraordinary cost and from the FSA statistics recording the levels of redress paid each month. These costs have been observed to be very substantial; by way of example, Lloyds TSB plc reported they would be providing a £3,200m provision for the costs of the PPI decision and subsequent discussions with the FSA (Lloyds TSB, 2011), Barclays plc has a PPI redress provision of £1,000m (Barclays, 2011) and Royal Bank of Scotland Group a total provision for PPI redress of £950m (Royal Bank of Scotland, 2011). These costs vary due to the degree of 'inappropriate' sales undertaken and subsequently the response of individual banks to complaints handling. From a sample of just eight large UK banks to date, provision of over £6bn has been recorded for this issue. Further details are provided in Table 1.5. Further, the cumulative total of redress payments actually made to PPI customers has been recorded by the FSA. At the time of writing, the latest month recorded is October 2011, at which point the level of redress actually paid to customers has exceeded £1bn. These values are recorded in Figure 1.3.

Table 1.5 Levels of PPI 'mis-selling' redress stated in Annual and Interim Reports and Accounts – sample of eight large UK banks

	Stated redress for PPI mis-selling (from 2011 annual and interim accounts)
Lloyds TSB PLC	£3,200m
Barclays PLC	£1,000m
Royal Bank of Scotland	£950m
Santander	€620m (or £516m at €-£of 1.2)
Cooperative Bank	£90m for PPI redress
HSBC PLC	£332m for all customer redress programmes including the PPI judicial review issues
Nationwide Building Society	£15m of which £10m related to claims processing
National Australia Bank	£102m for PPI redress
Total for this sample	£6,205m

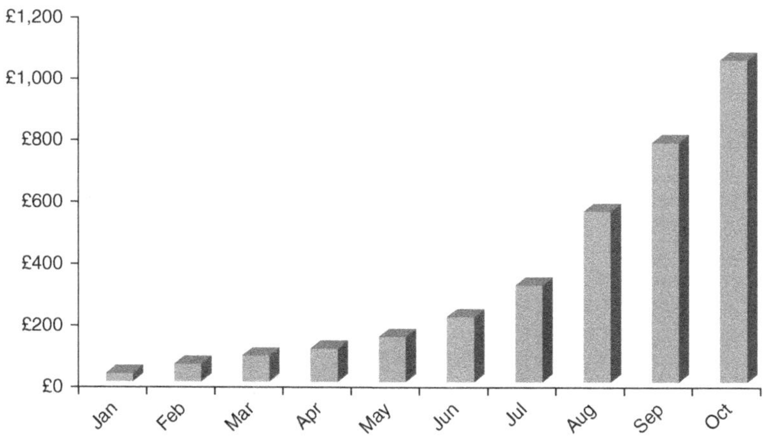

Figure 1.3 Cumulative total payments for redress of PPI mis-selling 2011 (£m)
Source: FSA.

1.6 Conclusions

This study examines the causes and consequences of the PPI mis-selling, the subsequent prohibition of joint sales with credit in 2010 and the consequences of this event for the UK financial services industry. This examination has outlined the scope and focus of these markets, the cause of complaints as to the operation of these markets, the empirical evidence regarding the justification for the regulatory judgement made, the nature of the regulatory judgement, and lastly the outcome of this judgement for firms.

We conclude that this is a very large market which has had a range of problems, particularly in the sales of this financial service. Equally we have also observed the costs of this judgement, which are very large indeed and will clearly run into many billions of pounds for the financial firms which sold this insurance product. Despite the apparently clear-cut nature of these conclusions, it is also important to state that this outcome has clearly helped none of the key participants involved in this mis-selling episode; customers have been mis-sold a financial service, some firms have had to pay vast sums in fines and customer redress, and regulators have been obliged to dedicate substantial resources to this market at a time when the needs for financial regulation in many areas have been high. In light of such a sober reflection we strongly advocate further academic work as to the causes and consequences of financial mis-selling, and recommend a requirement for new regulatory solutions for these concerns.

Notes

1. The Department of Trade and Industry (hereafter DTI) was renamed the Department of Business, Enterprise and Regulatory Reform (BERR) in 2007. In 2009, this department was renamed again, as the Department for Business, Innovation and Skills.
2. Under the Enterprise Act (2002), a consumer body such as the CAB may make a super-complaint as to their concerns with a market to the competition authorities. In this case the super-complaint by the CAB initiated the OFT investigation into PPI, which in turn triggered the CC investigation of this market.

References

Allen, D. S. and Chan, T. S. (1997). 'The Efficiency of Residential Mortgage Guarantee Insurance Markets', *The Federal Reserve Bank of St. Louis Working Paper Series*, 1997–013A, The Federal Reserve Bank of St. Louis.

Ashton, J. K. and Hudson, R. (2011a). 'Should the Joint Provision of Credit Insurance with Unsecured Lending be Prohibited? An Examination of the UK Payment Protection Insurance Market', *Bangor Business School Working Paper*, No. BBSWP/11/008, Bangor University.

Ashton, J. K. and Hudson, R. (2011b). 'The Price, Quality and Distribution of Mortgage Payment Protection Insurance: A Hedonic Pricing Approach', *Bangor Business School Working Paper*, No. BBSWP/11/010, Bangor University.

Barron, J. M. and Staten, M. E. (1995). 'Coercion in the Selling of Credit Life Insurance', *Psychology and Marketing*, vol. 12, no. 8, pp. 765–787.

BERR (Department for Business, Enterprise and Regulatory Reform) (2007). *Tackling Over-Indebtedness. Annual Report*, London.

Borenstein, S. (1989). 'The Economics of Costly Risk Sorting in Competitive Insurance Markets', *International Review of Law and Economics*, vol. 9, pp. 25–39.

Burchardt, T. and Hill, J. (1998). 'From Public to Private: The Case of Mortgage Payment Insurance in Great Britain', *Housing Studies*, vol. 13, no. 3, pp. 311–323.

Chiu, W. H. and Karni, E. (1998). 'Endogenous Adverse Selection and Unemployment Insurance', *The Journal of Political Economy*, vol. 106, no. 4, pp. 806–827.

Citizens Advice Bureau (CAB) (2005). *Protection Racket. CAB Evidence on the Cost and Effective of Payment Protection Insurance*, Citizens Advice Bureau, September.

Commission of the European Communities (2005). *Modified Proposal for a Directive of the European Parliament and the Council on Credit Agreements for Consumers Amending Council Directive 93/13/EC*, Brussels.

Competition Commission (2007). *Market Investigation into Payment Protection Insurance*, Emerging Thinking, London.

Competition Commission (2008). *Market Investigation into Payment Protection Insurance*, Provisional findings report, London.

Competition Commission (2009). *Market Investigation into Payment Protection Insurance*, London.

Competition Commission (2010). *Payment Protection Insurance Market Investigation: Remittal of the Point-of-Sale Prohibition Remedy by the Competition Appeal Tribunal*, London.

Consumer Credit Act (2006). Chapter 14. The Stationery Office, London.

De Meza, D., Irlenbusch, B., and Reyniers, D. (2007). 'Information versus Persuasion: Experimental Evidence on Salesmanship: Mandatory Disclosure and the Purchase of Income and Loan Payment Protection Insurance', *Working Paper*, Financial Services Authority, London.

Department for Business, Enterprise and Regulatory Reform (BERR) (2007). *Tackling Over-Indebtedness. Annual Report*, London.

Department for Environment, Transport and the Regions (2000). *Quality and Choice: A Decent Home for All. The Green Paper*, HMSO, London.

Department of Trade and Industry (DTI) (2003). *Fair, Clear and Competitive. The Consumer Credit Market in the 21st Century*, CM 6040, The Stationery Office, London.

Diaz-Serrano, L. (2005). 'Income Volatility and Residential Mortgage Delinquency across the EU', *Journal of Housing Economics*, vol. 14, pp. 153–177.

Durkin, T. A. (2002). 'Consumers and Credit Disclosures: Credit Cards and Credit Insurance', *Federal Reserve Bulletin*, April pp. 201–213.

European Commission (2005). Mortgage Credit in the EU. Green Paper, 327, Brussels.

Federal Reserve Board (2007). 94th Annual Report, Federal Reserve Board, Washington.
Federal Trade Commission (2001). *Prepared Statement of the Federal Trade Commission before the California State Assembly Committee on Banking and Finance on Predatory Lending Practices in the Home-Equity Lending Market.* Federal Trade Commission, Washington.
Financial Services Authority (2000). 'Informing Consumers: A Review of Product Information at the Point of Sale', DP4, *The Financial Services Authority Discussion Papers*, The Financial Services Authority, London.
Financial Services Authority (2005). *The Sale of Payment Protection Insurance – Results of Thematic Work*, November, London
Financial Services Authority (2006). *Financial Capability in the UK: Establishing a Baseline.* The Financial Services Authority London.
Financial Services Authority (2007a). *The Sale of Payment Protection Insurance. Thematic Update*, September, London.
Financial Services Authority (2007b). 'The Sale of Payment Protection Insurance – Phase III Mystery Shopping Results' *Consumer Research* 61, September, London.
Financial Services Authority (2007c). 'Insurance Selling and Administration. Feedback on CP07 and Final Rules', *Policy Statement* 07/24, December, London.
Financial Services Authority (2008). 'Consumer Responsibility', *Discussion Paper*, 08/5, London.
Financial Services Authority (2010). *The Assessment and Redress of Payment Protection Insurance Complaints,* Consultation Paper 10/6, London.
Financial Services Authority (2011). *Product Intervention,* DP 11/1, London.
Ford, J. and England, J. (2000). *Data and Literature on Mortgage Interest: State Provision and Private Insurance*, Department for Social Security, In-House Report 65, ref. 962–8557.
Ford, J. and Quilgars, D. (2000). *Financial Intermediaries and Mortgage Payment Protection Insurance*, Joseph Rowntree Foundation, York.
Ford, J. and Quilgars, D. (2001). 'Failing Home Owners? The Effectiveness of Public and Private Safety-nets', *Housing Studies*, vol. 16, no. 2, pp. 147–162.
Ford, J., Quilgars, D., Burrows, R. and Rhoades, D. (2004). *Home Owners Risk and Safety-Nets. Mortgage Payment Protection Insurance (MPPI) and Beyond*, Office of the Deputy Prime Minister, London.
Grey, J. (2011). 'Legality of Payment Protection Insurance Compensation Arrangements Examined on Judicial Review', *Journal of Financial Regulation and Compliance*, vol. 19, pp. 396–406.
Lacko, J. M. and Pappalardo, J. K. (2007). 'Improving Consumer Mortgage Disclosures: An Empirical Assessment of Current and Prototype Disclosure Forms', *Department of Economics Staff Report*, Federal Trade Commission.
Miles, D. (2005). 'Incentives Information and Efficiency in the UK Mortgage Market', *The Economic Journal*, vol. 115, pp. C82–98.
Office of Fair Trading (OFT) (2006). 'Payment Protection Insurance', October, OFT 869, London.
Polden, D. J. (1983). 'The Antitrust Implications of Credit Insurance Tying Arrangements', *Drake Law Review*, vol. 32, pp. 861–912.

Pryce, G. and Keoghan, M. (2002). Theory and Estimation of the Mortgage Payment Protection Insurance Decision', *Scottish Journal of Political Economy*, vol. 49, no. 2, pp. 216–234.
Ross, S. L. and Tootell, G. M. B. (2004). 'Redlining, and the Community Reinvestment Act, and Private Mortgage Insurance', *Journal of Urban Economics*, vol. 55, pp. 278–297.
Scanlon, K., Lunde, J. and Whitehead, C. M. E. (2008). 'Mortgage Product Innovation in Advanced Economies: More Choice, More Risk', *European Journal of Housing Policy*, vol. 8, no. 2, pp. 109–131.
Spahr, R. W. and Escolas, E. L. (1986). 'Mortgage Guaranty Insurance: A Unique Style of Insurance', *Journal of Risk and Insurance*, vol. 53, no. 2 pp. 308–319.
Stephens, M. and Quilgars, D. (2008). 'Sub-prime Mortgage Lending in the UK', *European Journal of Housing Policy*, vol. 8, no. 2, pp. 197–215.

2
The Relationship between Mortgage Credit and Property Prices: The Chinese Case

Santiago Carbó-Valverde, Francisco Rodríguez-Fernández and Ming Qi

2.1 Introduction

Over the past decade, both the mortgage market and real estate sector have experienced a dramatic growth. The current financial crisis, which started in 2008 and significantly affecting the whole banking industry, has been attributed largely to the excessive growth of the mortgage and property markets. It started with the US subprime mortgage meltdown, but other countries (principally Ireland and Spain) experienced similar problems. The rapid growth of real estate prices and mortgage loans was extensively documented across many countries. (Wolswijk, 2006; Miles and Pillonca, 2008). In an international context, bank lending and property prices have a strong correlation . This stylized fact is supported by abundant cross-country evidence (Égert and Mihaljek, 2007; Lacoviello and Minetti, 2008; Goodhart and Hofmann, 2008; Davis and Zhu, 2010), as well as the indications from individual countries such as the USA (Capozza et al., 2002), Spain (Gimeno and Martinez-Carrascal, 2006; Carbó-Valverde and Francisco Rodriguez, 2010) and Ireland (Fitzpatrick and McQuinn, 2007). China has also witnessed rapid growth in the real estate industry. The percentage of real estate investment to GDP rose sharply, from 5 per cent in 1999 to 12 per cent in 2010 (see Figure 2.1). Meanwhile we also document the soaring property prices and the mortgage credit boom in the domestic market. At the same time, China experienced a substantial reform in both the banking and the mortgage financing systems. In this chapter, we investigate the relationship between the evolution of mortgage loans and house prices in China.[1] In addition, we test to what extent sociodemographic characteristics and monetary policies can affect the mortgage and property market.

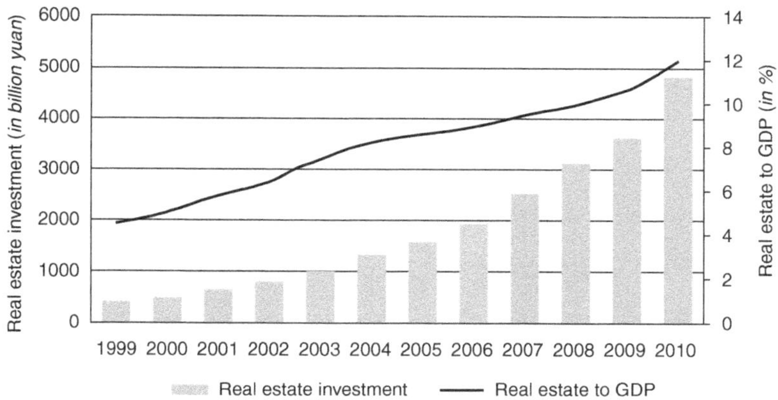

Figure 2.1 The development of real estate investment in China
Source: National Bureau of Statistics of China.

2.2 The development of China's housing finance system

The development of the Chinese commercial mortgage market began to accelerate in 1998, when the People's Bank of China authorized all the domestic commercial banks to grant household mortgage loans. From then on, the Chinese government embarked upon an effort to introduce into the property financing system a number of market-oriented mechanisms such as financial leverage through banks. These measures have promoted and contributed to housing reform in mainland China. On the other hand, commercial banks also recognize residential mortgage credit as healthy assets in their loan portfolio, given the lower default rate of household mortgage loans compared to that of state-owned entrepreneurs (Deng and Fei, 2008). Figure 2.2 illustrates the change in mortgage loans and the proportion of mortgages in household loans and new annual loans. By the end of 2010, the outstanding mortgage loans had soared from (Chinese yuan) ¥51bn in 1999 to ¥6060bn. Mortgage loans account for 80 per cent of total household loans (see Figure 2.2).

Unlike the US market, which is characterized by diversified financing channels, the mortgage market in China is dominated by banks. The total mortgage credit of commercial banks covers more than 80 per cent of the total mortgages outstanding. In addition, banks under different ownership contribute different proportions of the total mortgage lending. We find that most of mortgage loans are issued by state-owned banks (SOBs), which play a dominant role in the Chinese banking industry.

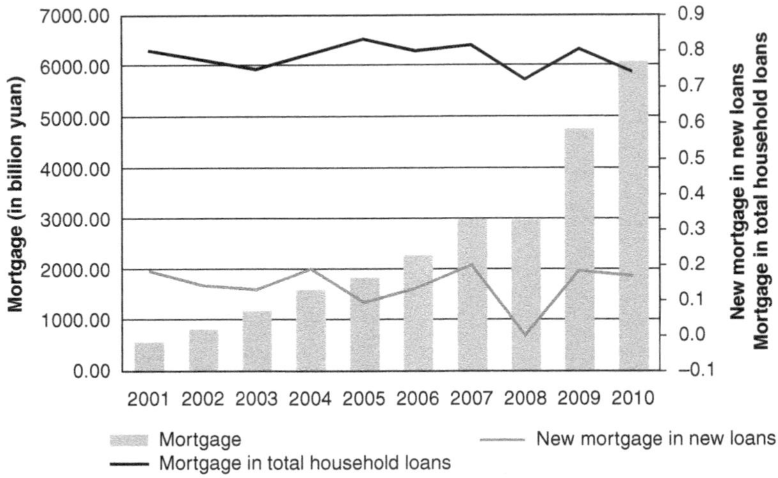

Figure 2.2 The movements of mortgage loans in China
Source: People's Bank of China.

But their market share has been gradually eroded by other bank groups. In 2004, over 96 per cent of total mortgage loans were issued by SOBs; however, in 2009 their market share had decreased to 74 per cent. Joint stock banks (JSBs) keep expanding their mortgage origination, and also make up a significant part of the total credits; they expanded their mortgage business, raising their market share from 3 per cent in 2004 to over 22 per cent in 2009. The market share of city commercial banks (CCBs) became relevant after 2005 (see Figure 2.3). They issued almost no mortgage loans in 2004, but accounted for over 3 per cent of total mortgage market in 2009.

Two characteristics of the Chinese mortgage market are critical to the understanding of it. First, the People's Bank of China, the central bank, sets a uniform mortgage rate by for all banks that provide mortgage loans.[2] This rate is adjustable, and once a new mortgage rate is announced it applies to all types of mortgage loans, including existing ones. Excluding commercial mortgage loans from financial institutions, an alternative method is the Housing Provident Fund (HPF), which provides the participants with a lower interest rate than that of the commercial mortgage rate from banks.[3] Second, the Chinese mortgage market is not mature, since it has a very limited secondary market. At the time of writing, only two mortgage-backed securities (MBS) have been issued in China.[4]

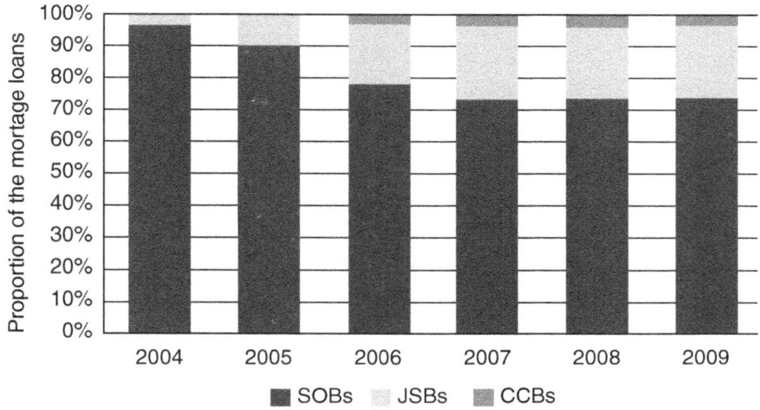

Figure 2.3 The decomposition of mortgage loans by different bank ownership
Source: Compiled by authors, data from the annual report of banks.

2.3 Factors explaining the mortgage and property price movements

We aim to investigate the relation between bank mortgage loans and property prices. In addition, we test the actual effects of monetary policies and sociodemographic change. Theoretical research into the mortgage and property markets suggests that if we maximize the borrower's utility under the constraint of disposable income, mortgage demand increases with house price and borrower's income, and decreases with intention to purchase a house purchase and the interest rate. In addition, inflation has a positive impact on the demand for mortgages. On the other hand, the bank allocates a proportion of its total deposits on mortgage loans and thus maximizes its profits. The optimal mortgage supply provided by the bank increases with its net interest margin (NIM), the number of mortgage banks and house prices, but decreases with its loan-to-deposit ratio.

In our analysis we include several impact factors. The growth in the prices of four different types of house is employed in our framework. They are: condominium price, which is the average real estate price and an indicator of the property market as a whole; residential price, that is the indicator of solo residential market; high-grade house price, a measure of luxury and high-end real estate; and economical house price, which is the value of affordable houses. Figure 2.4 illustrates the movements of property prices in four separate real estate markets. During the

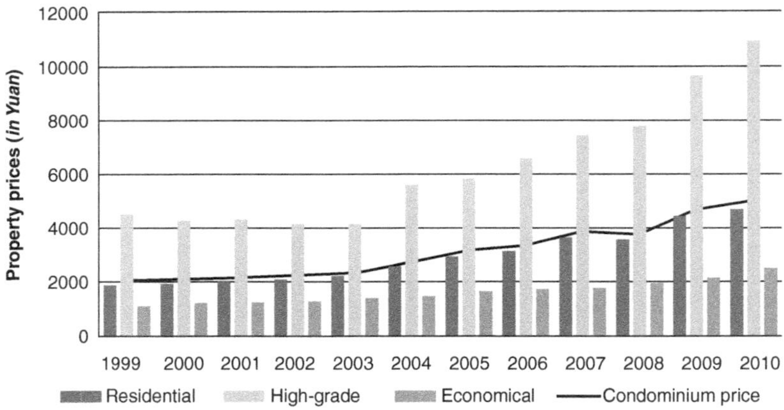

Figure 2.4 The movements of property prices
Source: National Bureau of Statistics of China.

sample period, property prices increased with the volume of outstanding mortgage loans during the period 1999 to 2010, except for 2008, when the effects of the financial crisis hit China. In addition, the condominium and residential prices illustrate a similar movement during this period; this is because after the housing reform in 1998 work units were no longer allowed to provide welfare houses to employees. As a result, the fully market-oriented residential houses contributed to the majority of condominium supply in the property market, so the movement of their prices follows a similar pattern. The prices of high-grade and economic houses move in the same direction as condominium prices, but in either a more volatile or smoother way. We assume both house prices and mortgage loans are endogenous variables and we employ a simplified version of the inverted demand model to estimate the house prices.[5]

Urbanization is an important indicator of sociodemographic change and another impact factor on both property and mortgage markets. Over the past decade, China has experienced a dramatic process of industrialization and urbanization. More and more internal immigrants moved into cities and settled down. The percentage of China's urban population rose from 34.78 per cent to 49.95 per cent between 1999 and 2010 (see Figure 2.5). It implies that more than 15 per cent of the total population moved into the cities in 10 years. It is expected that if the population grows, this will push up the demand for local housing and hence the property prices. Taking into account the higher number of potential home buyers, a higher volume of mortgage loans can be expected. We use

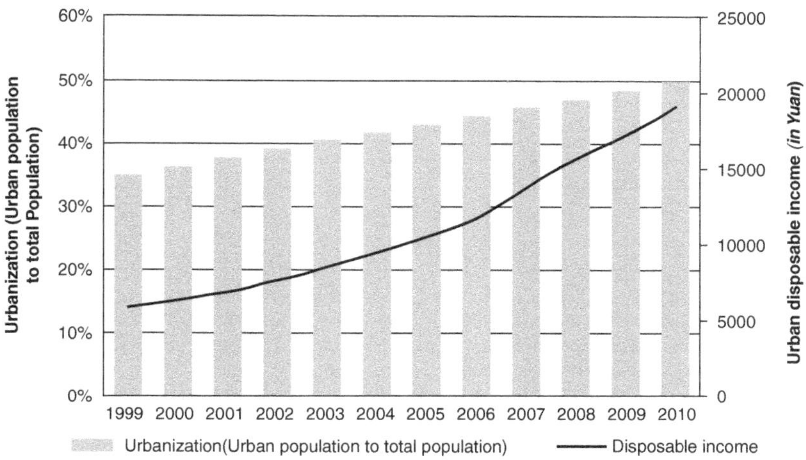

Figure 2.5 The process of urbanization and the rise of dispensable income
Source: National Bureau of Statistics of China.

the percentage of urban population against total population to capture the effect of sociodemographic change.

Urban disposable income was another important factor influencing the movement of property prices. With the rapid economic growth in mainland China, the per capita disposable income of residents also increased substantially – from ¥5,854 in 1999 to ¥19,019 in 2010 (see Figure 2.5). We employ the national average deposable income for SOBs and JSBs, given their nationwide business line, and local average disposable income for CCBs, taking into account their local market focus.

The expected rate of house price appreciation reflects the intention of consumers to purchase a house; the price index of real estate sales rose more quickly than the rent and leasing price index, reaching a peak in 2004, from which year the value of the price/rent index remained higher than 1.04 (see Figure 2.6). This reflects the strong and inflexible demand for house occupation in China. We use the ratio of house price index to rental price index to proxy the house price appreciation. In addition, consumer price index (CPI) is also included, as a measure of the inflation rate. An increased CPI implies higher living expenditure, which undermines the individual's intention to undertake the risk of a mortgage loan.

The interest rate, as an indicator of monetary policy, is a widely accepted explanatory variable for the analysis of the house financing

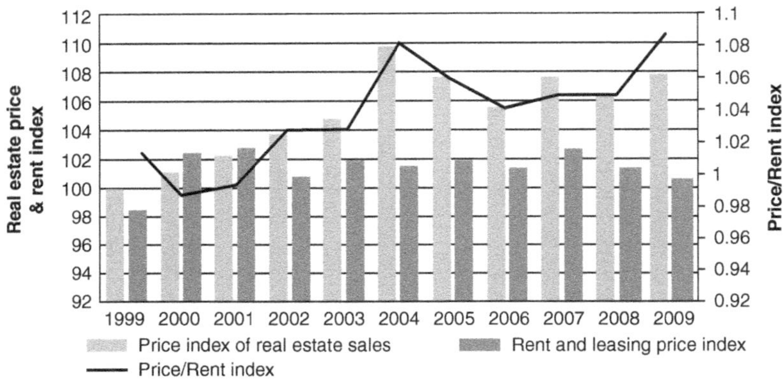

Figure 2.6 The price index and rent index of the real estate market
Source: National Bureau of Statistics of China.

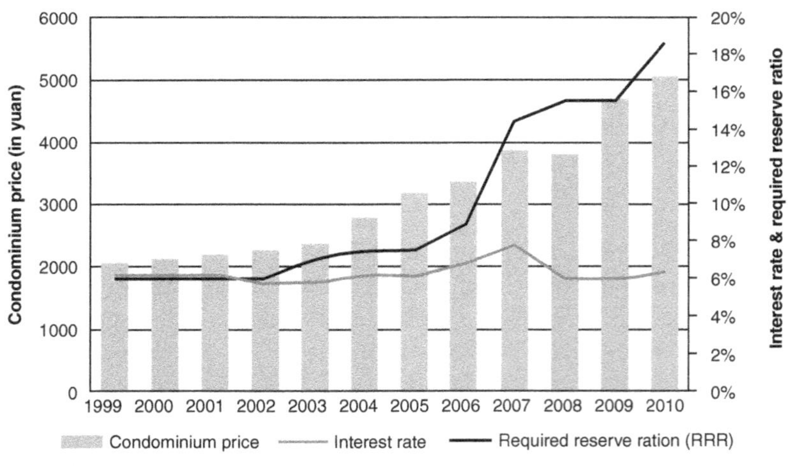

Figure 2.7 The movement of condominium price, interest rate and RRR
Source: National Bureau of Statistics of China and People's Bank of China.

system. A rising interest rate environment will curb the credit expansion and the demand for mortgage loans. Between 1999 and 2005 the interest rate changed very little. Then, after rapid growth till 2007, it began to decrease because of the financial crisis (see Figure 2.7). In 2007, the five-year interest rate rose from 6.84 per cent to 7.83 per cent to restrain the growing credit demand. However in 2008 there was a sharp drop in interest rates to 5.94 per cent in order to overcome the impact of the financial crisis (see Appendix). By including the interest rate, we investigate to what extent it can affect the mortgage credit boom and property prices.[6]

The required reserves ratio limits banks' lending to a certain proportion of their demand deposits. A high deposit reserve ratio contributes to the restraint of excessive money supply and overheated investment. Over the past decade, with the soaring property prices and mortgage credit boom, the central bank has raised the required reserve ratio (RRR) several times, from 6 per cent in 1999 to 20 per cent in 2011 (see Figure 2.7); in China, this is viewed as another frequently used instrument of monetary policy, as well as the interest rate. But in 2007 the RRR was raised 10 times, from 9.5 per cent to 14.5 per cent. Then, with the defusing of the financial crisis, the central bank cut down the RRR four times in the first quarter of 2008 to stimulate domestic economic growth (see Appendix). We explore whether the change of banks' reserve ratio has had a significant impact on the movements of properties and mortgage credit. Then we compare the real effects of the interest rate and the RRR.

The bank-specific factors also play a significant role in mortgage lending. The loan-to-asset ratio is a measure to indicate the balance sheet risk of individual banks. Since banks can not grant credit at all prices, they need to conduct a credit audit and to monitor effectively in order to maintain low levels of non-performing loans and increase margins (Abreu and Mendes, 2002). In spite of a positive relationship between loan-to-deposit ratio and bank profitability, a high loan ratio is a warning sign of a bank's credit risk, hence should be a discouragement to credit expansion. The NIM is referred to as the net yield on interest-earning assets and hence an indicator of the profitability of a bank's lending activities. In addition, the NIM is also a proxy of bank performance and profitability for the Chinese banking sector (Matthews, 2009). We would like to test the attitude of individual banks towards mortgage profits.

2.4 Data description

Compared with those of developed countries, the Chinese mortgage market has a relatively short history, and therefore limited data is available. In our analysis an unbalanced panel of annual mortgage loans of commercial banks is employed. Our sample consists of all SOBs, JSBs and major CCBs. The variables included in the empirical framework are described in groups as follows: the house prices, disposable income, urban and total population, inflation rate and appreciation indices were collected from the National Bureau of Statistics of China. Mortgage loans and bank-specific variables were collected from the Bureau van Dijk's BankScope database, as were the annual reports of individual banks. Taking into account the endogeneity of mortgage and house prices, a simultaneous equation system is employed to estimate mortgage loans and endogenous house prices. A panel data approach and two-stage least squares/instrument variable method are appropriate for our estimation.

2.5 Evidence of China's mortgage and property market

Our findings suggest that the mortgage credit and house prices are closely associated with each other. An increased property price has positive impacts on the mortgage credit boom. In addition, we find the elasticity of condominium (and residential) price to mortgage loans is much higher than that of other countries,[7] reflecting a higher dependence of the property market on mortgage loans in China. However, the rising price of economical houses exerts a negative influence on the mortgage market; the reason being that the market for economical houses consists mainly medium- and low-income households and internal migrants.[8] Increased prices will weaken the resolve of some potential buyers, and naturally lower prices are favoured by more potential buyers, most of whom need to rely on mortgages to finance their purchase.

In addition, neither the NIM nor the loan-to-deposit ratio affects the banks' mortgage loans. It implies that the lending behaviour of Chinese commercial banks is more demand-oriented than risk- or profit-adjusted. On the other hand, a higher volume of mortgage issuance accelerates soaring property prices. It implies a procyclical behaviour of credit boom and indeed of condominium prices in general. However, the prices of economical houses illustrate a negative response to mortgage credit. This is because the prices of economical houses in China, also referred to as capped-price houses, are more a response to administrative interference than fully market-driven. The movements of these two special property markets does not match the boom in mortgage credit.

In terms of monetary policies, we find that the rising interest rate has little effect on controlling the credit boom in China, whereas a negative correlation between banks' mortgage loans and required reserves is observed in general. On the other hand, interest rates move counter to condominium prices. Then we argue that the RRR is a relatively effective instrument in controlling the mortgage credit boom; and the interest rate plays an active role in restraining house prices. Meanwhile, the impact of urbanization is also appreciable, reflected in the stronger correlation between urban population and mortgage loans than between other variables in our analysis. Another interesting feature is that the change of urban population has a more significant impact on the economical houses. Since the purchasing power of new migrants is not as strong as city natives, the economical housing market is more sensitive to the sociodemographic change.

2.6 Conclusion

We use bank-level data to gain insight into the factors determining the growth of mortgage credit and house prices. We find evidence of a significant and positive relationship between house prices and mortgage loans. Rising property prices stimulate the demand of mortgage loans. In addition, credit expansion also contributes to soaring property prices. We document a positive impact of urbanization effect on the growth of mortgage lending. In terms of monetary policy, the RRR is more effective in controlling the mortgage credit boom; and the interest rate plays an active role in controlling house prices. Our findings have important policy implications and account for the existing monetary policies which are being implemented. With the explosively growing mortgage market in China, there is still room for improvement in the housing financial system. First, a diversified repayment pattern needs to be introduced to meet the demands from households with steady incomes or fluctuating ones. Second, it is necessary to establish a residential mortgage loan insurance and a mortgage-backed security (MBS) market.

Appendix

Chronological changes in interest rates

Time	Commercial loans	HPF loans
21-Feb-2002	5.76%	4.05%
29-Oct-2004	6.12%	4.23%
17-Mar-2005	6.12%	4.41%
28-Apr-2006	6.39%	4.59%
19-Aug-2006	6.84%	4.59%
18-Mar-2007	7.11%	4.77%
19-May-2007	7.20%	4.86%
21-Jul-2007	7.38%	4.95%
22-Aug-2007	7.56%	5.04%
15-Sep-2007	7.83%	5.22%
21-Dec-2007	7.83%	5.22%
16-Sep-2008	7.74%	5.13%
9-Oct-2008	7.47%	4.86%
27-Oct-2008	7.47%	4.59%
30-Oct-2008	7.20%	4.59%
27-Nov-2008	6.12%	4.05%
23-Dec-2008	5.94%	3.87%
20-Oct-2010	6.14%	4.05%
27-Dec-2010	6.40%	4.30%

Chronological changes of the RRR

Time	Required Reserve Ratio (RRR)	Change
21-Nov-1999	6.0%	−2
21-Sep-2003	7.0%	1
25-Apr-2004	7.5%	0.5
5-Jul-2006	8.0%	0.5
15-Aug-2006	8.5%	0.5
15-Nov-2006	9.0%	0.5
15-Jan-2007	9.5%	0.5
15-Feb-2007	10.0%	0.5
16-Apr-2007	10.5%	0.5
15-May-2007	11.0%	0.5
5-Jun-2007	11.5%	0.5
15-Aug-2007	12.0%	0.5
25-Sep-2007	12.5%	0.5
25-Oct-2007	13.0%	0.5
26-Nov-2007	13.5%	0.5
25-Dec-2007	14.5%	1
25-Jan-2008	15.0%	0.5
18-Mar-2008	15.5%	0.5
25-Apr-2008	16.0%	0.5
20-May-2008	16.5%	0.5
7-Jun-2008	17.5%	1
25-Sep-2008	Large 17.5%	–
	Small 16.5%	−1
15-Oct-2008	Large 17.0%	−0.5
	Small 16.0%	−0.5
5-Dec-2008	Large 16.0%	−1
	Small 14.0%	−2
25-Dec-2008	Large 15.5%	−0.5
	Small 13.5%	−0.5
18-Jan-2010	Large 16.0%	0.5
	Small 13.5%	–
25-Feb-2010	Large 16.5%	0.5
	Small 13.5%	–
2-May-2010	Large 17.0%	0.5
	Small 13.5%	–
10-Nov-2010	Large 17.5%	0.5
	Small 14.0%	0.5

Note: 'Large' is referred to large (or systemically significant) financial institutions, e.g. SOBs. 'Small' is referred to small-sized financial institutions, e.g. JSBs, CCBs and credit cooperatives.

Notes

1. Liang and Cao (2007) investigate the case of China and suggest a unidirectional causality from bank lending to property prices. In contrast to their previous work, we employ bank-level mortgage data, rather than bank lending, to study the relationship between the mortgage credit and property prices.
2. Since 2005, commercial banks have been authorized to set individual rates, which, however, cannot be lower than 90 per cent of the benchmark rate set by The People's Bank of China.
3. Most house purchasers apply for both HPF and commercial mortgage loans due to the insufficiency of a single HPF loan.
4. According to the report proposed by The People's Bank of China, only the China Construction Bank (CCB) was authorized to issue MBS in the domestic inter-bank bond market, amounting to ¥3.018 billion and ¥4.16 billion in 2005 and 2007 respectively.
5. The inverted demand model, proposed by Muellbauer and Murphy (1997), is more appropriate for those countries in which the housing supplies rocket.
6. We employ the individual bank's interest rate, which is calculated as the ratio of total interest revenue over the interest-bearing assets of individual banks.
7. In our analysis the impact of house price on mortgage credit is 1.7 (for condominium price), and this elasticity is 0.5 for Ireland, 0.62 for Spain and 0.75 for the European area (Fitzpatrick and McQuinn, 2007; Carbó-Valverde and Francisco Rodriguez, 2010; Annett, 2005).
8. During the sample period, the internal immigrants were eligible to purchase properties without any restrictions. From the last quarter of 2010, with the introduction of a property purchasing limitation policy, the demand of houses from internal immigrants has fallen sharply.

References

M. Abreu and V. Mendes (2002) Commercial bank interest margins and profitability: Evidence from EU countries, *Porto Working Paper Series.*

A. Annett (2005) House prices and monetary policy in the euro area. Chapter III in Euro area policies: selected issues. *IMF Country Report*, No. 05/266.

D. Capozza, P. Hendershott, C. Mack and C. Mayer (2002) Determinants of real house price dynamics. *NBER Working Paper*, No. W9262.

S. Carbó-Valverde and F. Francisco Rodriguez (2010) The relationship between mortgage markets and house prices: Does financial instability make the difference? *CenFIS Working Paper*, No. 10–02.

E.P. Davis and H. Zhu (2010) Bank lending and commercial property cycles: Some cross-country evidence. *Journal of International Money and Finance*, 30: 1–21.

Y. Deng and P. Fei (2008) The emerging mortgage markets in China. In D. Ben-Shaher, C.K.Y. Leung and S.E. Ong (eds), *Mortgage Market Worldwide*. Blackwell Publishing Ltd.: Oxford, UK, pp. 1–33.

B. Égert and D. Mihaljek (2007) Determinants of house prices in central and eastern Europe. *Comparative Economic Studies*, 49: 367–88.

T. Fitzpatrick and K. McQuinn (2007) House prices and mortgage credit: Empirical evidence for Ireland. *Manchester School*, 75 (1): 82–103.

R. Gimeno and C. Martinez-Carrascal (2006) The interaction between house prices and loans for house purchase: The Spanish case. *Banco de Espana Research Paper*, No. WP-0605.
C. Goodhart and B. Hofmann (2008) House prices, money, credit, and the macroeconomy. *Oxford Review of Economic Policy*, 24: 180–205.
M. Lacoviello and R. Minetti (2008) The credit channel of monetary policy: Evidence from the housing market. *Journal of Macroeconomics*, 30: 69–96.
Q. Liang and H. Cao (2007) Property prices and bank lending in China. *Journal of Asian Economics*, 18 (1): 63–75.
K. Matthews (2009) Bank productivity in China 1997–2007: An exercise in measurement. *HKIMR Working Paper*, No. 25/2009.
D. Miles and V. Pillonca (2008) Financial innovation and European housing and mortgage markets. *Oxford Review of Economic Policy*, 24 (1): 145–75.
J. Muellbauer and A. Murphy (1997) Booms and busts in the UK housing market. *The Economic Journal*, 107: 1701–27.
G. Wolswijk (2006) Determinants of mortgage debt growth in EU countries. *European Journal of Housing Policy*, 6 (2): 131–49.

3

Bank Restructuring and Bank Stability in Latin America

Ngoc Vo and Jonathan Williams

3.1 Introduction

The objective of this chapter is to examine whether or not banking sector restructuring produces significant improvements in bank stability. Restructuring is targeted at distressed banks, and common resolution strategies include injecting liquidity and/or capital, sanitizing bank balance sheets, and consolidating troubled banks with healthier banks through a process of mergers and acquisitions (M&A). Restructuring is often accompanied by legal reforms to strengthen the competitive environment facing banks. Repeal of restrictions on foreign banks is one example. Withdrawing the influence of government in the banking sector through privatization is another. These reforms are expected to increase banking sector stability, because the performance of non-intervened banks should improve – otherwise market share can be lost to resolved incumbents and/or new foreign entrants. An assessment of the effectiveness of bank restructuring must evaluate the impact of legislative changes upon the banking sector per se as well as analysing the post-resolution performance of resolved banks.

We consider the bank restructuring processes adopted in the largest Latin American economies to resolve the regional banking crises of the mid-1990s. For this task, we construct a panel dataset of 379 commercial banks from Argentina, Brazil and Mexico over 1985 to 2010, giving a total of 4254 observations. Intervened banks are identified according to three resolution strategies: privatization, acquisition by foreign bank, and consolidated via M&A. We date each case of resolution to give periods before and after the change. The timing of legislative reforms is dated to enable us to identify the impact of reforms on banking sectors.

The chapter has two aims. First, we review the existing frameworks of bank resolution prior to crises, and identify the legislative changes that were deemed necessary to implement bank restructuring. This will include dating the privatization programmes and the repeals of restrictions on foreign banks. The second aim is to determine the effect of the different resolution strategies on bank stability. A difference-in-differences methodology is used because it identifies treatment groups: (1) privatized banks; (2) foreign-acquired banks; (3) consolidated banks via M&A – and a control group of non-resolved banks. The approach identifies if restructuring impacts bank stability in a significantly different way from the overall trend in bank stability.

The research design is expected to answer policy-relevant questions to provide a clean and easy test of public policy. First, and given the fiscal expenditure associated with resolution, policymakers are interested to know if their actions realize improvement in bank stability once the policy is enacted; different policies may produce different outcomes. We investigate if there is a dominant resolution policy amongst the three under investigation. We consider the possibility that the impact of resolution may exhibit intertemporal differences, and divide the post-resolution period into three sub-periods: an immediate post-crisis period, when the effects of resolution may not be observable (1996–2001); a second period of economic stability, when we expect potential benefits to arise (2002–2006); and a third period, coinciding with the transmission of the global banking crisis to the region (2007–2010). For each sub-period we can identify the impact of each of the three resolution strategies on bank stability and determine whether or not the outcome exceeds the overall trend in stability.

The remainder of the chapter is structured as follows. Section 2 discusses bank restructuring, and includes a detailed section on resolution programmes by country. In Section 3 we present the difference-in-differences methodology. whilst Section 4 presents the data and variables. The empirical results are shown in Section 5 by country and Section 6 offers some conclusions.

3.2 Bank restructuring in Latin America

This section begins with a brief synopsis of developments in Latin American banking, to place the mid-1990s restructuring within an historical context. Carvalho et al. (2010) explain that the process of change was essentially the same across the various countries of Latin America and took place in similar time periods. In general, countries across the region had financially repressed banking sectors as governments sought to engineer economic growth through control of the banking sector. This established a precedent for state involvement in banking that ended only in the 1990s, when the fiscal cost of maintaining public ownership of banks became too onerous. Until then, directed lending had been imposed on even privately owned banks to finance sectors of purported strategic interest. Latin America was hit hard by the oil shocks of the 1970s and then national governments increased reliance on short-term foreign debt, culminating in the 1980s debt crisis. The liberal reforms of the 1990s are due in part to the clauses contained in the resolution packages negotiated with international creditors and multilateral agencies. Common features of these reforms were the liberalization of interest rates, the elimination of entry barriers to the provision of banking services, large-scale privatization of state-owned banks and the facilitation of entry for foreign banks (see Singh et al., 2005; Carvalho et al., 2009).

3.2.1 Resolution programmes

In the mid-1990s, the tools for resolving banking crises were very limited and were in the case of one country described as 'bare bones' (De la Torre, 2000). Governments had to legislate and amend existing laws before the resolution process could begin. This section reviews the mechanisms for resolution on a country-by-country basis and at the same time highlights the important legal reforms that facilitated privatization, foreign bank entry, and consolidation through M&A. In summary, restructuring and privatization ushered in a new wave of cross-border (and domestic) M&A activity. Cross-border bank M&A partially reflect country-specific factors positively related to shared language (Spanish bank entry, Sebastián and Hernansanz, 2000) and geographical proximity (North American bank entry; Buch and DeLong, 2001), and the availability of access to large, relatively poor countries with widely-spaced populations and underdeveloped financial sectors (Buch and DeLong, 2001; Focarelli and Pozzolo, 2001).

Argentina

In 1991, the Convertibility Plan adopted a more radical liberalization strategy, including opening the domestic banking market to competition from foreign banks. Foreign penetration of the Argentinean banking system increased dramatically as it was promoted by a restructuring and concentration policy which had been implemented after the contagion of Mexico's Tequila crisis.

The central bank was charged with managing bank resolution, but the lack of a coherent resolution policy required legal reforms before the central bank could begin its task. The reforms were enacted in 1995; the Financial Institutions Law No. 21526 (Article 35) was amended to enable the central bank to implement the good bank/bad bank model that transfers assets and liabilities between distressed and healthy banks. Article 44 of the law permits the closure of non-viable banks. Law 24485 established a Deposit Guarantee Scheme (*Sistema de Seguro de Garantía de los Depósitos Bancarios*) comprising a Deposit Guarantee Fund (*Fondo de Garantía de Depósitos*), which is managed by the deposit insurance agency (*Seguro de Depósitos Sociedad Anónima, SEDESA*). The objective of the scheme was to protect depositors and to halt bank runs;. under its terms, depositors were insured for US$30,000, to be paid out in cash in the event of bank failure. A third pillar of the resolution process was the Bank Capitalization Trust Fund (*Fondo Fiduciario de Capitalización Bancaria*) that was introduced in 1995 by Decree 445/95. Finances for this fund were raised via a bond issue (*Bono Argentina 1998*) and from loans made by multilateral agencies under the 1995 Argentina Bank Reform Law. The trust fund could inject capital into distressed banks, either directly, by making loans convertible into equity, or indirectly, by buying the illiquid assets of troubled banks. The fund was used to facilitate banking sector consolidation in a process that included M&A and capitalization. In cases where the distressed bank was deemed non-viable, the trust fund was used to construct a good bank under Article 35 (De la Torre, 2000).

In the 1980s, each Argentine province owned a public bank that in many cases dominated the local banking sector. Provincial-owned banks held between 40 and 70 per cent of banking sector assets in each province. In November 1991 the province of Corrientes passed a law to enable privatization of its provincial bank. Then in 1995, the Tequila crisis had spread to Argentina, by which time six provinces had authorized bank privatization (Clarke and Cull, 2000). Publicly owned banks had tended to serve political and social purposes, and their loan quality, cost control, and overall performance were weak; in fact, privatization was deemed a cheaper option than restructuring and recapitalization (Carvalho et al., 2009). In Argentina, as in Mexico, the privatization process was flawed – the sale of the provincial banks contained conditions that restricted the operational management of the new, private owners. For instance, in some provinces, clauses forbade the firing of staff and the closure of bank branches; in other cases, lengthy service contracts with the public sector sweetened deals (Clarke and Cull, 2000). Between

1993 and 1999, the number of provincial banks fell from 25 to 10, and their asset share decreased from 21.6 to 13 per cent (Clarke et al., 2005). In summary, the resolution measures were used to resolve 18 bank failures between mid-1995 and the first half of 1999. In 12 cases, the resources of the deposit insurance agency were used to construct good banks, and the Capitalization Trust Fund provided resources in more than 10 cases.

Brazil

A new stabilization plan called the Real Plan was introduced in July 1994, and its success in controlling inflation is well documented. The loss of inflationary revenues from index-linked public securities threatened bank profitability and the stability of the banking sector. Estimates had put average inflationary gains to banks at around 2 per cent of GDP per annum since the 1940s (Mendonça de Barros and Almeida, 1997); but then, as the share of float income in GDP grew to 4 per cent in 1991 and 1992, inflationary revenues to total revenues exceeded 40 per cent (Baer and Nazmi, 2000). Policymakers expected banks to make good the loss of float income by diversifying into other lines of business including increasing the amount of credit. The success of the Real Plan fuelled the demand for credit, and bank lending increased by around 44 per cent over the first eight months of the Plan. Whilst the loss of float income was offset partially by revenues from increased lending, banks became more vulnerable as new first-time customers entered financial markets, making the assessment of credit risk more difficult. In the second half of 1995 the ratio of non-performing loans to total loans increased to approximately 17 per cent (Baer and Nazmi, 2000), setting the scene for the 1995 banking crisis.

Though dealing with troubled banks did not pose a new problem for the central bank, the legal framework needed amending before it could administer distressed banks. Law 6024/74 enabled the liquidation of insolvent non-federal financial institutions, and it was the legal instrument used to liquidate both private and publicly owned banks. In 1985, Decree-Law 1342 gave legal responsibility to the central bank to intervene in distressed institutions. In February 1987, and due to distress at publicly owned banks, Decree-Law 2321 established a Special Temporary Administration Regime (RAET) that allowed the central bank to take over and administer distressed financial institutions, and also to transform, expropriate and/or liquidate institutions under intervention. In 1995, the central bank had four means to deal with distressed banks: liquidation; recapitalization; M&A; and restructuring the bank before privatizing it. By mid-1995, 21 banks had been placed under RAET: the central bank took action in 48 banks, and liquidated 31 banks between 1994 and 1998 (Baer and Nazmi, 2000).

In November 1995, Resolution 2208/95 introduced an extensive restructuring programme to facilitate M&A amongst privately owned banks, called the Program of Incentives for the Restructuring and Strengthening of the National Financial System (PROER – Programa de Estímulo à Reestruturação e ao Fortalecimento do Sistema Financeiro Nacional). Distressed institutions participating in PROER could access different types of support: lines of credit to ease liquidity problems; deferral of bank restructuring costs for up to five years; and reception of temporary exemption from the Basel capital requirements. M&A were sweetened by tax subsidies. Resolution 2211/95 established Brazil's deposit insurance scheme (FGC – Fundo Garantidor de Créditos). The scheme protects small depositors (up to R$20,000), and all financial institutions except credit unions are compulsory members, contributing 0.025 per cent of deposits monthly to the fund. Whereas PROER targeted privately owned banks, more acute difficulties existed in the public banks. Before the 1995 crisis, each state in the Federation had owned a bank.

The problems of public ownership are more apparent when we note that public banks were the main supplier of bank loans (57 per cent of banking sector assets in 1993 as against 41 per cent for privately owned banks). The problems were especially apparent when governments received the bulk of those loans (Ness, 2000). Administrative inefficiencies, and what Ness (2000) terms a conflict between the government's economic and political goals and banks' business goals, had pushed the public bank sector close to insolvency by the late 1980s/early 1990s. Public banks relied more on float income than did private banks: in 1994, bank revenue-to-GDP equaled 4 per cent, with public banks appropriating 63 per cent of this revenue (Makler, 2000). Compared to private banks, public banks had failed to keep abreast of technological advances due to high staff costs and over-lending. Finally, political ties, a soft-budget constraint, and the relative size of public banks had combined to confer a too-big-to-fail status, illustrated by the frequent financial support given to states by the central bank to support ailing public banks.

The challenge of restoring credibility after the 1987 default on foreign loans prompted a major privatization program. Resolution 155 of March 1990 established the legal base for the National Privatization Program (PND – Programa Nacional de Desestatização). Privatization played an increasing role between 1995 and 2003. In 1995, the National Council for Privatization (CND – Conselho Nacional de Desestatização) was created, with direct accountability to the President.

Reforms of the public banking sector took place in two phases. First, interventions of distressed public banks through RAET occurred at the end of 1994 and in early 1995. Second, provisional measure 1514 and Resolution 2365/97 of 28 February 1997 established a program similar to to PROER but for public banks. This was PROES (Programa de Incentivo á Redução do Setor Público Estadual na Atividade Bancária – PROES, Program of Incentives to the Reduction of the State Banking Sector in Banking Activities); its objective was to reduce the role of the states in the banking system. Although the scheme was not compulsory, the availability of federal government funds to restructure public banks acted as an incentive to banks to participate in it. A state participating in PROES had four options: to privatize the public bank; liquidation; transform the public bank into a non-banking financial institution or development bank; or restructure and recapitalize the public bank under new management (Maia, 1999; Baer and Nazmi, 2000; Beck et al., 2005). The number of public banks fell from 35 to 10 between 1996 and 2003.

Bank Reform Law 4595/64 had stipulated that foreign bank entry must be authorized by the central bank or congressional decree (Puga, 1999). This limited foreign banks to owning minority stakes in investment banks and leasing companies in the 1960s, 1970s and 1980s (Paula, 2003), although it did not prevent establishment of representative offices (Puga, 1999). Despite explicit entry rules, foreign bank penetration did in fact increase, because the central bank operated a process of bilateral agreements which allowed entry according to a reciprocity principle at a time when Brazilian banks were expanding into foreign markets (Puga, 1999). The 1988 Constitution introduced a transitory rule explicitly prohibiting the expansion of foreign banks. However, a clause prevented the rule from applying to authorizations resulting from international agreements, reciprocity, or decisions made in the interests of the Brazilian government. Hence, foreign bank entry was made on a case-by-case basis (Fachada, 2008).

In August 1995 as the banking crisis intensified, Legislative Intent 311 deemed increasing foreign bank entry or participation to be in the interests of the country. Several factors influenced this policy: a shortage of domestic capital; perceived higher operating efficiencies and financial capacity of foreign banks; expectations of competition driving down costs and prices in banking, and a desire to bring foreign bank technologies to the domestic market. Legal amendments in November 1995,

Resolution 2212/95, eradicated the requirement that the minimum capital of a foreign bank must be double that of a domestic bank (Puga, 1999). These changes stimulated the privatization program.

Mexico

The Mexican default on its external obligations in August 1982 set in motion a process beginning with the nationalization of banks, and culminating a decade later in the bank privatization programme of 1991 to 1992. Nationalization was taken ostensibly on the grounds that 'private banks had generated excessive profits from bank operations, created monopolistic markets through concentration, and facilitated massive capital flight' (Unal and Navarro, 1999, p. 63). Despite the rhetoric against bank management, the government dismissed only the boards of directors; most of the rest of the incumbent management remained (Gruben et al., 1994). In order to implement bank nationalization, Articles 28 and 123 of the Constitution were amended to prohibit private ownership of banks (Montes-Negret and Landa, 2001).

Liberalization measures began towards the end of the 1980s, setting the stage for the privatization of state-owned enterprises including the 18 state-owned banks. Privatization provided the government with the income necessary to achieve the much-needed reduction in government expenditure at a more politically manageable pace. Thus the government's principal objective was to maximize the price received for the privatized banks (Haber, 2005). Although banking was a profitable activity, large capital investment was needed to modernize the sector (Unal and Navarro, 1999). Before the commercial banks could be privatized, however, a new legal framework for private institutions had to be designed. A bill was submitted to Congress on 2 May 1990 requesting amendment to Articles 28 and 123, which led to the passage of two laws in July 1990: the Credit Institutions Law, which allowed the private ownership of banks and established the terms under which government regulates and supervises the banking sector; and the Financial Groups Law, facilitating the emergence of universal banking as the main organizational structure of the financial sector. Bank privatization commenced in June 1991 and ended in July 1992: the sale of 18 banks raised US$13.5bn (Barnes, 1992). Foreign investors were prevented from participating in the auctions selling off the privatized banks.

In response to the 1994 crisis, the Mexican government floated the exchange rate and restructured the banking sector (Graf, 1999; Krueger and Tornell, 1999). Restructuring included a dollar liquidity bailout programme. In early 1995, 75 per cent of the banks' international debts were short-term and unlikely to be rolled over by international creditors. Under the terms of the programme, the government acquired, partially or totally, the non-performing loans of banks in exchange for promissory notes or zero coupon dollar-denominated 10-year bonds (*tesobonos*). Dollar credits could also be acquired by banks at below market rates of interest (Krueger and Tornell, 1999; Graf, 1999). Due to the deleterious effect of the crisis on bank capitalization, banks were required to convert debt into common shares to restore capital-to-asset ratios under a capitalization programme. A trust fund was introduced to lend to insolvent banks, to help them meet capital requirements. Between December 1994 and 1997, the government acquired 12 distressed banks, and this set the stage for a second round of privatization. In contrast to the earlier round, this time foreign banks were allowed to participate in the auctions to buy Mexican banks, which were reconstituted as universal banks (McComb et al., 2002). Restrictions on foreign bank entry were abolished in 1995, with effect from 1997.

3.3 Methodology

In order to explicitly consider the impact of changes on the structure of bank governance that are associated with the resolution processes in Latin America, we use a difference-in-differences (DiD) approach. This enables the identification of the effects of privatization, foreign acquisition, and M&A on bank stability. The DiD approach identifies a treatment group – in this case, banks – that undergoes a change which does not impact directly upon a control group. A time variable captures the before and after treatment periods. A basic DiD specification is shown in Equation 3.1 below for the purpose of illustration:

$$y_{it} = \beta_0 + \delta_0 d2_t + \beta_1 dT_i + \delta_1 d2_t{}^* dT_i + X_{it}\gamma + \mu_{it} \tag{3.1}$$

where y_{it} is the preferred dependent variable; dT_i is the treatment dummy that controls for differences in outcomes of the treatment and control groups prior to the treatment; $d2_t$ is a time dummy that controls for the aggregate factor which causes the dependent variable to change even without the treatment; δ_0 identifies how each group was impacted by time or aggregate factors that are affected only with time; β_1 accounts for differences in the means of the treatment and control groups; and δ_1 is the estimate of the effect of the treatment on the treated banks. X_{it} contains covariates, and γ is a vector of coefficients to be estimated on these variables.

There are three treatment groups in the preferred DiD model specification: banks that were (1) privatized, (2) acquired by foreign banks, and

(3) consolidated using M&A. This lets us identify effects for individual policy treatments that can be used to rank the policies, at least in terms of their impact on bank stability. Since the policies were enacted in the mid-1990s, we should expect intertemporal variation in bank stability. For reasons of precision, we sub-divide the post-resolution period into three components. The first sub-period is from 1995 (1996 in the case of Brazil) to 2000, because we hypothesize that the treatments may be effective with a lag. We consulted the database of Laeven and Levine (2010) to date the length of crisis episodes. The period also contains the majority of cases of foreign bank entry into the region. The second sub-period runs from 2001 to 2006, which provides a medium-term outlook on each of the treatments. Generally speaking, the period is characterized by stronger economic fundamentals. The final sub-period is from 2007 to 2010, and it covers the era of the recent global banking crisis.

Equation 3.2 shows the specification of the preferred DiD model:

$$\begin{aligned} Y_{i,t} = {} & \alpha_0 + \beta_1 D1 + \beta_2 D2 + \beta_3 D3 + \beta_4 PRI_i + \beta_5 FOR_i + \beta_6 MA_i \\ & + \beta_7 D1 * PRI_i + \beta_8 D1 * FOR_i + \beta_9 D1 * MA_i + \beta_{10} D2 * PRI_i \\ & + \beta_{11} D2 * FOR_i + \beta_{12} D2 * MA_i + \beta_{13} D3 * PRI_i + \beta_{14} D3 * FOR_i \\ & + \beta_{15} D3 * MA_i + \beta_{16} SIZE_{i,t} + \beta_{17} CAP_{i,t} + \beta_{18} LLR_{i,t} \\ & + \beta_{19} HHI_t + \beta_{20} GDP_t + \beta_{21} INF_t + \varepsilon_{i,t} \end{aligned} \tag{3.2}$$

where: Y_{it} = natural logarithm of Z score of bank *i* at time *t*; D1 = one for years from 1995 and 2000 for Argentine and Mexican banks, and 1996 to 2000 for Brazilian banks, and zero otherwise; D2 = one for years from 2001 to 2006 and zero otherwise; D3 = one for years from 2007 to 2010 and zero otherwise; PRI_i = dummy for banks selected for privatization, = one for all periods, zero otherwise; FOR_i = dummy for banks selected for acquisition by foreign banks, = one for all periods, zero otherwise; MA_i = dummy for banks selected for M&A, = one for all periods, zero otherwise; $SIZE_{it}$ = natural logarithm of total assets of bank *i* at time *t*; CAP_{it} = capitalization indicator, ratio of equity-to-assets, of bank *i* at time *t*; LLR_{it} = asset quality indicator, ratio of loan loss reserves to loans of bank *i* at time *t*; HHI_t = Herfindahl–Hirschman index to proxy concentration in assets markets at time *t*; GDP_t = gross domestic product growth to proxy the business cycle at time *t*; INF_t = inflation measured as the change in the GDP deflator to proxy management of monetary policy at time *t*; and ε_{it} = error term.

In the model, each treatment is interacted with each time period to control for intertemporal variations in bank stability that are associated with the short-, medium- and long-term effects of bank resolution. This

Table 3.1 Number of observations by variable

Variable	Argentina	Brazil	Mexico	Total
D1 (1995–2000)	496	393	225	1114
D2 (2001–2006)	385	906	187	1478
D3 (2007–2010)	194	343	106	643
PRI	251	252	262	765
FOR	181	386	156	723
MA	456	555	206	1217
D1PRI	43	14	48	105
D1FOR	21	23	17	61
D1MA	58	43	36	137
D2PRI	59	87	7	153
D2FOR	33	131	44	208
D2MA	91	139	26	256
D3PRI	35	26	0	61
D3FOR	20	42	19	81
D3MA	55	45	16	116
Pre Policy (1985–1994)	274	598	147	1019
Post Policy (1995–2010)	1075	1642	518	3235

allows us to consider, for instance, if privatized banks outperform other banks during periods of growth, or if foreign-acquired banks were more or less stable than other banks during the recent global banking crisis. The model is completed by a vector of covariates as controls for bank specific and economic wide factors. These variables are described below.

Table 3.1 shows the number of observations of the time, policy and interaction variables by country. In total, there are 1019 observations across the period from 1985 to 1994, and 3235 observations between 1995 and 2010.

In what follows, we use random effects generalized least squares (RE-GLS) estimation with robust clustered standard errors, and estimate the model by country.

3.4 Data and variables

A unique feature of this chapter is the construction of panel data covering a quarter of a century from 1985 to 2010 for 116 banks from Argentina, 200 from Brazil, and 61 from Mexico. The number of observations are 1326, 2250 and 665, respectively. Financial statements data are sourced from the IBCA (Intervest Bancshares Corp) and BankScope databases. Data are deflated by national GDP deflators and converted in US $ millions at 2000 prices. The dimension of the dataset is 377 banks and 4241 observations over 26 years. We date interventions, privatizations, foreign acquisitions, and M&A from several sources including BankScope, central bank reports, academic papers, newswire services, and bank websites. The macroeconomic data are from the World Bank Financial Indicators and World Economic Outlook databases.

Bank stability is a concern for bank regulators and policymakers alike because of the intended (and unintended) effects associated with changes in public policy (Laeven and Levine, 2009). To proxy stability we calculate the Z score of each bank for all periods the bank is in the sample (Hannan and Hanweck, 1988), and we use the Z score as the dependent variable. Z measures bank stability or the probability of insolvency. Since the aim of bank restructuring is to lower the likelihood of the latter, we consider Z to be an appropriate choice. Z is constructed as follows:

$$Z\ score = \frac{ROA + E/A}{\sigma_{ROA}} \tag{3.3}$$

where *ROA* is the pre-tax return on assets; *E* is the ratio of equity-to-assets; *A* is total assets; and σ_{ROA} is the three year rolling standard deviation of ROA. The *Z* score combines a performance measure (ROA), a volatility measure to capture risk ($\sigma_{\downarrow} ROA$), and book capital as proxy for soundness or prudence of bank management. As Z is expressed in units of standard deviation of ROA, it shows the extent to which earnings can be depleted until the bank has insufficient equity to absorb further losses. Higher values of Z indicate stability, and lower values imply higher probability of bankruptcy (Nash and Sinkey, 1997).

The covariates in X_{it} give an approximation of bank size, capitalization, and asset quality. Total assets (*A*) measures bank size to control for the possibility that larger banks might be more stable because the too-big-to-fail status may reduce systemic risk potential via diversification benefits (Demsetz and Strahan, 1997). Capitalization is measured by the ratio of equity to assets. We expect capitalization is positively related to stability because better capitalized banks are less susceptible to losses arising from unanticipated shocks (Sanya and Wolfe, 2011). Asset quality is indicated by the ratio of loan loss reserves to gross loans; a higher ratio implies that a bank's portfolio is weaker and so there is a greater likelihood of anticipated losses.

The economic wide covariates are the Herfindahl–Hirschman index of assets concentration in each country by year, and it is specified to control for the effects of increases in market concentration on stability. Under the franchise value hypothesis, there is less incentive for banks to assume unnecessary risks in more concentrated markets (Keeley, 1990). Business

Table 3.2 Descriptive statistics

Country		Argentina	Brazil	Mexico
Number of banks		*N = 116*	*N = 200*	*N = 61*
No. of observations		*N = 1326*	*N = 2250*	*N = 665*
Z score	Mean	21.97	20.34	19.97
	Std dev.	72.11	37.49	33.18
Size (US$ m)	Mean	1786.92	5243.90	6570.46
	Std dev.	4520.30	16834.75	11795.38
Asset quality	Mean	0.19	0.17	0.17
	Std dev.	0.18	0.17	0.18
Capitalization	Mean	0.09	0.08	0.06
	Std dev.	0.12	0.52	0.21
HHI (Herfindahl–Hirschman Index)	Mean	11.27	10.10	14.95
	Std dev.	12.2	4.57	4.44
GDP	Mean	3.53	2.85	2.54
	Std dev.	5.83	2.48	3.64
Inflation	Mean	69.94	310.80	16.93
	Std dev.	373.00	688.76	19.32

cycle effects are captured by the annual growth in gross domestic product, whilst inflation, measured as the change in annual GDP deflators, is proxy for the stance of monetary policy. Whereas one may expect economic growth to be positively correlated with bank stability (King and Levine, 1993; Grossman, 1994) there is some evidence of an inverse relationship, which suggests that banks may become insolvent during boom periods (Nilsen and Rovelli, 2001). De Nicoló et al. (2004) find that bank insolvency risks tend to rise during episodes of macroeconomic volatility, including periods of inflation.

Table 3.2 shows the descriptive statistics for the variables. There is little to distinguish the mean Z score by country, though we note the large standard deviation for Argentine banks, which is unsurprising given the country's recent economic record. On average, banks in Mexico and Brazil are comparable in terms of size, and they are much bigger than their counterparts in Argentina. Whilst asset quality is comparable across country, Mexican banks are undercapitalized. Mexico has the most concentrated banking sector and the best record on inflation.

3.5 Empirical results

This section reports the estimated coefficients from Equation 3.2 to show the relationship between bank stability and resolution across discrete time intervals in each country. The results are presented in Table 3.3.

3.5.1 Argentina

The variables D1, D2 and D3 show the overall trend in bank stability for all banks in each sub-period. Between 2000 and 2006 there is a significant reduction in bank stability at the 5 per cent level of significance. This result is unsurprising because of economic and financial sector difficulties in Argentina during parts of the period. The variables PRI, FOR and MA identify banks that were privatized, acquired by foreign banks and consolidated using M&A. The estimated coefficient on PRI reveals that the banks chosen for privatization were significantly less stable than the control group at the 1 per cent level of significance. This result is expected. The weak condition of the provincial-owned banks in terms of profitability, asset quality and cost control is documented in the literature (Clarke and Cull, 2000; Berger et al., 2005). The stability of those banks acquired by foreigners and banks consolidated via M&A is not significantly different from the stability of the control group.

The interactions of the resolution policies within the first time period D1*PRI (1995–2000) show privatized banks to be significantly less stable, with an increased probability of bankruptcy compared to the control group. Though the short-term impacts of foreign acquisition and M&A raised the probability of bankruptcy, the coefficients are statically insignificant at conventional levels. The unfavourable short-term impact of bank privatization is reversed in the second sub-period, D2*PRI from 2001 to 2006. A possible explanation for this finding is that the privatized provincial banks which ran into difficulties in the mid-1990s had been intervened and restored to health. In contrast, foreign-acquired banks became less stable in this period, D2*FOR, which caused a number of foreign operators to abandon Argentina during the early 2000s. Bank privatization appears to be the most successful resolution policy in the Argentine case. In sub-period D3 (2007–10), privatized banks (D3*PRI) are significantly more stable than the control group at the 10 per cent level of significance. Foreign-acquired banks participating in M&A are less stable than the trend, but not significantly so. The evidence tentatively suggests that the experience gained from bank privatization may have benefited those banks when dealing with the transmission of the recent global banking crisis.

An examination of the coefficients on the control variables shows that bank stability is significantly related to asset quality at the 10 per cent significance level. Banks with poorer quality assets exhibit a higher

Table 3.3 Estimated relationship between bank stability and resolution from eqn [2]

	Argentina			Brazil			Mexico		
Variable	Coef.	SE	Z	Coef.	SE	Z	Coef.	SE	Z
D1	0.0128	0.0208	0.62	0.0124	0.0145	0.85	−0.1421**	0.0649	−2.19
D2	−0.0434**	0.0219	−1.99	0.0325	0.0230	1.41	−0.0481	0.0709	−0.68
D3	−0.0019	0.0291	−0.06	0.0443	0.0342	1.29	−0.0952	0.0718	−1.33
PRI	−0.0824***	0.0158	−5.20	−0.0538*	0.0331	−1.62	−0.1237*	0.0672	−1.84
FOR	0.0152	0.0278	0.55	−0.0116	0.0245	−0.47	−0.0511**	0.0247	−2.07
MA	−0.0062	0.0192	−0.32	−0.0186	0.0243	−0.77	−0.0202	0.0251	−0.81
D1*PRI	−0.0327**	0.0183	−1.78	−0.0269	0.0190	−1.41	0.0788	0.0651	1.21
D1*FOR	−0.0440	0.0544	−0.81	−0.0365	0.0429	−0.85	0.1648***	0.0600	2.75
D1*MA	−0.0113	0.0278	−0.41	−0.0098	0.0284	−0.34	0.0206	0.0407	0.51
D2*PRI	0.0734**	0.0289	2.54	0.0537	0.0432	1.24	−0.0258	0.0840	−0.31
D2*FOR	−0.1141***	0.0319	−3.58	−0.0736**	0.0285	−2.58	0.0662	0.0745	0.89
D2*MA	−0.0105	0.0266	−0.40	−0.0562*	0.0345	−1.63	0.0819	0.0997	0.82
D3*PRI	0.0700*	0.0365	1.92	−0.0316	0.0514	−0.61			
D3*FOR	−0.0750	0.0723	−1.04	−0.0317	0.0678	−0.47	0.1134	0.0772	1.47
D3*MA	−0.0420	0.0322	−1.30	−0.1273***	0.0454	−2.81	0.0607	0.0608	1.00
SIZE	0.0034	0.0044	0.79	0.0235***	0.0056	4.17	0.0369***	0.0124	2.99
CAP	−0.0047	0.0139	−0.34	0.1484***	0.0201	7.38	0.1137***	0.0407	2.79
LLR	−0.0205*	0.0107	−1.92	−0.0374***	0.0117	−3.21	−0.0509	0.0522	−0.98
HHI	0.0013	0.0009	1.44	−0.0003	0.0011	−0.25	−0.0014	0.0016	−0.87
GDP	−0.0025**	0.0010	−2.37	0.0004	0.0014	0.31	0.0019	0.0015	1.25
INF	0.0000	0.0000	−0.89	0.0000**	0.0000	2.06	0.0001	0.0003	0.49
Constant	4.8388***	0.0822	58.89	4.2368***	0.0996	42.54	4.4055***	0.1831	24.06
N			*1349*			*2250*			*665*

Note: ***, **, * statistical significance at 1, 5 and 10 per cent.

probability of bankruptcy. During years of higher GDP growth, Argentine banks are significantly less stable at the 5 per cent level.

3.5.2 Brazil

The time variables D1, D2 and D3 show a positive trend in bank stability for the Brazilian banking sector, albeit insignificantly so. Consistent with the evidence from Argentina and also Mexico, the privatized Brazilian banks were significantly less stable than the control group in the pre-privatization period. The preponderance of state-owned banks and their characteristics of weak profitability, low asset quality, and poor cost control can explain the finding. Indeed, all banks that participated in either foreign acquisition or M&A underperformed in terms of stability but the coefficients are insignificant. The underperformance of each resolution type continues into the sub-period D1, from 1996 to 2000. Again, the results are not significant.

During the second sub-period, from 2001 to 2006, the Brazilian economy entered an expansionary phase based largely on price movements in primary products. Whilst the trend in bank stability, D2, was upward, foreign-acquired banks suffered a significant decrease in stability at the 5 per cent significance level. As in the case of Argentina, some foreign-owned banks considered the future of their Brazilian operations, and some sold their operations to other banks (Fachada, 2008). Anecdotal evidence suggests that foreign owners faced difficulties in dealing with the local operating environment, which led to underperformance (Carvalho, 2000). In contrast to the overall trend over 2007 to 2010, which was positive, the three resolved cohorts became less stable in the period with banks that had participated in M&A significantly less stable at the 1 per cent level.

In contrast to the evidence from Argentina, all the bank-specific control variables significantly impact bank stability in Brazil. Larger banks and well capitalized banks are significantly more stable at the 1 per cent level. Like the Argentine case, banks with poorer quality assets show a higher probability of bankruptcy. Of the economic controls, only inflation, INF, is significant – but the magnitude of the coefficients implies its economic significance is low.

3.5.3 Mexico

The probability of bankruptcy for the entire Mexican banking sector significantly increased at the 5 per cent level between 1995 and 2000, the sub-period that coincided with bank intervention and the immediate post-resolution era, D1. The privatized banks, PRI, like their counterparts in Argentina and Brazil, were significantly less stable in the period before privatization and in comparison to the control group at the 10 per cent level. Foreign-acquired banks also had a higher probability of bankruptcy, FOR, but at the 5 per cent level. This is unsurprising, since foreign banks were used to recapitalize distressed large Mexican banks following the Tequila crisis.

Resolution appears to have had an immediate and positive effect in Mexico. Foreign-acquired banks became significantly more stable than the control group in the sub-period, D1, at the 1 per cent level. The magnitude of the coefficient suggests the economic significance of this result to be important. In subsequent sub-periods, D2 and D3, the sign on foreign bank acquisitions is positive, albeit insignificant, but the magnitude of the coefficients remains relatively large. Similar to the evidence from Brazil, larger and better capitalized banks in Mexico are significantly more stable at the 1 per cent level. Yet each macro-level control variable is insignificant in the Mexican case.

3.6 Conclusions

The chapter has considered the bank restructuring processes implemented in Argentina, Brazil and Mexico in the mid-1990s to resolve banking crises. Although legal structures to resolve troubled banks did exist prior to the crises, they were minimal and insufficient to deal with the problems facing central banks. Legislative reforms allowed central banks to use the good bank/bad bank model of resolution in which assets and liabilities are transferred between banks. Governments repealed restrictions on foreign entry, and foreign bank acquisition of local banks became a tool to recapitalize banking sectors. Privatization was used to roll back the involvement of the State in banking and to transfer public banks to the private sector, which was expected to realize efficiency gains based on the assumption that privately owned banks are less susceptible to agency problems than are public-sector banks. The net result of restructuring has been to increase both the level of consolidation and the foreign ownership of national banking sector assets (Gelos and Roldós, 2004).

We also investigated the effect of restructuring on bank stability that is measured by a bank's Z score. A DiD model provides a clear test of the effectiveness of discrete resolution policies. The approach lets us disentangle the impact of resolution strategies from the overall trend in bank stability. We suggest that there is intertemporal variation in bank stability, and this is incorporated in the modelling framework through the interaction of three post-resolution sub-periods of time with the resolution policies of privatization, foreign bank acquisition, and consolidation via M&A.

It is not possible to determine if there is a preferred resolution strategy, because the empirical evidence varies across the three countries. However, there is consistent cross-country evidence showing that privatized banks were significantly less stable prior to the onset of the privatization processes, supporting evidence provided elsewhere in the literature (see, for instance, Berger et al., 2005; Carvalho et al., 2010). Yet the impact of privatization has been mixed. After an initial deterioration in bank stability in the post-restructuring period, privatization produced significantly more suitable banks in subsequent periods in Argentina. This finding cannot, however, be generalized to Brazil and Mexico; whilst privatization seems to have produced a result in Brazil that is similar to Argentina, the estimated coefficients are not statistically significant. The evidence suggests that foreign acquisition weakened bank stability during the more economically stable period from 2001 to 2006, at least in Argentina and Brazil. Stability deteriorated in the 2007 to 2010 period, albeit not in a statistically meaningful manner. In contrast, foreign acquisition has proved to be very effective in significantly improving bank stability in Mexico in the immediate post-resolution sub-period, in spite of the fact that the acquired banks were significantly less stable in the pre-restructuring period. Finally, consolidation via M&A has significantly lowered stability in the 2001 to 2006 and 2007 to 2010 sub-periods in Brazil.

References

W. Baer and N. Nazmi (2000) Privatization and restructuring of banks in Brazil. *The Quarterly Review of Economics and Finance*, 40: 3–24.

G. Barnes (1992) Lessons from bank privatization in Mexico. *Policy Research Working Papers WPS1027*, World Bank.

T. Beck, J.M. Crivelli and W. Summerhill (2005) State bank transformation in Brazil – choices and consequences. *Journal of Banking and Finance*, 29: 2223–57.

A.N. Berger, G.R.G. Clarke, R. Cull, L. Klapper and G.F. Udell (2005) Corporate governance and bank performance: A joint analysis of the static, selection, and dynamic effects of domestic, foreign, and state ownership. *Journal of Banking and Finance*, 29: 2179–221.

C.M. Buch and G.L. DeLong (2001) Cross-border bank mergers: What lures the rare animal? Kiel Institute of World Economics, *Working Paper*, No. 1070.

F. Carvalho (2000) New competitive strategies of foreign banks in large emerging economies: The case of Brazil. *Banca Nazionale del Lavoro Quarterly Review*, 213: 135–70.

F.J.C. Carvalho, L.F. Paula and J. Williams (2010) Banking in Latin America. In A. Berger, P. Molyneux and J.O.S. Wilson (eds), *The Oxford Handbook of Banking*. Oxford: Oxford University Press, pp. 868–902.

G.R.G. Clarke, J.M. Crivelli and R. Cull (2005) The direct and indirect impact of bank privatization and foreign entry on access to credit in Argentina's provinces. *Journal of Banking and Finance*, 29: 5–29.

G.R.G. Clarke and R. Cull (2000) 'Why privatize? The case of Argentina's public provincial banks. *World Development*, 27: 865–86.

A. De la Torre (2000) Resolving bank failures in Argentina: Recent developments and issues. *World Bank Policy Research Working Paper Series*, No. 2295.

G. De Nicoló, P. Bartholomew, J. Zaman and M. Zephirin (2004) Bank consolidation, internationalization, and conglomeration: Trends and implications for financial risk. *Financial Markets, Institutions and Instruments*, 13 (4): 173–217.

R. Demsetz and P. Strahan (1997) Diversification, size, and risk at bank holding companies. *Journal of Money, Credit and Banking*, 29 (3): 300–13.

P. Fachada (2008) Foreign banks' entry and departure: The recent Brazilian experience (1996–2006). *Banco Central do Brasil Working Paper Series*, 164, June.

D. Focarelli and A.F. Pozzolo (2001) The patterns of cross-border bank mergers and shareholdings in OECD countries. *Journal of Banking and Finance*, 25: 2305–37.

R.G. Gelos and J. Roldós (2004) Consolidation and market structure in emerging market banking systems. *Emerging Markets Review*, 5: 39–59.

P. Graf (1999) Policy responses to the banking crisis in Mexico. *BIS Policy Papers*, No. 6, *Bank Restructuring in Practice*, 164–82.

R. Grossman (1994) The shoe that didn't drop: Explaining banking stability during the great depression. *The Journal of Economic History*, 54 (3): 654–82.

W.C. Gruben, J.H. Welch and J.W. Gunther (1994) U.S. banks, competition, and the Mexican banking system: How much will NAFTA matter? Federal Reserve Bank of Dallas, *Research Department Working Paper* 94–10.

S. Haber (2005) Mexico's experiments with bank privatization and liberalization, 1991–2003. *Journal of Banking and Finance*, 29: 2325–53.

T. Hannan and G. Hanweck (1988) Bank insolvency risk and the market for large certificates of deposit. *Journal of Money, Credit and Banking*, 20 (2): 203–11.

M. Keeley (1990) Deposit insurance, risk, and market power in banking. *American Economic Review*, 80 (5): 1183–200.

R. King and R. Levine (1993) Finance and growth: Schumpeter might be right. *The Quarterly Journal of Economics*, 108 (3): 717–37.

A. Krueger and A. Tornell (1999) The role of bank restructuring in recovering from crises: Mexico 1995–1998. *NBER Working Paper*, No. 7042. Cambridge, Mass.: National Bureau of Economic Research, March.

L. Laeven and R. Levine (2009) Bank governance, regulation, and risk taking. *Journal of Financial Economics*, 93 (2): 259–75.

L. Laeven and F. Valencia (2010) Resolution of banking crises: The good, the bad, and the ugly. *IMF Working Paper*, No. WP/10/146, 1–35.

G. Maia (1999), Restructuring the banking system – the case of Brazil. Bank restructuring in practice. *BIS Papers*, No. 6, 106–23.

H. Makler (2000) Bank transformation and privatization in Brazil: Financial federalism and some lessons about bank privatization. *The Quarterly Review of Economics and Finance*, 40: 45–69.
R.P. McComb, W.C. Gruben and J.H. Welch (2002) Privatization and performance in the Mexican financial services industry. *The Quarterly Review of Economics and Finance*, 34 (1): 217–35.
J.R. Mendonça de Barros and M.F. Almeida Jr (1997) Restructuring Brazil's financial system. Secretariat of Economic Policy, Ministry of Finance, Brazil.
F. Montes-Negret and and L. Landa (2001) Interest rate spreads in Mexico during liberalization. In G. Caprio, P. Honohan and J.E. Stiglitz (eds), *Financial Liberalization: How Far? How Fast?* Cambridge: Cambridge University Press.
R. Nash and J. Sinkey (1997) On competition, risk, and hidden assets in the market for bank credit cards. *Journal of Banking and Finance*, 21: 89–112.
W.L. Ness (2000) Reducing government bank presence in the Brazilian financial system: Why and how. *The Quarterly Review of Economics and Finance*, 40: 71–84.
J.H. Nilsen and R. Rovelli (2001) Investor risk aversion and financial fragility in emerging economies. *Journal of International Financial Markets Institutions and Money*, 11: 443–7.
L.F. Paula (2003) The determinants of recent foreign bank penetration in Brazil. *CEPAL Review*, 79: 159–76.
F.P. Puga (1999) The Brazilian financial system: Recent restructuring, international comparisons, and vulnerability to a foreign exchange crisis. *Discussion Paper*, No. 68, National Bank for Economic and Social Development, Rio de Janeiro.
S. Sanya and S. Wolfe (2011) Can banks in emerging economies benefit from revenue diversification? *Journal of Financial Services Research*, 40 (1–2): 79–101.
M. Sebastián and C. Hernansanz (2000) The Spanish banks strategy in Latin America. *SUERF Working Paper*, No. 9, Paris.
A. Singh, C. Belaisch, C. Collyns, P. de Masi, R. Krieger, G. Meredith and R. Rennhack (2005) Stabilization and reform in Latin America: A macroeconomic perspective on the experience since the early 1990s. *IMF Occasional Paper*, No. 238.
H. Unal and M. Navarro (1999) The technical process of bank privatization in Mexico. *Journal of Financial Services Research*, 16 (1): 61–83.

4
Monetary Policy and Trade Credit: Evidence for Spain

Santiago Carbó-Valverde, José Manuel Mansilla-Fernández and Francisco Rodríguez-Fernández

4.1 Introduction and motivation

Trade credit is one of the most important financial sources for Spanish firms. It facilitates trade between firms and diversifies their funding sources. One of the main objectives of trade credit is to permit sellers to delay payment to their customers, depending on their financial needs. On the other hand, customers are able to operate with higher liquidity margins.

In quantitative terms, trade credit is one of the most important financial sources for Spanish firms, although this form of financing for firms has not been broadly studied like other forms of funding (such as bank financing) since the information provided is sparser. The Bank of Spain reported that the outstanding balance of trade credit represents 55 per cent of Spanish GDP and 92 per cent of bank lending. Trade credit may become more relevant in times of crisis, because it is expected to follow a procyclical behaviour.

The recent economic literature has shown the importance of trade credit, particularly in times of crisis, as well as the importance of the credit channel which operates in addition to the interest rate channel in the transmission of monetary policy to the real economy. Economic literature frequently analyses these monetary policy transmission channels separately (see Clauss, 2011). Moreover, economic literature has traditionally focused on the transmission of monetary policy to bank prices and credit availability. In this chapter we examine the effects of changes in monetary policy interest rates on the price of trade credit.

The remainder of the chapter proceeds as follows. Section 2 shows the background literature. Section 3 formally discusses the empirical approach and the database. Section 4 presents the main empirical analysis for this research. Finally, Section 5 offers the main conclusions and policy implications.

4.2 Background literature

The interest rate channel results from the central bank's response to target objectives, and the central bank's adjustments in the price of bonds. Therefore, changes in interest rates are transmitted to the real sector (Clauss, 2011).

Market imperfections play a specific role in the transmission of monetary policy (see Romer and Romer, 1990, 1994; Hubbard, 1998). They also depend on factors related to the strength of firm's balance sheet (Mateut et al., 2006). The bank lending channel was introduced by Bernanke and Blinder (1988), based on the view that banks play a special role in the financial system because they have an advantage in solving the asymmetric information problem in credit markets (Bernanke and Blinder, 1992; Bernanke and Gertler, 1995; Kashyap and Stein, 2000).[1] The main implication for the bank lending channel for a firm's credit investment is that variations in monetary policy have more repercussions on more bank-dependent firms (Kashyap and Stein, 2000). In this sense, Huang (2003) shows that the dynamic behaviour between bank debt and non-bank debt influences credit availability, especially for small firms rather than larger ones. Carbó and López (2009) analyse the empirical relationship between liquidity and firm structure in order to assess the importance of monetary policy; they find that when interest rates increase, firms reduce their dependence on bank credit and maintain higher levels of liquidity.

As the bank lending channel is declining in importance, the Bernanke and Gertler (1995) balance sheet channel becomes more relevant. Important theoretical papers demonstrate that capital market imperfections condition the access to bank lending for firms with lower financial heath (see Diamond, 1984, 1991; Hoshi et al., 1990, 1991; Bolton and Freixas, 2000; Repullo and Suarez, 2000). Bernanke and Gertler (1989, 1995) show that a tightening in monetary policy might damage a firm's creditworthiness, and then this could diminish said firm's ability to raise funds from financial institutions. The empirical work of Gertler and Gilchrist (1993, 1994) finds that the sharpest distinction between small and large borrowers is opposed between bank and non-bank credit: small firms are more affected by an increase in interest rates.[2] Ashcraft (2006) and Ashcraft and Campello (2007) demonstrate that borrowers' creditworthiness influences the response of bank lending to monetary policy. Bougheas et al. (2006, 2009) find that smaller and younger firms are more affected by tight monetary conditions.

The broad credit channel approach introduced by Oliner and Rudebusch (1995) suggests that the main ingredient of the broad credit channel is the opposition between internal and external funds. This is because of the existence of informational asymmetries which are more relevant to smaller firms than to larger ones. In this way, Oliner and Rudebusch (1996) show that the broad credit channel operates through small firms and those asymmetries of information induce to a higher-cost premium for external funds as compensation for monitoring cost; this premium depends on the stance of monetary policy which could damage the borrower's balance sheet and reduce the collateral.

Moreover, a trade credit channel might be a substitute for the bank lending channel presented above. The trade credit channel considers all the implications for trade credit that are considered in the broad credit channel approach. Nielsen (2002) shows that monetary contractions induce firms to increase the use of trade credit, suggesting that credit and trade credit channels operate in UK, and the latter channel tend to weaken the former one – whereas Choi and Kim (2005) show that accounts payable and accounts receivable increase in times of monetary tightening. Atanasova and Wilson (2002, 2004) find that corporate demand for bank financing might be reduced during monetary contractions, and that the supply of bank loans also decreases.

We also study the effects of monetary policy on the behaviour of working capital financing. Several papers advocate the complementarity hypothesis between the availability of bank lending and trade credit when a financial constraint is imposed by credit institutions (Petersen and Rajan, 1994, 1995, 1997; Danielson and Scott, 2004; Burkart and Ellingsen, 2004; Burkart et al., 2006; Cull et al., 2009). The most recent studies supporting complementarity hypothesis find that trade creditors are willing to provide more financing when customers are rationed in the bank loan market (see Boissay and Gropp, 2007; Cuñat, 2007). Carbó et al. (2009) find evidence of the importance of trade credit in substituting bank lending at self-constrained firms. Love and Zaidi (2010), however, find evidence that does not support the hypothesis that trade credit could substitute bank credit in times of crisis. De Blasio (2005) and Fukuda (2006) argue that the substitutability of trade credit acts during times of financial instability. Tsuruta (2007, 2010) argues that during economic recession the amount of trade credit is reduced. Finally,

Huang et al. (2011) find the existence of substitution between trade credit and bank lending but suggests that the pattern of substitution is procyclical and infrequent.

4.3 Methodology and data

4.3.1 Description of the variables

We propose several measures for the cost of trade credit, bank financing and the effects of transmission of monetary policy on the cost of trade credit. Table 4.1 shows the definitions of the variables used in this chapter as well as the sources employed. The main interest rate variable in this research is the implicit interest rate (IIR hereafter) of trade credit measured as the ratio financial expenses minus interest rate over accounts payable. This variable represents the interest rate paid by the firm for the use of trade credit.

We also study the role of monetary policy on the firm's financing position. Therefore, we construct the relative net trade credit variable (RNTC hereafter) as the difference between accounts payable and accounts receivable over the sum of both of them. If the RNTC is negative (positive), then the firm is a net credit extender (recipient). The main point of interest in the RNTC is the normalization of the traditional net trade credit proposed by the financial literature, since the ratio ranges from -1 to 1, which means that the firm is purely a trade debtor or purely a trade creditor respectively.

In order to study the bank lending channel, we consider the interest rates paid (r_{it}^{TC}) by the firm for bank loans measured as interest paid over total assets. We also consider the amount of bank debt (B_{it}) as the leverage ratio, and this is measured as the ratio of bank lending over firm's total assets. As for the transmission of monetary policy through the trade credit channel, we consider the amount of trade credit (TC_{it}) maintained in the firm's balance sheet. In particular we compute the the ratio accounts payable over firm's total assets. In the same way, the amount of trade debit (TD_{it}) is measured as the ratio accounts receivable over the firm's total assets.

As for the variable that shows the stance of monetary policy, we consider three standard measures in the economic literature: three-month EURIBOR_t, EONIA_t, and lending facilities (LF_t). Additionally, in order to further analyse the transmission of monetary policy through the bank lending channel, we also consider the average price that credit institutions set for their loans (P_{ijt}) measured as the interest–income

Table 4.1 Description of the variables

Variables	Definition	Source
r_{it}^{TC}	This variable represents the implicit interest rate of trade credit (IIR). This variable is proxy for the ratio *financial expenses* minus *interest paid* over *accounts payable*.	SABI (2010)
r_{it}^{B}	This variable measures the amount of interest rate paid by the firm for bank financing. This variable computed as *interest paid* over *firm's total assets*.	SABI (2010)
$RNTC_{it}$	The relative net trade credit measures the net trade financing position. This variable is computed as the difference between trace credit and trade debit over the sum of both.	SABI (2010)
$r_{it}^{TC} - \overline{r_{kt}^{TC}}$	This variable measures the competition effect and is proxy for the difference between the implicit interest rate of trade credit paid by firm *i* and the average interest trade credit for each period *t* and industrial sector *k* which firm belongs to.	SABI (2010)
$r_{it}^{TC} - r_{it}^{B}$	This variable measures the complementarity effect and is proxy for the difference between the implicit interest rate of trade credit and the price paid by firm for bank financing.	SABI (2010)
TC_{it}	This indicator measures the proportion of trade credit maintained by the firm in its balance sheet. This variable is measured as the ratio *accounts payable* over *firm's total assets*.	SABI (2010)
TD_{it}	This variable measures the amount of trade debit in firm's balance sheet computed as the ratio *accounts receivable* over *firm's total assets*.	SABI (2010)
B_{it}	This variable represents the leverage ratio proxy as the ratio *bank debt* over *firm's total assets*.	SABI (2010)
$EURIBOR_t$	This variable represents the three-month *Euribor* yearly measured from 1998 until 2009.	Bank of Spain
$EONIA_t$	This variable represents the three-month *Eonia* yearly measured from 1998 until 2009.	Bank of Spain
LF_t	This variable represents the *Lending facilities* yearly measured from 1998 until 2009.	Bank of Spain
P_{jit}	This variable approximates to the price that banks establish for their loans measured as *interest income* plus *other operating income* over *bank's total assets* (Maudos and Fernández de Guevara, 2004, 2007; Fernández de Guevara et al., 2007).	AEB-CECA-UNACC (2010)
$Crisis_t$	This dummy variable takes on the value one for periods higher than 2007, and zero otherwise.	

ratio plus other operating income over the bank's total assets (Maudos and Fernández de Guevara, 2004, 2007; Fernández de Guevara et al., 2007).

We study the competition effects among firms in order to analyse how firms set the price of trade credit relative to their competitors. We proxy the competition effect as the difference between firm's IIR and the average IIR established by each industrial sector $\left(r_{it}^{TC} - \overline{r_{kt}^{TC}}\right)$. Then we consider the existence of convergence (divergence) among firms if the indicator is lower (higher) than zero. Similarly, we analyse the substitution effects between trade credit and bank financing by computing the difference between r_{it}^{TC} and r_{it}^{B} $\left(r_{it}^{TC} - r_{it}^{B}\right)$. We assume a competition (substitution) effect if the indicator is higher (lower) than zero.

Finally, we are interested in analysing the divergences in the cost and the amount of trade credit, and other form of firm financing during the crisis, by considering a crisis dummy variable ($crisis_t$) which takes on the value one from 2007 onwards, and zero otherwise.

4.3.2 Database construction

The dataset employed in this chapter combines three sources of data: for firms, financial institutions and macroeconomic variables, respectively. Figure 4.1 summarizes these sources. We extracted firm-level information from Bureau van Dijk's SABI (2010). The sample consists of a panel data of 13,634 firms for the period 1998 to 2009, which results in 145,514 firm-year observations.

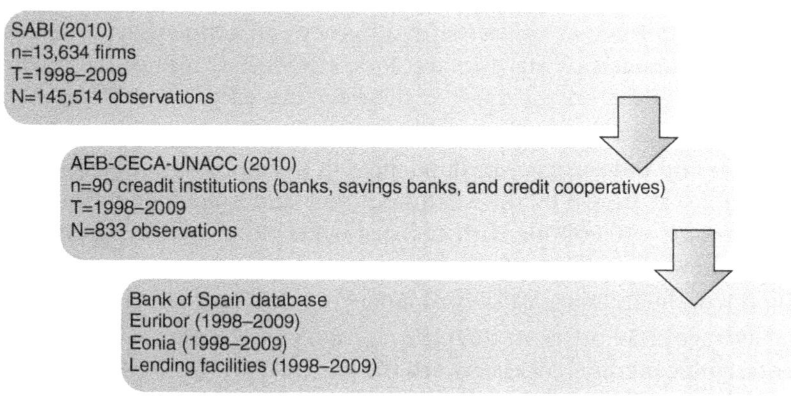

Figure 4.1 Sample construction

The second set of variables provides information about the Spanish financial institutions. This second panel dataset is based on balance sheet and income statement information obtained from the Spanish Banking Association (AEB) for the whole population of commercial banks which operate in Spain, from the Spanish Savings Banks Association (CECA) for all savings banks, and from the National Union of Credit Cooperatives (UNACC) for the three larger Spanish credit cooperatives. The SABI (2010) database contains information on the main bank which has a relationship with each firm (from survey data), and this permits the matching of each firm's data with information from its correspondent financial institution.

Finally, the third set of variables corresponds with the stance of monetary policy, including EURIBOR, EONIA and the lending facilities, and it is obtained from the Bank of Spain.

4.4 Results

4.4.1 How has the financial crisis affected trade and bank financing?

The recent financial literature shows that the evolution of trade credit has changed with the financial crisis (Love and Zaidi, 2010). The monetary policy response of the European Central Bank and the other major central banks to the financial crisis, especially during October 2008, was labelled as unprecedented because of the size of monetary policy quantitative easing, the liquidity provided to the financial system, and the use of non-standard measures to provide central bank liquidity and support the provision of credit to the private sector. Table 4.2 represents the main summary statistics, as well as Mann–Whitney and Kolmogorov–Smirnov tests and parametric *t*-statistics test for differences of means, taking the beginning of the crisis ($crisis_t$) as the reference date. We find that the IIR $\left(r_{it}^{TC}\right)$ that Spanish firms pay is around 1.77 per cent on average. We also find the existence of differences in the cost of trade credit after the crisis – as shown by the Mann–Whitney and Kolmogorov–Smirnov test (*p-value* = 0.000 for both cases) – while the negative sign of the *t*-test shows that the cost of trade credit is higher after the crisis. As expected, the interest rate of bank financing paid by firms $\left(r_{it}^{B}\right)$ is lower on average (1.59 per cent) than the rate shown for trade credit. We also find significant differences between the pre-crisis and post-crisis periods.

As for the outstanding value of trade credit (TC_{it}) and trade debit (TD_{it}), we find that both variables have also changed considerably since

Table 4.2 Main statistics

	Summary statistics		Non-parametric test Crisis dummy		
	Observations	Mean (Std dev.)	Mann–Whitney test [p-value]	Kolmogorov–Smirnov test [p-value]	t-test for comparison of means [t-statistics]
			z-statistics H0: Diff. = 0	Diff.: F(z) –G(z) H0: Diff. = 0	Diff. = mean (0) – mean (1) H0: Diff. = 0
r_{it}^{TC}	88,488	0.0177	11.065	0.0556	−0.0077***
		(0.0749)	[0.000]	[0.000]	(−14.9249)
r_{it}^{B}	110,730	0.0159	−26.450	0.0882	−0.0021***
		(0.0185)	[0.000]	[0.000]	(−17.9239)
$RNTC_{it}$	92,469	−0.2545	36.163	0.1114	0.0889†††
		(0.3895)	[0.000]	[0.000]	(33.8649)
$r_{it}^{TC} - \overline{r_{kt}^{TC}}$	88,488	−0.0073	−4.028	0.0272	−0.0018***
		(0.0219)	[0.000]	[0.000]	(−12.1903)
$r_{it}^{TC} - r_{it}^{B}$	88,942	−0.0043	17.196	0.0868	0.0001
		(0.0261)	[0.0000]	[0.000]	(0.3883)
TC_{it}	92,563	0.2209	51.871	0.1435	0.0589†††
		(0.1669)	[0.000]	[0.000]	(48.0394)
TD_{it}	117,720	0.3735	21.078	0.0616	0.0297†††
		(0.2314)	[0.0000]	[0.000]	(20.4410)
B_{it}	78,744	0.1364	−12.814	0.0637	−0.0088***
		(0.1300)	[0.000]	[0.000]	(−9.1250)
$EURIBOR_t$	145,514	3.0894	10.679	0.3339	0.1898†††
		(1.1246)	[0.0000]	[0.000]	(28.1804)
$EONIA_t$	145,514	2.8246	52.309	0.3339	0.7881†††
		(1.0798)	[0.000]	[0.000]	(128.2343)
LF_t	145,514	3.7429	95.830	0.4128	0.6838†††
		(1.0646)	[0.000]	[0.000]	(110.1067)
P_{jit}	143,123	4.7291	−57.385	0.2372	−0.2532***
		(1.2791)	[0.000]	[0.000]	(−32.8215)

Source: SABI (2010), AEB-CECA-UNACC (2010), Bank of Spain database and own elaboration.
Notes: *, **, *** statistically significant at the 10, 5 and 1 per cent level, respectively under H0: Diff. <0
†, ††, ††† statistically significant at the 10, 5 and 1 per cent level, respectively under H0: Diff. > 0

the start of the financial crisis. Trade credit represents 22.09 per cent of firms' liabilities, whilst trade debit represents 33.35 per cent. The Mann–Whitney and Kolmogorov–Smirnov test suggests differences between the pre- and post-crisis periods. The positive sign for the *t*-test for mean differences shows that the use of trade financing was higher before the financial crisis, The net position of current assets, that is whether the firm is a net trade creditor or debtor, is reflected by the RNTC. The results suggest that Spanish firms are net trade debtors, and the value computed is 25.45 per cent on average. The non-parametric tests reflect differences before and after the financial crisis in the RNTC values and, as expected, t with the positive sign, and the significance of t-test shows that firms became trade borrowers only after the crisis.

The amount of bank lending maintained by firms is around 13.64 per cent, which is lower than the amount of trade credit. This result reveals that firms use more intensive trade credit rather than bank financing. The parametric t-test shows a negative and significant sign, in contrast to the case of trade credit, which indicates that firms have not significantly changed the amount of bank lending in their balance sheets over time.

As for the competition effect $(r_{it}^{TC} - \overline{r_{kt}^{TC}})$, the negative and significant sign of the t-test reveals convergence among firms towards the mean value of each sector after the crisis. However, no empirical significance evidence is found for the complementarity effect $\left(r_{it}^{TC} - r_{it}^{B}\right)$.

Finally, we also analyse the effect of the financial crisis on monetary policy variables. Contrary to our expectations, P_{ijt} shows a significant and negative sign which suggests a delay in the transmission of the effects of monetary policy to interest rates for bank loans set.

4.4.2 Evolution of trade credit and bank financing

Figure 4.2 represents the evolution of average trade credit and bank lending in our sample of Spanish firms. The weight of trade credit on the liability side followed an increasing path until the start of the crisis in 2007, reaching a maximum of 25.05 per cent in 2002. The beginning of the financial crisis then led to a drastic fall in 2008 and 2009, where the weight of trade credit was 17.34 and 15.90 per cent, respectively. We find that the amount of bank lending overall is lower than the volume of trade credit maintained by firms before the crisis. However, with the financial crisis, the weight of both forms of financing converged to approximately 15 per cent.

Figure 4.3 analyses the evolution of trade credit, trade debit and the RNTC. We find that trade debit is higher than trade credit in every period; the RNTC index has changed from 22.57 per cent in 2007 to 35.35 per cent in 2009.

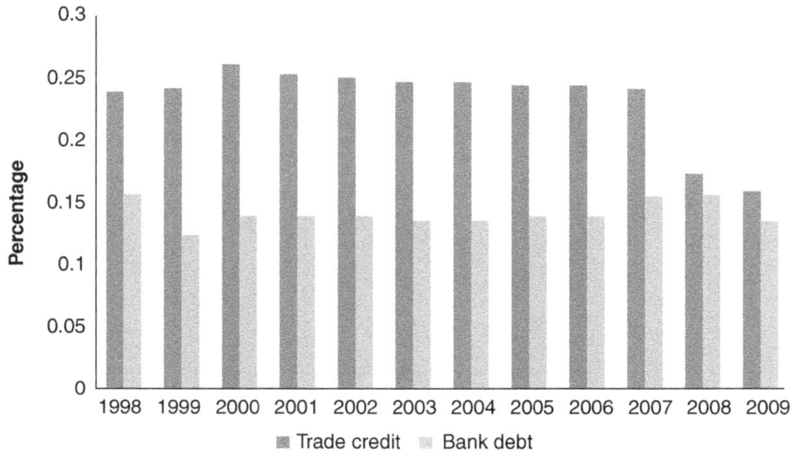

Figure 4.2 Trade credit and bank lending
Source: SABI (2010) and own elaboration.

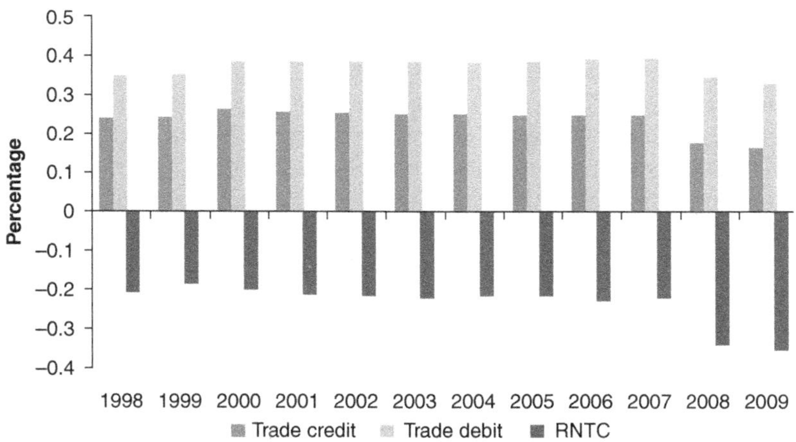

Figure 4.3 Trade credit, trade debit and relative net trade credit
Source: SABI (2010) and own elaboration.

4.4.3 Monetary policy transmission: evidence, competition and the complementarity effect

The main interest of this chapter is to study if the changes in monetary policy are transmitted to the interest rates collected by firms that grant

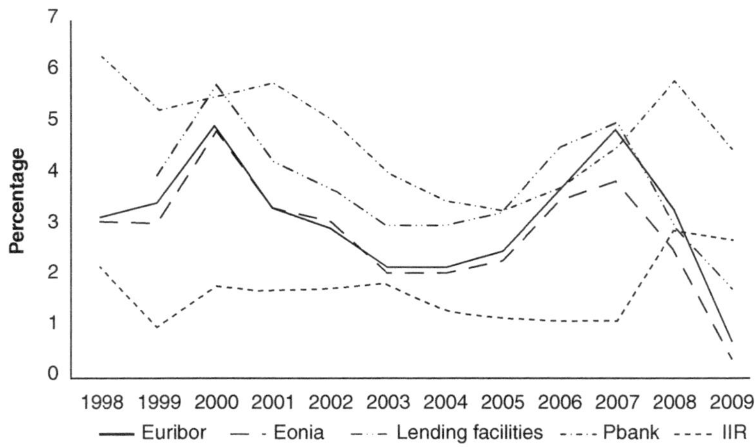

Figure 4.4 Evolution of European Central Bank interest rates and the average cost of trade credit and bank average prices: evidence of transmission
Source: SABI (2010), AEB-CECA-UNACC (2010), Bank of Spain database and own elaboration.

trade credit. Figure 4.4 plots EURIBOR_t, EONIA_t, and LF_t, set by the European Central Bank, as well as the average loan rate set by banks, and the evolution of the IIR. The time series for EURIBOR_t, EONIA_t, and LF_t, describes a decreasing curve from 1998 to 2006, all of them reaching a maximum in 2007. After the financial crisis, these indicators rapidly decreased to 0.71, 0.35, and 1.75 per cent, respectively. The average price for bank loans follows a similar trend, as expected for the bank lending channel. We find that the IIR of trade credit also follows a path similar to the previous indicators, which suggests that the whole range of changes of monetary policy considered are transmitted to the price of trade credit.

Figure 4.5a analyses the existence of a competition effect among firms represented by the difference between the IIR for each firm *i* and the average interest rate for the correspondent industrial sector *k* to which firm *i* belongs $(r_{it}^{TC} - \overline{r_{kt}^{TC}})$. The indicator shows that as macroeconomic interest rates increase (in the periods 1998–1999 and 2003–2007), $tr_{it}^{TC} - \overline{r_{kt}^{TC}}$ is lower, which shows the existence of convergence among firms when they decide to establish the price of trade credit. Moreover, we also study the existence of competition effects between trade and bank financing given by the difference between the cost of trade credit and the price paid by firms for bank financing $\left(r_{it}^{TC} - r_{it}^{B}\right)$ represented by Figure 4.5b.

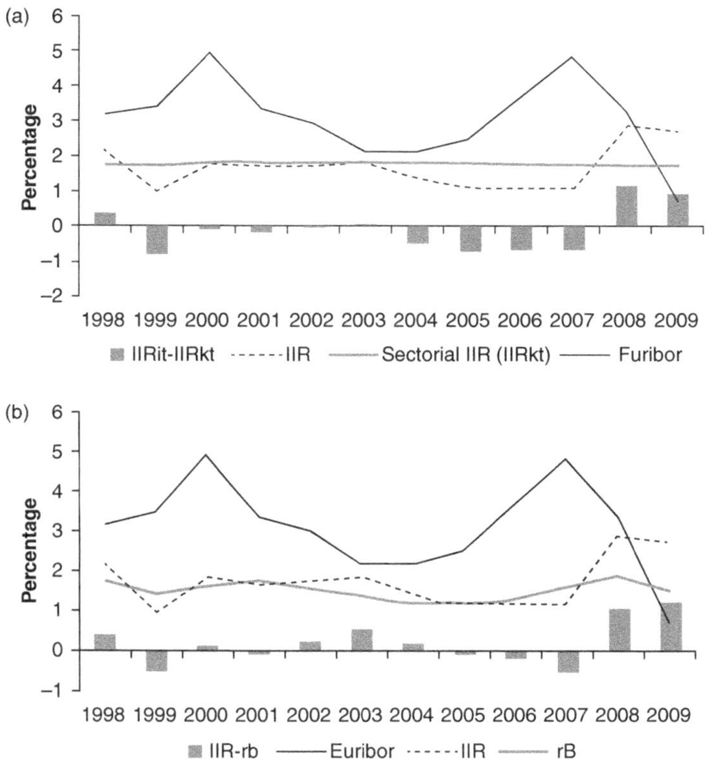

Figure 4.5 Competition and complementarity effect (a) Competition effect (5b) Complementarity effect differences between IIR and sectorial IIR differences between IIR and RB
Source: SABI (2010), Bank of Spain database and own elaboration.

Overall, our results suggest the existence of complementarity in prices between trade credit and bank financing.

4.5 Conclusions

In this chapter, we have analysed the effects of changes in the stance of monetary policy on the interest rates of trade credit, and firms' financing behaviour. We have also studied whether these relationships have an impact on the competition among firms within the same sector and on the complementarity between trade credit and bank financing.

The results reveal that the pattern of trade credit changed after the crisis began in 2007. We observed that the volume of trade credit decreased after the financial crisis started, though trade credit became more expensive. Moreover, while bank financing also experimented with similar behaviour, we find that trade credit shows a more abrupt change because of its expected short-term flexibility and adaptation.

We find that the interest rates set by the European Central Bank and the IIR of trade credit follow a similar trend for the entire period examined. Finally, we find that changes in monetary policy led to convergence in the price established by firms within the same industrial sector (what we call the 'competition effect'). and we also suggest the existence of a 'complementarity effect' between trade credit and bank financing in an environment of increasing interest rates.

Notes

1. Stein (1998) develops a model in which information problems make it difficult for banks to raise funds with instruments other than deposits.
2. See Black and Rosen (2007) who show that during periods of monetary tightening, banks adjust their stock of credit, reducing the maturity of loans and reallocating short-term credit to large firms.

References

A.B. Ashcraft (2006) New evidence on the lending channel. *Journal of Money, Credit, and Banking*, 38 (3): 751–75.

A.B. Ashcraft and M. Campello (2007) Firm balance sheets and monetary policy transmission. *Journal of Monetary Economics*, 54: 1515–28.

C.V. Atanasova and N. Wilson (2004) Disequilibrium in the UK corporate loan market. *Journal of Banking and* Finance, 28: 595–614.

—— (2002) *Borrowing Constraints and the Demand for Trade Credit: Evidence from UK Panel Data*. Leeds University Business School: Mimeo.

B.S. Bernanke and A.S. Blinder (1992) The federal funds rate and the channels of monetary transmission. *American Economic Review*, 82: 901–21.

—— (1988) Credit, money, and aggregate demand. *American Economic Review*, 78 (2): 435–9.

B.S. Bernanke and M. Gertler (1995) Inside the black box: The credit channel of monetary policy transmission. *Journal of Economic Perspectives*, 9 (4): 27–48.

—— (1989) Agency cost, net worth, and business fluctuations. *American Economic Review*, 79 (1): 14–31.

L.K. Black and R.J. Rosen (2007) How the credit channel works: differentiating the bank lending channel and the balance sheet channel. Federal Reserve Bank of Chicago *Working Paper 2007–13*.

F. Boissay and R. Gropp (2007) Trade credit defaults and liquidity provision by firms. ECB *Working Paper Series*, No. 753.

P. Bolton and F. Xabier (2000) Equity, bonds, and bank debt: Capital structure and financial market equilibrium under asymmetric information. *Journal of Political Economy*, 108 (2): 324–51.
S. Bougheas, S. Mateut and P. Mizen (2009) Corporate trade credit and inventories: New evidence of a trade-off from accounts payable and receivable. *Journal of Banking and* Finance, 33: 300–7.
S. Bougheas, P. Mizen and C. Yalcin (2006) Access to external finance: Theory and evidence on the impact of monetary policy and firm-specific characteristics. *Journal of Banking and Finance*, 30: 199–227.
M. Burkart and T. Ellingsen (2004) In-kind finance: A theory of trade credit. *American Economic Review*, 94 (3): 569–90.
M. Burkart, T. Ellingsen and M. Gianneti (2006) What you sell is what you lend? Explaining trade credit contract. *Finance Working Paper*, No. 71/2005.
S. Carbó and L. Rafael (2009) Bank-lending channel and non-financial firms: Evidence for Spain. *Spanish Economic Review*, 11: 125–40.
S. Carbó, F. Rodríguez and G.F. Udell (2009) Bank market power and SME financing constraints. *Review of Finance*, 13: 309–40.
W. Choi and Y. Kim (2005) Trade credit and the effect of monetary macro-financial shocks: Evidence from U.S. panel data. *Journal of Financial and Quantitative Analysis*, 40 (4): 897–925.
I. Clauss (2011) Inside the black box: How important is the credit channel relative to the interest and exchange rate channels? *Economic Modelling*, 28: 1–12.
R. Cull, L.C. Xu and T. Zhu (2009) Formal finance and trade credit during China's transition. *Journal of Financial Intermediation*, 18: 173–92.
V. Cuñat (2007) Trade credit: Suppliers as debt collectors and insurance providers. *Review of Financial Studies*, 20 (2).
M.G. Danielson and J.A. Scott (2004) Bank loan availability and trade credit demand. *Financial* Review, 39: 579–600.
G. De Blasio (2005) Does trade credit substitute for bank credit? Evidence from firm-level data. *Economic Notes*, 34 (1): 85–112.
D.W. Diamond (1991) Monitoring and reputation: The choice between bank loans and directly placed debt. *Journal of Political Economy*, 99 (4): 689–721.
—— (1984) Financial intermediation and delegated monitoring. *Review of Economic Studies*, 51 (3): 393–414.
J. Fernández de Guevara, J. Maudos and F. Pérez (2007) Integration and competition in the European financial markets. *Journal of International Money and Finance*, 26: 26–45.
S. Fukuda, M. Kayusa and K. Akashi (2006) The role of trade credit for small firms: An implication for Japan's banking crisis. *Bank of Japan Working Paper Series* 06-E18.
M. Gertler and S. Gilchrist (1994) Monetary policy, business cycles, and the behavior of small manufacturing firms. *Quarterly Journal of Economics*,109 (2): 309–40.
—— (1993) The role of credit market imperfections in the monetary transmission mechanism: Arguments and evidence. *Scandinavian Journal of Economics*, 95 (1): 43–64.

T. Hoshi, A. Kashyap and D. Scharftein (1991) Corporate structure, liquidity, and investment: Evidence from Japanese industrial groups. *Quarterly Journal of Economics*, 106 (1): 33–60.
—— (1990) The role of banks in reducing the cost of financial distress in Japan. *Journal of Financial Economics*, 27: 67–88.
Z. Huang (2003) Evidence of a bank lending channel in the UK. *Journal of Banking and Finance*, 27: 491–510.
H. Huang, S. Xiaojun and S. Zhang (2011) Counter-cyclical substitution between trade credit and bank credit. *Journal of Banking and Finance*, 35: 1859–78.
R.G. Hubbard (1998) Capital-market imperfections and investment. *Journal of Economic Literature*, 36 (1): 193–225.
A.K. Kashyap and J.C. Stein (2000) What do a million observations on banks say about the transmission of monetary policy? *American Economic Review*, 90 (3): 407–28.
I. Love and R. Zaidi (2010) Trade credit, bank credit, and financial crisis. *International Review of Finance*, 10 (1): 125–47.
S. Mateut, S. Bougheas and P. Mizen (2006) Trade credit, bank lending and monetary policy transmission. *European Economic Review*, 50: 603–29.
J. Maudos and J. Fernández de Guevara (2007) The cost of market power in banking social welfare loss vs. cost inefficiency. *Journal of Banking and Finance*, 31: 2103–25.
—— (2004) Factors explaining the interest margins in the banking sectors of European Union. *Journal of Banking and Finance*, 28: 2259–81.
J.H. Nielsen (2002) Trade credit and the bank lending channel. *Journal of Money, Credit, and Banking*, 34 (1): 226–53.
S.D. Oliner and G.D. Rudebusch (1996) Is there a broad credit channel for monetary policy? *FRBSF Economic* Review, 1: 3–13.
—— (1995) Is there a bank lending channel for monetary policy? *Economic Review-Federal Reserve Bank of San Francisco*, 2: 3–20.
M.A. Petersen and R.G. Rajan (1997) Trade credit: Theories and evidence. *Review of Financial Economics*, 10 (3): 226–53.
—— (1995) The effect of credit market competition on lending relationships. *Quarterly Journal of Economics*, 110: 407–43.
—— (1994) The benefits of lending relationships: Evidence from small business data. *Journal of Finance*, 49 (1): 3–37.
R. Repullo and J. Suarez (2000) Entrepeneurial moral hazard and bank monitoring: A model of the credit channel. *European Economic Review*, 44: 1931–50.
C.D. Romer and D.H. Romer (1994) Monetary policy matters. *Journal of Monetary Economics*, 34: 75–88.
—— (1990) New evidence on the monetary transmission mechanism. *Brookings Papers on Economic* Activity, 1: 149–213.
J.C. Stein (1998) An adverse-selection model of bank asset and liability management with implication for the transmission of monetary policy. *RAND Journal of Economics*, 29 (3): 466–86.
D. Tsuruta (2010) How does small businesses finance their growth opportunities? The case of recovery from the lost decade in Japan. *GRIPS Policy Information Center*. Discussion Paper No. 09–19.
—— (2007) Credit contagion and trade credit supply: Evidence from small business data in Japan. *RIETI Discussion Paper Series* 07-E-043.

5

The Assessment of the Net Stable Funding Ratio (NSFR) Value. Evidence from the Financial Crisis

Laura Chiaramonte, Barbara Casu and Roberto Bottiglia

5.1 Introduction

The recent financial crisis has shown how rapidly and acutely liquidity risk, in terms of both market liquidity risk and funding risk, can manifest itself in financial markets and how it can affect banks' stability and indeed the entire financial system. This has highlighted the need to pay more attention to liquidity risk and its interactions with other banking risks.

Basel I and II managed liquidity risk with non-harmonized procedures, based on strict rules which proved inadequate in the face of the degree of market sophistication. To fill this gap, following the crisis a series of normative measures to regulate liquidity risk were proposed both by the Basel Committee on Banking Supervision (BCBS)[1] and by European Commission and Committee of European Banking Supervisors (CEBS).[2] In particular, the Basel Committee, in the December 2010 final document (Basel III), set the gradual introduction of two internationally harmonized global liquidity standards for banks: the Liquidity Coverage Ratio (LCR) and the Net Stable Funding Ratio (NSFR). The LCR (short-term rule) is intended to promote resilience to potential liquidity disruptions over a 30-day horizon. It aims to ensure that global banks have sufficient unencumbered high-quality liquid assets to offset the net cash outflows they could encounter under an acute short-term stress scenario. After an observation period that began in 2011, the LCR will be introduced on 1 January 2015. The NSFR (structural rule) requires a minimum amount of stable sources of funding relative to the liquidity profiles of the assets, as well as the potential for contingent liquidity needs arising from off-balance-sheet commitments, over a one-year horizon. The NSFR aims to limit over-reliance on short-term wholesale funding during times of buoyant market liquidity and to encourage better assessment of liquidity risk across all on- and off-balance-sheet items. The NSFR will move to a minimum standard by 1 January 2018. Both liquidity ratios will be equal to at least 100 per cent.

Although the Basel Committee outlined these two liquidity standards, this research focuses on the NSFR only, since publicly available information does not allow assessment of the value of LCR. In addition, good management of structural liquidity would avoid any negative effect in the short term.

In particular, this chapter assesses, on the basis of available data and simplified hypothesis,[3] the value of the NSFR on a sample of top-tier international banks operating in five areas of specialization (bank holding and holding companies, commercial banks, cooperative banks, savings banks and real estate and mortgage banks – the latter principally English building societies) both in the pre-crisis period (2005–2007), during the crisis and in the post-crisis period (2008–2009), in order to identify which sample banks comply with the new structural liquidity risk measure in the dual time horizon considered. Our results highlight that the banks with structural liquidity furthest from the minimum requirements are those that would probably be included in the systemic risk list drawn up by the Group of Governors and Head of Supervision, and tend to be bank holding and holding companies or commercial banks. Conversely, the sample banks with liquidity structures in line with the new NSFR liquidity requirement are cooperative banks, saving banks, or real estate and mortgage banks; these banks operate on a smaller geographical scale and so have lower total assets.

5.2 The Basel III NSFR

The Basel Committee on Banking Supervision (BCBS, 2010a) has defined the NSFR as the ratio of available stable funding (ASF) to required stable funding (RSF).[4] This ratio must be greater than 100 per cent (see Equation 5.1).

$$NSFR = \frac{(ASF)}{(RSF)} \geq 100\% \tag{5.1}$$

ASF is defined as the total amount of a bank's: (a) capital; (b) preferred stock with maturity equal to or greater than one year; (c) liabilities with effective maturities of one year or greater; (d) the portion of demand deposits and/or term deposits with maturities of less than one year that would be expected to stay with the institution for an extended period in an idiosyncratic stress event; and (e) the portion of wholesale funding with maturities of less than one year that is expected to stay with the institution for an extended period in an idiosyncratic stress event.

The amount assigned to each category is to be multiplied by an ASF factor ranging from 100 per cent for more stable funding to 50 per cent for less stable funding. In this way, ASF categories are biased to a greater extent by more stable funding and to a lesser extent by less stable funding. Table 5.1 summarizes the components of each of the ASF categories and the associated maximum ASF factor.

The RSF imposed by supervisors is calculated as the sum of the value of the assets held and funded by the institution, multiplied by a specific RSF factor assigned to each particular asset type. The RSF factor applied to the reported values of each asset is the amount of that item that supervisors believe should be supported with stable funding. Assets that are more liquid and more readily available to act as a source of extended liquidity in the stressed environment receive lower RSF factors (and require less stable funding) than assets considered less liquid in such circumstances and, therefore, require more stable funding. Hence, more liquid assets (even in conditions of stress) are weighted by a lower RSF factor; in fact, asset components are weighted inversely to their degree of liquidity.

Table 5.1 summarizes the specific types of assets to be assigned to each asset category and their associated RSF factor.

This table summarizes the balance sheet weighting used to calculate NSFR as defined in the Basel III Accords 2010.

- ASF denotes Available Stable Funding, while RSF denotes Required Stable Funding.
- Short- and long-term is defined as less and more than one year respectively.
- Stable deposits are those deposits that are fully covered by an effective deposit insurance scheme or by a public guarantee that provides equivalent protection and where: (a) the depositors have other established relationships with the bank that make deposit withdrawal highly unlikely; or, (b) the deposits are in transactional accounts.
- Less stable deposits are those deposits that are not covered by an effective deposit insurance scheme or by sovereign deposit guarantee; they include high-value deposits, deposits from sophisticated or high net worth individuals, deposits that can be withdrawn quickly and foreign currency deposits, as determined by each jurisdiction.

Table 5.1 Summary of NSFR (Basel III)

ASF categories (Liabilities)	ASF Factor	RSF categories (Assets)	RSF factor
Capital long-term debt	100%	Other assets	100%
Stable short-term deposits of retail and small business customers	90%	Short-term loans to retail clients	85%
Less stable short-term deposits of retail and small business customers	80%	Unencumbered residential mortgage of any maturity with Basel II standardized risk weights of 35% or below	65%
Wholesale short-term funding from non-financial corporates	50%	Listed equity securities, single A-rated corporate and covered bonds Short-term loans to non-financial corporate clients	50%
		Highly rated corporate and covered bonds	20%
All other liabilities and equity not included above	0%	Sovereign debt	5%
		Off balance sheet exposures undrawn amount of committed credit and liquidity facilities	5%
		Cash and short-term securities	0%

(Left side, arrow pointing up: More stable funding; right side, arrow pointing down: More liquid assets)

Source: Adapted from BCBS (2010a) and Bank of England (2010).

Some detail of the NSFR has been omitted for simplicity. See Basel Committee on Banking Supervision (BCBS, 2010a) for full details.

5.3 The Quantitative Impact Studies and literature results

Empirical studies that attempt to assess the NSFR value are limited. Table 5.2 shows that there are two groups of studies that have tried to

Table 5.2 QIS and academic studies

	Sample	Year	NSFR
QIS studies:			
BCBS (2010b)	91 Group 1 international banks	2009	Group 1: 93% (average)
	158 Group 2 international banks		Group 2: 103% (average)
CEBS (2010)	48 Group 1 European banks	2009	Group 1: 91% (average)
	182 Group 2 European banks		Group 2: 94% (average)
Academic studies:			
King (2010)	6844 banks from 13 OECD countries	1993–2007	86% (average)
Angora and Roulet (2011)	781 US and European commercial banks	2005–2008	93.6%: entire sample (average) 114.2%: vulnerable banks (average) 94.5%: non-vulnerable banks (average)
Lusignani and Zicchino (2011)	31 Italian banks	2009	99%: entire sample (average) 97.8%: major banks (average) 102.6%: medium banks (average) 110.5%: small banks (average)
Giordana and Schumacher (2011)	Luxembourg banks (for a maximum of 157 banks and a minimum of 68 banks)	2003q1–2010q4	Median of the NSFR (entire sample): above 100% before 2005 80% at the start of the crisis

Notes: Group 1 banks are those that have Tier 1 capital in excess of €3bn, are well diversified and are internationally active. All other banks are considered Group 2 banks.

Only Lusignani and Zicchino (2011) and Giordana and Schumacher (2011) used the weighting of the December 2010 final document. The other studies showed in the table used the December 2009 Consultative Document.

assess the NSFR using simplified hypothesis: the Quantitative Impact Studies (QIS) of the Basel Committee on Banking Supervision (BCBS, 2010b) and Committee of European Banking Supervisors (CEBS, 2010), on the one hand, and the academic studies by King (2010), Angora and Roulet (2011), Lusignani and Zicchino (2011), and Giordana and Schumacher (2011), on the other.

Both QIS studies were conducted after the December 2009 publication of the Basel Committee's Consultative Document. For this reason, the weighting used by the Committee and the CEBS are slightly different from those of the December 2010 final document. Moreover, the two impact studies divided the sample banks (European banks for the CEBS and international banks for the Basel Committee) into two groups. In Group 1 we find banks with Tier 1 capital in excess of €3bn, well diversified and internationally active. All other banks were allocated to Group 2.

In terms of NSFR results, the CEBS QIS highlighted an average NSFR in 2009 of 91 per cent for Group 1 banks and 94 per cent for Group 2 banks. Conversely, the Basel Committee QIS results showed a slightly higher average NSFR for both groups in the international sample. Only Group 2 banks had an average NSFR slightly in excess of the 100 per cent threshold. In fact, the average NSFR for Group 1 banks was 94 per cent and for Group 2 banks was 103 per cent. Moreover, 43 per cent of Group 1 and 2 banks met or exceeded the minimum NSFR requirement, 67 per cent having an NSFR of 85 per cent or above.

NSFR have been analysed not only by the Committee and the CEBS, but also by a limited number of very recent academic studies. In particular, Lusignani and Zicchino (2011) and Giordana and Schumacher (2011) used the weighting of the December 2010 final document on a sample of Italian banks and on a sample of Luxembourg banks respectively. Lusignani and Zicchino demonstrated that the average NSFR of the major five Italian banking groups was 97.8 per cent, while the average NSFR of the medium and small banks was 102.6 and 110.5 per cent respectively. Giordana and Schumacher found that the median of the NSFR of a sample of Luxembourg banks for the period spanning 2003 to 2010 was above 100 per cent before 2005, but from then until the start of the crisis declined continuously, to a level of 80 per cent. Giordana and Schumacher demonstrated also that there were significant differences in the median of the NSFR between large and small banks; in particular, large banks fare worse in terms of the NSFR.

Conversely King (2010) and Angora and Roulet (2011) used the weighting of the December 2009 consultative proposal on a sample of banks from 13 OECD countries and on a sample of US and European publicly traded commercial banks, respectively. King showed an average NSFR over the period 1993 to 2007 of 86 per cent for the 6844 banks from 13 OECD countries. Angora and Roulet showed an average NSFR over the period 2005 to 2008 of 93.6 per cent for the US and European commercial banks.

5.4 Data description and the NSFR construction

This study considers only top-tier international banks (with total assets greater than US$10bn) operating in five areas of specialization: bank holding and holding companies, commercial banks, cooperative banks, savings banks, and real estate and mortgage banks.

The final sample is composed of 235 top-tier international banks, 141 of which are European (Austria: 6, Belgium: 2, Denmark: 17, France: 10, Germany: 11, Ireland: 4, Italy: 14, the Netherlands: 4, Norway: 21, Portugal: 4, Spain: 26, Sweden: 9, Switzerland: 4, and the United Kingdom: 9), 10 are Australian, 12 are Canadian, and there are 72 US banks. Since top-tier banks in the Asian countries did not experience liquidity problems during the recent financial crisis, we decided to not consider such banks in the study. See Table 5.3 for sample distribution by specialization in each country.

The overall time horizon considered comprises the period from January 2005, the year in which the International Accounting Standard (IAS/IFRS) became mandatory for the preparation of the consolidated financial statements of European banks, to December 2009, the latest data available at the time of this study. This time period is then divided into two sub-periods. The first sub-period, pre-crisis, prior to the onset of the subprime crisis, covers January 2005 to December 2007; it is widely accepted that the outbreak of the subprime crisis occurred in the summer of 2007. A second sub-period, the crisis and post-crisis periods, is from January 2008 to December 2009, covering the acute and less acute phases of the crisis.

For each bank in the sample, we calculated the NSFR value on the basis of BankScope database information. Since the BankScope database does not contain all the detailed information specified in the Basel Committee December 2010 final document, in the study we assessed the NSFR values using a simplified version (see Equation 5.2) that is similar to the NSFR observed by King (2010).

Our simplified version was based on three assumptions. The first assumption was related to deposits. In BankScope there is no distinction between stable and less stable deposits. For this reason, the only way to determine the NSFR value was to use one of the supervisors' assumptions indicated in King's paper: for the supervisors, 75 per cent of deposits are stable and 25 per cent are less stable.

Table 5.3 Sample distribution by specialization in each country

Country/Specialization	Bank holding and holding companies	Commercial banks	Cooperative banks	Saving banks	Real estate and mortgage banks	Total
Austria	4	2				**6**
Belgium	2					**2**
Denmark		11	1	5		**17**
France	1	5	2	1	1	**10**
Germany	3	5	1	2		**11**
Ireland		3			1	**4**
Italy	1	5	8			**14**
Netherlands	1	2	1			**4**
Norway	1	1		18	1	**21**
Portugal	1	2		1		**4**
Spain		8	2	16		**26**
Sweden	3	3		2	1	**9**
Switzerland	2	1	1			**4**
United Kingdom	4	2			3	**9**
Australia	1	7	1		1	**10**
Canada		9	2	1		**12**
USA	68	4				72
Total	**92**	**70**	**19**	**46**	**8**	**235**

Source: BankScope database, authors' calculations.

The second assumption relates to corporate loans. In the BankScope database there is no distinction between corporate loans with less than one year to maturity and corporate loans with more than one year to maturity. For this reason, in order to determine the short-term loans to corporate clients required by Basel for the calculation of the NSFR, this study used one of the supervisors' assumptions indicated in King's paper: for the supervisors, 25 per cent of corporate loans are less than one year to maturity.

The third assumption relates to retail loans. In the BankScope database it is not possible to distinguish between the two types of retail loans required by Basel III: unencumbered residential mortgages of any maturity weighted at 65 per cent, on the one hand, and retail loans with less than one year to maturity weighted at 85 per cent, on the other hand. For this reason the only way to determine the NSFR value was to use a simplified assumption based on a prudential perspective. In particular, retail loans used in this study are retail loans of any maturity (short and long-term) funded at 85 per cent, in other words the higher of the two weightings established for retail loans.

$$NSFR = \frac{ASF}{RSF} = \frac{\begin{array}{l} Equity + Liabs > 1yr + (StableDeposits < 1yr * 90\%) + \\ (LessStableDeposits < 1yr * 80\%) \end{array}}{\begin{array}{l} (GovtDebt * 5\%) + (CorpLoans < 1yr * 50\%) + \\ (RetLoans * 85\%) + (OtherAssets) \end{array}} \tag{5.2}$$

The NSFR described in Equation 2 was calculated for the 235 banks in our sample.

Figure 5.1 shows the results of the NSFR of sample banks in each year. The results, despite the fact that we adopted a simplified version of NSFR, show for the period 2005 to 2009 an average NSFR of nearly 97 per cent for the 235 international banks in the sample, close to the minimum requirement of 100 per cent. In particular, the sample banks' average NSFR reached its highest average value, 98.80 per cent, in 2006. In subsequent years, the NSFR gradually decreased; in 2009 the average NSFR had dropped to 95.94 per cent, a little higher than the average 2005 NSFR, 95.49 per cent.

Figure 5.2 also shows that banks with structural liquidity furthest from minimum requirements, regardless of their geographical area, belonged to the category of bank holding and holding companies or commercial banks. In comparative terms, the total assets of these banks were higher, well diversified and internationally active. In short, however, owing to their funding characteristics, these banks would probably be included in the systemic risk list, the so-called too big to fail (TBTF), drawn up by

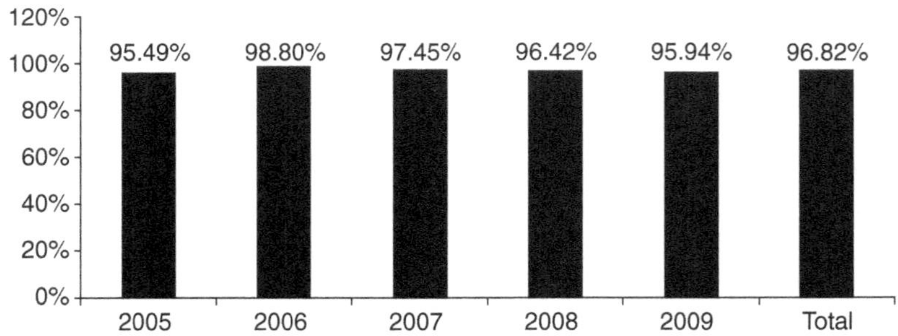

Figure 5.1 NSFR of sample banks in each year
Source: BankScope database, authors' calculations.

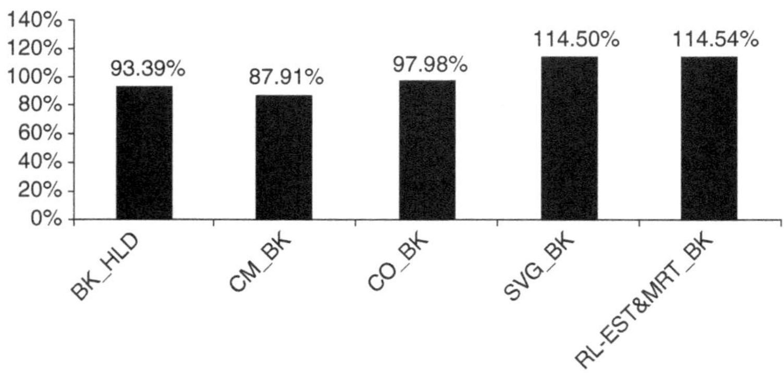

Figure 5.2 NSFR distribution by specialization on the whole period
Source: BankScope database, authors' calculations.
Notes: BK_HLD: Bank holding & holding Companies; CM_BK: commercial banks; CO_BK: cooperative banks; SVG_BK: saving banks; RL-EST&MRT_BK: real estate & mortgage banks.

the Group of Governors and Head of Supervision (GHOS). In the period 2005 to 2009, the commercial banks and the bank holding and holding companies exhibited an average NSFR below the minimum requirement: 87.91 per cent and 93.39 per cent respectively.

Conversely, the sample banks with liquidity structures in line with the new liquidity requirement NSFR, are s cooperative banks, saving banks, or real estate and mortgage banks. These banks operate on a smaller geographical scale, and so have lower total assets, high capitalization and capital requirements in line with traditional standards. In particular, saving banks and real estate and mortgage banks in the period considered showed structural liquidity in excess of the minimum requirement principally on account of a stable funding structure and a typically stable retail deposit base. Finally, the average NSFR of cooperative banks was 97.98 per cent, slightly below the minimum requirement, due to balanced funding and lending activity.

5.5 Conclusions

This study assessed, on the basis of available data and hypothesis, the value of the NSFR on a sample of top-tier international banks both in the pre-crisis period and in the crisis period (acute and less acute). This analysis shows the presence of a negative relationship between bank size (in terms of total assets) and the NSFR value. In particular, the study highlighted how the structural liquidity of systemic banks, typically bank holding and holding companies or commercial banks, is furthest from minimum requirements. Underlying the NSFR values below minimum requirements, there appears to be a tendency towards a high degree of maturity transformation. Banks that are below the 100 per cent required minimum have until 2018 to meet the standard, and can take a number of measures to do so, including lengthening the term of their funding, reducing maturity mismatching and scaling back activities which are most vulnerable to liquidity risk in periods of stress. Unlike the bank holding and holding companies and the commercial banks, banks that operate on a smaller geographical scale and so have lower total assets, such as cooperative banks, saving banks, or real estate and mortgage banks, are generally characterized by NSFR values above the minimum requirements due to lower maturity transformation.

Notes

1. See Basel Committee on Banking Supervision (BCBS, 2008a, 2008b, 2009, 2010a, 2010b).
2. See Committee of European Banking Supervisors (CEBS, 2008, 2009) and European Commission (2010).
3. Underlying this chapter is an awareness that publicly available information does not provide the level of detail required to ensure full application of the new structural rule.
4. 'Stable funding' is defined as the portion of those types and amounts of equity and liability financing expected to be reliable sources of funds over a one-year time horizon under conditions of extended stress.

References

A. Angora and C. Roulet (2011) Liquidity assessment and the use of liquidity ratio as defined in the Basel III accords to identify bank distress. *Working Papers* – Université de Limoges.

Bank of England (2010) *Financial Stability Report* (London), December.

Basel Committee on Banking Supervision (BCBS) (2010a) *Basel III: International Frame work for Liquidity Risk Measurement, Standards and Monitoring*, December.

—— (2010b) *Results of the Comprehensive Quantitative Impact Study*, December.

—— (2009) *International Framework for Liquidity Risk Measurement, Standards and Monitoring* – consultative document, December.

—— (2008a) *Liquidity Risk: Management and Supervisory Challenges*, February.

—— (2008b) *Principles for Sound Liquidity Risk Management and Supervision*, September.

Committee of European Banking Supervisors (CEBS) (2010) *Results of the Comprehensive Quantitative Impact Study*, December.

—— (2009) *Guidelines on Liquidity Buffers*, December.

—— (2008) *Second Part of CEBS' Technical Advice to the European Commission on Liquidity Risk management*, June.

European Commission (2010) *Consultation Regarding Further Possible Changes to the Capital Requirements Directive (Crd)*, February.

G. Giordana and I. Schumacher (2011) The impact of the Basel III liquidity regulations on the bank lending channel: A Luxembourg case study. *Cahier D'Etudes Working Paper*, No. 61, June.

M.R. King (2010) Mapping capital and liquidity requirements to bank lending spreads. *BIS Working Papers*, No. 324, November.

G. Lusignani and L. Zicchino (2011) Convergenza a Basilea 3: un tetto alla crescita del credito? *Bancaria*, 3: 2–10.

6
Distance and Efficiency in the Italian Banking System

Cristina Bernini and Paola Brighi

6.1 Introduction

During recent decades, banks have progressively moved towards larger, centralized and hierarchical organizational structures. An increased investment in non-interest-generating activities has also implied performance vulnerability, whose effects have been particularly destabilizing during the recent financial crisis. In this economic and financial contest, several banks have become increasingly concerned with controlling and analysing their costs and revenues, as well as measuring the risks taken to produce acceptable returns.

In line with these developments, literature has evolved examining alternative banking organizational models, and risk and efficiency issues (Kano et al., 2011; Berger and Black, 2011; Fiordelisi et al., 2011). With reference to efficiency, the level of attention has increased due to the growing complexity and competitiveness of the market, and different methodological approaches have been proposed to investigate financial bank efficiency (Bos et al., 2009; Fiordelisi et al., 2011).

Among efficiency determinants, size, capital, risk and environmental factors turn out to be the most investigated; conversely to our knowledge no empirical studies have analysed whether relationship lending features influence bank efficiency levels. In the literature, distance, size and attitudes towards bank diversification are used as proxy for different bank organization structures, and indirectly for alternative relationships between banks and customers.

Several factors – innovation, consolidation and regulation – have recently changed bank organizational structure, making banks larger and more complex. Small business lending has also been affected. Technological innovations, such as credit scoring, make SMEs' evaluation easier;

moreover, consolidation means that SMEs interact with larger and more complex financial institutions differently than they do with smaller and less complex institutions. Large and complex institutions are usually more distant and are characterized by a wider and more sophisticated product diversification. The effects of both these aspects on efficiency depend, as suggested by Udell (2009, p. 16), 'on the extent to which hard information about borrower quality is a good substitute for soft information. On the one hand, hard information is quantifiable and easily stored and can be produced and communicated over long distances. ... On the other hand, soft information cannot be easily stored; and it can neither be easily generated over long distances, nor be easily communicated over long distances or within large and complex banking organizations' (on this point see also Stein, 2002).

As for distance, we refer to the so-called Church Tower Principle (CTP), proposed by Carling and Lundberg (2005, p. 40), affirming that 'the bank is the church tower and from its outlook it can screen and monitor firms in its proximity'. The authors refer to this as asymmetric information, which increases with distance. This principle appears to be particularly relevant to the Italian banking system, whose lending service is mainly addressed to SMEs that are highly opaque. The distance between the bank headquarters (HQ) and its branches could complicate the loan evaluation process, affecting overall bank efficiency negatively. The rationale is that as the distance between the borrowing firm and the bank loan decision unit increases, the relationship lending weakens and the credit evaluation process of the firm in question becomes problematic.

Even if the relationship between distance and efficiency has not, to our knowledge, been investigated, a considerable stream of the literature has, conversely, analysed the relation between organizational structure, distance and lending conditions. As suggested by Alessandrini et al. (2009c, p. 1) 'technological progress, deregulation, and consolidation have deeply changed the geography of the banking industry in many countries'. In this respect it becomes important to understand the role of functional distance – defined as the separation gap between the decision centre of a bank from its operational branches – in explaining the relationship lending between banks and borrowers. Functional distance and bank size can explain differences between bank organization structures and the consequent different impacts on their efficiency. Relationship lending is mainly based on the accumulation of soft information over time, and empirical evidence suggests that as the relationship grows in strength then borrowers benefit from better credit terms and credit availability (Petersen and Rajan, 1994, 1995). As expected, the lending relationship becomes easier if loan officers can personally interact with their borrowers. Moreover, it is less expensive to collect soft information if the bank is part of the local community, having the opportunity to use its knowledge to better evaluate the borrowers (Hauswald and Marquez, 2006).

Although the recent technological changes have strongly reduced the operational distance – defined as the physical gap separating banks from customers – many authors show that distance still matters. Degryse and Ongena (2004, p. 573) underline that 'current technological and regulatory developments may to a large extent remain impotent to further dismantling the various residual but mutually reinforcing frictions in the retail banking markets in Europe'.

Furthermore, the different banking attitudes to business may be analysed in respect of the degrees of income and asset diversification. Since the early 1990s, in Italy as well as in the USA and in other European countries, the banking industry has been moving from interest income models towards non-interest ones. Although financial assets diversification policies aim to increase the return, they may also generate both higher risk and destabilizing effects, affecting overall bank performance. Whether this strategy positively influences the risk-adjusted bank profitability, or, conversely, the strong increase in non-interest income causes a problematic growth of profit instability is an empirical question.

Bank income and asset diversification are also of interest in the banking efficiency literature. In this respect, Akhigbe and Stevenson (2010) show that an increase in non-interest income, especially underwriting/brokerage income, negatively influences profit efficiency. The effect is less evident for medium and large banks that can offset the decrease in cost efficiency with an increase in revenue efficiency.

With reference to European small banks, Mercieca et al. (2007) find that the higher volatility of net-interest income outweighs diversification benefits. As regards Italy, Chiorazzo et al. (2008) evidence that the shift toward activities that generate non-interest income has beneficial effects.

Within this framework, the originality of this chapter relies on the analysis of the relationship between bank business models and efficiency. The chapter extends previous literature by investigating the intertemporal relationship between bank efficiency and some key variables, such as distance, size and income diversification, used as proxies of different organizational banking models. In particular, the effects of the distance between bank local branches and its HQ on cost efficiency are examined. Quality and riskiness of bank loans are also considered to control for other sources of bank efficiency variability.

6.2 Relationship lending and bank efficiency: a literature review

6.2.1 What is the role of distance on bank efficiency?

Several empirical studies have underlined the role of distance on bank performance. If a borrower is not located close to a bank, the distance between them can act as a physical gap affecting either credit price or quantity conditions. From a theoretical perspective, the distance influences lending conditions because of transportation costs and asymmetric information (Degryse and Ongena, 2005).

A similar result holds under the asymmetric information hypothesis. The evaluation process of the bank borrower becomes more imprecise as the distance between lender and borrower increases. In this respect, the bank operating at the local level can have an informational advantage, charging higher loan rates to closer firms (hold-up). Further investigations suggest that the distance can also imply spatial credit rationing problems; as Hauswald and Marquez (2006) evidence, distance aggravates the information asymmetry problem, implying credit rationing effects for distant firms.

Another stream of research has investigated the relationships between distance, bank internal organization and lending policies. Berger et al. (2005) show that large banks lend at greater distances than do small banks, being better equipped to collect and act on hard information. Mian (2006) finds that local banks are much more concentrated on borrowers displaying soft information.

As for the Italian banking system, Felici and Pagnini (2008) evidence that large banks, by using hard information, are more able to cope with distance-related entry costs than are small banks. The analysis suggests that due to the advent of information and communication technology, banks have become increasingly able to open branches in distant markets. Nevertheless, they say that distance continues to play a role: 'Yet the fall in trade costs due to distance brought about by the new technologies does not imply that they are about to disappear. In other words, we do agree with a recent remark by Degryse and Ongena [2004] that "distance dies another day"' (p. 527).

The complexity of the above-mentioned relations implies that the empirical evidence may produce results that are not uniformly shared over time and across space. Petersen and Rajan (2002) show that technological changes improve the monitoring process, and thus distance becomes less important in explaining spatial rationing. Other findings suggest that for large and distant banks, credit scoring models could improve SME evaluation, relaxing the necessity for relationship-based models (Berger and Frame, 2007). Recently, Berger et al. (2011) confirmed that community banks make large use of credit scores but not simply 'for automatic approval/rejection of loan applicants, suggesting that these institutions continue to stress relationship lending or other lending technologies' (p. 16). Because relationship lending largely relies on soft information that is typically collected and processed at local level and is not easily transferable, relationship lending becomes less feasible across large distances. Stein (2002) suggests that a bank, depending on its organizational structure, will use different types of information. For a large and hierarchically complex organization it could be too costly to collect soft information at the local level, because of high delegation costs;[1] a large and distant bank specializing in relationship loans would need to invest more in monitoring its loan officers than in the performance of its loans. Conversely, small decentralized banks, characterized by a short distance between HQ and branch, could have a comparative advantage in small business lending.

To better investigate the effects of the distance on the bank–borrower relationship, a more accurate definition of distance, suggested by Alessandrini et al. (2009a), is considered. They compute the functional distance as 'an index that takes account of the ownership structure of the local lending offices. Specifically, [they] calculate functional distance as the ratio of local branches weighted by, alternatively, the physical, economic and socio-cultural distance which separates them from the locus where their own bank is headquartered, to the total number of local branches' (p. 263). In this respect, a bank characterized by local branches has the lowest value of functional distance indicator; otherwise, two banks with equally functional distance may be characterized by a different intensity of concentration/diffusion of local branches across the territory.

6.2.2 Does bank size affect cost efficiency?

The literature has investigated the role of bank size in order to understand its impact on credit allocation, loan contract requirements and lending technologies (Alessandrini et al., 2009b). As previously discussed, several studies suggest that large and transparent firms appear to be more likely to borrow from large banks, while small and opaque firms borrow from small and local banks (DeYoung et al., 2004). More recently, however, this dichotomous behaviour has been confuted by Berger et al. (2007); the authors show that small firms have a greater opportunity to borrow from a large bank as long as the concentration degree of large banks in the local market increases, suggesting that small firms are not penalized by large banks.

In the efficiency literature, the relationship between size and efficiency in the banking sector has also been investigated. Part of the literature emphasizes the role of different production technologies based on different bank size; other studies focus on the role of size in the inefficiency model. Both approaches seem to suggest that an increase in size is important only in the case of smaller banks, and that smaller banks appear to be more efficient than larger ones.

Assuming that different size groups of banks – small, medium and large – use the same production technology, Akhigbe and McNulty (2003) show that small banks are more profit-efficient than large banks. Using a two-step profit-efficiency approach, the authors explore whether several factors related to banking structure, competition and location, as well as the bank's financial ratios, affect the efficiency scores of small banks. Some key results are gained: (i) efficiency increases with bank size (this result is not coherent with the so-called information asymmetry hypothesis, that is the smaller the banks the better their loan customer screening, with positive effects in terms of greater profit efficiency); (ii) efficiency is greater for banks operating in more concentrated markets; (iii) the profit efficiency of small banks is negatively affected by the market's non-performing loan ratio, but is not influenced by the bank's internal non-performing loan ratio. These results are not unequivocally confirmed in the case of other groups of banks, suggesting some degree of heterogeneity among different-size banking groups (cf. Akhigbe and McNulty, 2005).

As regards the Italian banking market, Girardone et al. (2004) propose a comparative X-efficiency and an economies of scale analysis for different bank groups classified with respect to size, type and geographical location. The analysis evidences that the highest cost efficiency, either in terms of X-efficiency or economies of scale, is reached by large and medium banks generally located in the northern regions. Among bank categories, the most efficient appears to be the mutual banks. Economies of scale and the power of local monopolies could explain this result. A negative relationship between size and inefficiency is found for only very small banks, evidencing the relevant role played by economies of scale within this group. Furthermore, very small banks are characterized by a positive and statistical significant relation between inefficiency and risk (as measured by the non-performing loans).

Following this stream of research, in this chapter we suggest investigating the relationship between banking business model and efficiency by also considering the effect that the bank size has on cost efficiency.

6.2.3 ...and what about diversification?

Another stream of research has evidenced the role of diversification strategy on the performance of the banking system. An asset and income diversification strategy may imply positive and negative effects on the overall risk-adjusted bank profitability. Some authors show that the higher volatility of net-interest income outweighs diversification benefits. Several studies have investigated the effects of banks' divergent strategies toward specialization and diversification of banking financial activities on bank performance, bank risk, bank stability for US and European countries.[2]

Other studies analyse the effect of diversification on bank efficiency. Among them, Lozano-Vivas and Pasiouras (2010) investigate the relevance of non-traditional activities on efficiency in the case of publicly listed commercial banks in 87 countries worldwide. The authors study the relevance of non-traditional activities in the cost/profit function. As a proxy of the non-traditional activities, the off-balance-sheet activities (OBS) and non-interest income are used interchangeably. The analysis suggests that cost efficiency increases on average if the OBS or non-interest income are considered as additional output in the cost function. With respect to profit efficiency, results are more ambiguous. Considering OBS as an additional output does not substantially change profit efficiency. Conversely, the non-interest-income based model determines higher profit efficiency scores.

Based on US annual bank holding company (BHC) data over the period 2003–2006, Akhigbe and Stevenson (2010) discuss the relevance of non-traditional activities on profit efficiency. In particular, the analysis investigates how 'the addition of underwriting/brokerage, venture capital, and insurance services to the commercial BHC's repertoire improves a BHC's ability to efficiently generate profit' (p. 134). In the study, a measure of BHC efficiency (obtained by using the stochastic frontier approach, SFA) is compared with an efficiency ratio (that is how much traditional and non-traditional banking profitability is consumed by non-interest expenses). The results suggest a negative correlation between the efficiency ratio and the efficiency scores: high levels in the efficiency ratio are associated with low levels of efficiency. Moreover, the authors find that an increase of alternative activities based on underwriting/brokerage, venture capital and insurance business do not create greater profit efficiency. The effect is less severe for larger banks that can offset the decrease in cost efficiency with an increase in revenue efficiency.

As for Europe, empirical findings on the role of diversification are reported in Mercieca et al. (2007). The analysis is based on annual data for small European banks for the period 1997–2003.[3] The authors explore the economic impact of diversification on average profitability by calculating the effect of an increase in the non-interest share. The analysis evidences that an increase in non-interest activities has two main effects: a direct impact from shifting into non-interest activities, and an indirect effect arising from changes in diversification. Moreover, a negative net effect on average profitability and a corresponding positive effect on volatility are detected. The results are robust with respect to several controls, suggesting that over the analysed period the higher volatility of net-interest income outweighs the diversification benefits.

Using annual data from Italian banks over the period 1993–2003, Chiorazzo et al. (2008) study the link between non-interest revenues and profitability. The study suggests that the shift toward activities that generate non-interest income is beneficial for the Italian banking system. Diversification gains associated with non-interest income also diminish with bank size, that is small banks with a low non-interest income share make gains in financial performance by increasing their non-interest income.

Following the above literature in the chapter, we consider the effects of asset diversification either in the cost function or in the inefficiency models. The aim is to investigate whether, and to what extent, bank propensity toward non-interest income affects cost efficiency.

6.3 The study method

6.3.1 The data

Data are provided by the balance sheets of individual Italian banks submitted to the Bank of Italy and collected by the Italian Banking Association over the period 2006–2009. An unbalanced panel of 2597 banks is used in the analysis. The coverage of our sample relative to the population of the whole Italian banking system is nearly 90 per cent, and it is quite stable over the period analysed (Table 6.1).

The panel is composed of several bank groups, differing in size and juridical category. The size classification distinguishes between minor, small and large banks. The thresholds are given by the Bank of Italy, and are based on the average amount of total intermediation assets.[4] Minor banks are defined as those with average total intermediation assets lower than €1.3bn; small banks are those with average total intermediation

Table 6.1 Sample size and population coverage

Size groups	2006	2007	2008	2009	Total
Large	45	46	46	46	183
	7%	*7%*	*7%*	*7%*	*7%*
Small	110	110	110	110	440
	18%	17%	17%	18%	18%
Minors	487	499	501	487	1,974
	75%	*75%*	*76%*	*75%*	*75%*
Juridical groups	**2006**	**2007**	**2008**	**2009**	**Total**
Cooperative & Saving	85	86	88	86	345
	13%	*13%*	*13%*	*13%*	*13%*
Other commercial banks	140	145	146	147	578
	22%	22%	22%	23%	22%
Mutual banks	417	424	423	410	1,674
	65%	*65%*	*64%*	*64%*	*64%*
Total unbalanced sample	642	655	657	643	2,597
Total sample over total national system	89%	90%	92%	90%	90%

assets between €1.3bn and €9bn; large banks comprise all banks with average total intermediation assets higher than €9bn. The juridical categories are mutual, cooperative, savings, and other commercial banks. The mutual banks are considered separately, being strictly linked to the local market and with a greater degree of capitalization. The cooperative group is based on the Italian Banking Association classification, and the savings group is identified by using the ACRI (Italian Association of Saving Banks) classification; the business model of these two bank groups is very similar, so they are considered jointly. The last group, the other commercial banks, is obtained as a residual. In Table 6.1, the sample data coverage by size and category over time is reported.

In the analysis, macro-environmental variables affecting banks' efficiency over the period 2006–2009 are also used. Information on GDP at the provincial level are provided by Istituto Tagliacarne (ISTAT), which provides data on the number of provincial firms that are established and registered. The number of branches (referred to each bank at the provincial level) are taken from the Bank of Italy, as well as a measure of credit risk (defined as the ratio of the flow of new-performing loans on the stock of performing loans at the end of the previous period).

6.3.2 The model

Evaluating the efficiency of a bank involves a comparison between actual and optimal values. It is specifically concerned with the comparison between observed outputs and maximum potential outputs obtained from given inputs, or observed inputs and minimum potential inputs producing a given amount of outputs. It is also possible to define efficiency in terms of behavioural goals, where efficiency is measured by comparing observed and optimal costs and profits, leading to cost and profit efficiencies respectively.

In this chapter, for measuring the cost efficiency of Italian banks we use the SFA (Battese and Coelli, 1995). This model incorporates the estimation of cost function and the determinants of efficiency at the same time, by parameterizing the mean of the efficiency term as a function of exogenous variables.

As for the cost function we consider:

$$\ln(TC_{it}) = X_{it}\beta + (V_{it} + U_{it}), \tag{6.1}$$

where $\ln(TC_{it})$ is the logarithm of total production cost for bank i at time t, X indicates the natural logarithm of input prices and output quantities, β is a vector of unknown parameters to be estimated; and the V_{it}s are random variables that are assumed to be independent and identically distributed, $N(0,\sigma_V^2)$. The non-negative random variables, (U_{it}), which account for cost inefficiency, are assumed to be independently distributed, such that U_{it} is the truncation (at zero) of the $N(\mu_{it},\sigma^2)$-distribution, where μ_{it} is a function of observable explanatory variables and unknown parameters, as defined below. We choose the truncated normal form because of the hypothesis that the market is competitive, that is the greater proportion of the enterprises operate close to efficiency. It is assumed that the V_{it}s and U_{it}s are independent random variables.

The parameters of the frontier production function are simultaneously estimated with those of the inefficiency model $(\beta,\delta,\sigma^2,\sigma_V^2)$, in which the cost inefficiency effects are specified as a function of other variables:

$$\mu_{it} = \delta_0 + \sum_{m=1}^{M} \delta_m \ln z_{mit}. \tag{6.2}$$

In Equation 6.2, the δs are parameters to be estimated. A positive parameter value of δ_m implies that the mean inefficiency increases as the value of the m-input variable increases.

Maximum-likelihood estimates of the model parameters are obtained using the program Frontier 4.1, written by Coelli (1996). The variance parameters are defined by $\sigma_S^2 = \sigma_V^2 + \sigma^2$ and $\gamma = \sigma^2/\sigma_S^2$, originally recommended by Battese and Corra (1977). The log-likelihood function of this model is presented in the appendix of Battese and Coelli (1993).

When the variance associated with the technical inefficiency effects converges towards zero ($\sigma^2 \rightarrow 0$) then the ratio parameter, γ, approaches zero. When the variance of the random error (σ_V^2) decreases in size, relative to the variance associated with the technical inefficiency effects, the value of γ approaches one.

The cost efficiency of a unit at a given period of time is defined as the ratio of the minimum cost to the observed cost needed to produce a given set of outputs. The technical efficiency of the *i*-unit in the year *t* is given by:

$$CE_{it} = \exp(U_{it}). \tag{6.3}$$

The cost efficiency of one unit lies between zero and one, and is inversely related to the inefficiency effect.

Hypotheses on the nature of the inefficiency can be tested using the generalized likelihood ratio statistic (LR test), λ, given by:

$$\lambda = -2\left[\ln(L(H_0)) - \ln(L(H_1))\right], \tag{6.4}$$

where $L(H_0)$ and $L(H_1)$ denote the value of the likelihood function under the null and alternative hypotheses respectively. If the given null hypothesis is true, then λ has approximately a chi-square (or a mixed chi-square) distribution. If the null hypothesis involves $\gamma = 0$, then the asymptotic distribution involves a mixed chi-square distribution (Coelli, 1995).

6.3.3 The cost function specification

In the literature, the definition of bank inputs and outputs varies across studies. This study follows the so-called value added approach, originally proposed by Berger and Humphrey (1992). This approach asserts that all liabilities and assets of banks have some output characteristics, rather than being categorized as either inputs or outputs only.[5] The econometric models are specified for panel data, with both stochastic frontier cost function and inefficiency model. A flexible functional form as the translog production function is used:

$$\begin{aligned}\ln(c_{it}) = {} & \alpha + \sum_{k=1}^{3} \beta_k \ln q_{kit} + \sum_{p=1}^{3} \beta_p \ln(p_{pit}) + \frac{1}{2}\sum_{j=1}^{3}\sum_{k=1}^{3} \beta_{jk} \ln q_{jit} \ln q_{kit} \\ & + \frac{1}{2}\sum_{m=1}^{3}\sum_{p=1}^{3} \beta_{mp} \ln(p_{mit}) \ln(p_{pit}) + \sum_{k=1}^{3}\sum_{p}^{3} \beta_{kp} \ln q_{kit} \ln p_{pit} \\ & + \beta_E \ln E_{it} + \beta_t t + \beta_{t2} t^2 + (V_{it} + U_{it}).\end{aligned} \tag{6.5}$$

where $\ln c_{it}$ is the natural logarithm of the operative cost of bank i in year t. According to the value added approach and following, among others, Akhigbe and McNulty (2003), we consider three outputs, $\ln q_{kit}(k = 1,2,3)$, that are: total net loans, retail deposits and fee-based financial services (that is non-interest income assets) respectively. $\ln p_{pit}(p = 1,2,3)$ is the logarithm of three prices: the price for wage rate for labour, the price of borrowed price of funds and the price of physical capital, respectively. We also consider a fixed input E, that is the equity capital defined at the bank level, controlling for differences in equity capital risk across banks. Banks with lower equity ratios are assumed to be riskier, in line with Mester (1996). The cost frontier may also shift over time according to the values of the parameters β_t and β_{t2}.

The conditions for ensuring that the cost function is linearly homogeneous in input price are:

$$\sum_{p=1}^{3} \beta_p = 1; \qquad \sum_{m=1}^{3} \beta_{mp} = 0; \qquad \sum_{k=1}^{3} \beta_{kp} = 0; \tag{6.6}$$

To meet these homogeneity conditions, Equation 6.6 is transformed into a normalized function. Specifically, costs and input prices are normalized by the price of wage rate for labour (p_1). Then, the normalized cost function to be estimated is:

$$\begin{aligned}\ln(c_{it}/p_{1it}) &= \alpha + \sum_{k=1}^{3} \beta_k \ln q_{kit} + \sum_{p=1}^{2} \beta_p \ln(p_{pit}/p_{1it}) \\ &+ \frac{1}{2}\sum_{j=1}^{3}\sum_{k=1}^{3} \beta_{jk} \ln q_{jit} \ln q_{kit} + \frac{1}{2}\sum_{m=1}^{2}\sum_{p=1}^{2} \beta_{mp} \ln(p_{mit}/p_{1it}) \ln(p_{pit}/p_{1it}) \\ &+ \sum_{k=1}^{3}\sum_{p}^{2} \beta_{kp} \ln q_{kit} \ln(p_{pit}/p_{1it}) + \beta_E \ln E_{it} + \beta_t t + \beta_{t2} t^2 + (V_{it} + U_{it}).\end{aligned} \tag{6.7}$$

Table 6.2 reports some statistics of the input and output variables used in estimating the cost functions, either for the whole bank sample or the bank groups.

6.3.4 What causes cost inefficiency?

We further investigate factors affecting bank efficiency in order to assess the importance of any (in)efficiency determinants. In particular, the main aim of the analysis is to examine whether bank organizational

Table 6.2 Descriptive statistics of input and output variables

	Mutual			Saving & cooperative			Other commercial banks			Total		
Variable	*Mean*	*Median*	*Se (mean)*	*Mean*	*Median*	*Se(mean)*	*Mean*	*Median*	*Se(mean)*	*Mean*	*Median*	*Se(mean)*
Cost (Profit) (in thousand €)												
Total cost (cit)	5,763	4,043	164	79,517	41,137	6,213	141,974	30,247	17,690	46,659	6,389	4,390
Output quantities (in thousand €)												
Loans(q1)	196,194	114,454	6,094	2,891,087	1,254,740	238,003	4,956,075	921,942	588,912	1,621,594	186,638	145,055
Demand deposits (q2)	132,434	85,739	4,625	1,799,412	864,407	148,637	2,949,291	443,790	357,097	1,009,855	122,762	90,978
Other earning assets (q3)	66,641	44,221	2,308	1,205,709	287,398	208,399	4,363,544	307,187	785,300	1,217,314	65,979	190,432
Equity (E)	30,696	19,643	866	439,517	145,465	50,553	860,114	129,041	156,369	275,178	31,484	38,055
Input prices												
Price of labour (p1)	50.348	49.323	0.403	50.039	4.3361	0.367	63.133	54.336	1.534	53.316	49.920	0.459
Price of funds (p2)	0.011	0.011	0.0	0.013	0.012	0.001	0.018	0.014	0.001	0.013	0.011	0.000
Price of fixed capital (p3)	1.105	0.692	0.053	1.409	0.706	0.140	10.623	1.889	1.357	3.349	0.760	0.327

(Continued)

Table 6.2 Continued

	Minor			Small			Large			Total		
Variable	*Mean*	*Median*	*Se (mean)*	*Mean*	*Median*	*Se(mean)*	*Mean*	*Median*	*Se(mean)*	*Mean*	*Median*	*Se(mean)*
Cost (Profit) (in thousand €)												
Total cost (cit)	5,934	4,213	125	50,790	39,494	1,721	440,291	229,486	49,314	46,659	6,389	4,390
Output quantities (in thousand €)												
Loans (q1)	173,788	114,216	3,807	1,668,936	1,312,245	54,930	15,700,000	9,663,200	1,563,880	1,621,594	186,638	145,055
Demand deposits (q2)	120,553	84,037	2,478	1,075,175	848,196	41,259	9,933,550	6,125,053	1,020,307	1,009,855	122,762	90,978
Other earning assets (q3)	66,734	45,833	1,624	640,517	364,463	36,213	13,900,000	4,279,767	2,315,034	1,217,314	65,979	190,432
Equity (E)	29,204	20,875	691	211,018	156,099	7,400	2,849,192	994,738	460,980	275,178	31,484	38,055
Input prices												
Price of labour (p1)	51.855	49.707	0.406	54.310	49.756	0.888	65.542	54.520	3.915	53.316	49.920	0.459
Price of funds (p2)	0.012	0.01	0.0	0.015	0.013	0.01	0.019	0.014	0.002	0.013	0.011	0.000
Price of fixed capital (p3)	2.480	0.742	0.331	3.828	0.729	0.658	11.210	1.192	2.332	3.349	0.760	0.327

structure – proxy by functional distance, size and income diversification – affects bank efficiency differently. In the inefficiency model, we also consider risk variables and macro-environmental factors in order to control for bank heterogeneity.

Supposing that internal and environmental economies factors impact on bank efficiency, we propose an innovative specification of the inefficiency model in which the means μ_{it} associated with the cost inefficiency of bank *i* at time *t* are assumed to be specified as a function of three different sets of variables. The variables of interest are obviously related to the business model strategy, depending on the distance between the headquarter and the branches spread over the territory (*HQ-DISTANCE*), its income diversification policy (DIV_{REV}) and its size (*SIZE*). Furthermore, to account for asset quality and bank micro credit risk conditions, a second group of variables has been included: (i) the loan loss provisions over total net loans (*LLP*); (ii) the traditional non-performing loans over total net loans ratio (*NPL*). Macro environmental effects are finally controlled by: (i) the standard provincial *GDP* annual growth rate; (ii) the provincial firm default rate; and (iii) a macro non-performing loans rate.

Then the inefficiency model is specified as follows:

$$\begin{aligned}\mu_{it} &= \delta_0 + \delta_{div} \ln DIV_{REV_it} + \delta_{fd} \ln HQ - DISTANCE_{it} + \delta_{size} \ln SIZE_{it} \\ &\quad + \delta_{llp} \ln LLP_{it} + \delta_{npl} \ln NPL_{it} + \delta_{gdp} \ln GDP\_RT_{it} + \delta_{dr} \ln DEF\_RT_{it} \\ &\quad + \delta_{npli} \ln NPL\_INDEX_{it}\end{aligned} \tag{6.8}$$

A novel measure of the functional distance (*HQ-DISTANCE*) between bank branches and its HQ is proposed. Our indicator is similar to the *F-DISTANCE* measure suggested by Alessandrini et al. (2009a). In contrast to the authors, we construct the indicator for the *i*-bank at the municipal level, as follows:

$$HQ - DISTANCE_i = \frac{\sum_{z_b=1}^{B_i} [Branches_{iz_b} \times \ln(1 + D_{iz_b})]}{\sum_{z_b=1}^{B_i} Branches_{z_b}}, \tag{6.9}$$

where $z_b = 1, \ldots, B_i$ are the municipalities where the *i*-bank has branches, with *i:1,..,I*. $D_{iz_b} = \sqrt{(X_{z_b} - X_{HQ_i})^2 + (Y_{z_b} - Y_{HQ_i})^2}$ is the Euclidean distance between the municipality z_b where the branch is located and the municipality where the *i*-bank HQ is located (HQ_i). The *HQ-DISTANCE* is calculated in respect to municipalities where at least one branch is present, that is for almost 5,900 Italian municipalities.[6]

Statistics reported in Table 6.3 show that the average functional distance of the Italian banking system is 40 km, but with large differences between bank groups. Large banks and other commercial banks have the highest value – 166 and 116 km respectively – whereas mutual and minor banks appear to be the most concentrated in their territories; the mean distance between their HQ and branches is 10 and 17 km respectively. The results may suggest that distance is correlated with bank size. The scatter plots of the size and distance for the different bank groups (Figure 6.1) confirm this relationship, being positive for large and other commercial banks and null for mutual and minor banks.

In Figure 6.2 the map of the *HQ-DISTANCE* and its dynamic are also reported. The average functional distance of the Italian banking system increases over the period by 4 per cent. The figure suggests that the operational units located in the south are the farthest from their *HQs*, mainly located in the centre and in the north of Italy.[7]

The bank organizational structure is also controlled by using a measure of bank size (*SIZE*) – that is, the natural logarithm of total asset. As banks become larger their organizational structure becomes more complex, hence 'gathering soft information [becomes] more costly and lending to informational opaque borrowers less profitable' (Alessandrini et al., 2009b, p. 4). In this sense the larger banks may be less efficient in SMEs lending operations.

The income diversification index (DIV_{REV}) measures for each bank the degree of diversification policy between traditional and non-interest income activities. Using the standard definition of *NET* (net interest income) and *NII* (net non-interest income) according to Chiorazzo et al. (2008), we compute the Herfindahl–Hirschman Index (HHI) revenue as follows:

$$HHI_{REV} = \left(\frac{NET}{NET+NII}\right)^2 + \left(\frac{NII}{NET+NII}\right)^2 \tag{6.10}$$

and then, following Stiroh and Rumble (2006), we define the income diversification measure as:

$$(10) \quad DIV_{REV} = 1 - HHI_{REV}. \tag{6.11}$$

As suggested by Chiorazzo et al. (2008), under the constraint that NET and NII have to assume positive values, this index varies from 0.0 to 0.5. It will be zero when the bank does not diversify its activity – because either it is strongly concentrated on traditional net-interest income or

Variable	Mutual			Saving & cooperative			Other commercial banks			Total		
	Mean	*Median*	*Std dev.*	*Mean*	*Median*	*Std. Dev.*	*Mean*	*Median*	*Std. Dev.*	*Mean*	*Median*	*Std. Dev.*
Banking business model												
Functional distance (HQ-DISTANCE)	1.625	1.742	0.019	2.793	2.769	0.053	2.950	3.187	0.071	2.083	2.009	0.025
Income diversification (DIV_{REV})	0.292	0.294	0.002	0.376	0.00	0.005	0.338	0.386	0.006	0.313	0.317	0.002
Total assets (in thousand €) (SIZE)	272,993	171,964	8,426	4,343,028	1,714,980	402,883	9,673,590	1,466,576	1,288,865	2,977,222	280,074	317,832
Micro risk conditions												
Loan loss provisions /Total net loans (LLP)	0.005	0.003	0.016	0.006	0.005	0.035	0.007	0.005	0.041	0.005	0.004	0.015
Non performing loans/Total net loans (NPL)	0.018	0.013	0.001	0.015	0.012	0.001	0.019	0.009	0.003	0.018	0.012	0.001
Macro environmental conditions												
GDP growth rate (GDP)	99.355	99.179	0.071	99.182	98.913	0.166	98.762	98.575	0.102	99.191	99.092	0.055
Firm default rate (DEF_RT)	2.370	2.110	0.042	2.680	2.465	0.075	3.176	2.600	0.066	2.602	2.190	0.033
Macro NPL (NPL_INDEX)	26.481	1.000	1.030	20.609	1.000	1.881	17.144	1.000	1.149	23.530	1.000	0.753

(Continued)

Table 6.3 Continued

Variable	Minor			Small			Large			Total		
	Mean	*Median*	*Std dev.*	*Mean*	*Median*	*Std dev.*	*Mean*	*Median*	*Std dev.*	*Mean*	*Median*	*Std dev.*
Banking business model												
Functional distance (HQ-DISTANCE)	1.675	1.753	0.022	3.091	2.969	0.056	4.003	4.097	0.091	2.083	2.009	0.025
Income diversification (DIV_{REV})	0.294	0.298	0.002	0.362	0.396	0.006	0.392	0.441	0.010	0.313	0.317	0.002
Total assets (in thousand €) (SIZE)	249,763	177,321	4,912	2,432,433	2,007,386	66,850	31,200	15,100,000	3,602,197	2,977,222	280,074	317,832
Micro risk conditions												
Loan loss provisions/Total net loans (LLP)	0.005	0.004	0.017	0.006	0.005	0.043	0.006	0.005	0.044	0.005	0.004	0.015
Non performing loans/Total net loans (NPL)	0.019	0.012	0.001	0.014	0.01	0.001	0.014	0.01	0.001	0.018	0.012	0.001
Macro environmental conditions												
GDP growth rate (GDP)	99.335	99.179	0.064	98.784	98.654	0.137	98.632	98.117	0.169	99.191	99.092	0.055
Firm default rate (DEF_RT)	2.536	2.160	0.040	2.673	2.335	0.065	3.107	2.605	0.106	2.602	2.190	0.033
Macro NPL (NPL_INDEX)	25.488	1.000	0.925	18.239	1.000	1.413	15.347	8.030	1.546	23.530	1.000	0.753

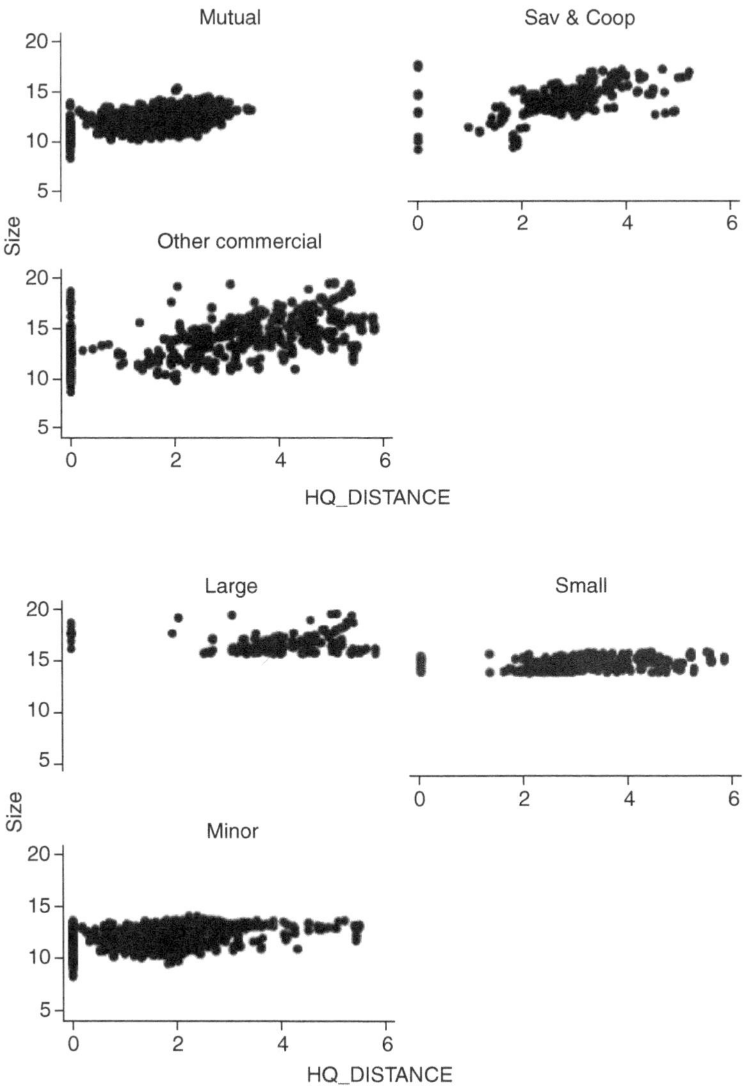

Figure 6.1 The relation between SIZE and HQ-DISTANCE

it has high non-interest income – and equals 0.5 when it is completely diversified.

According to the literature, a different bank organizational model also implies a different credit risk policy. Because of the relationship lending,

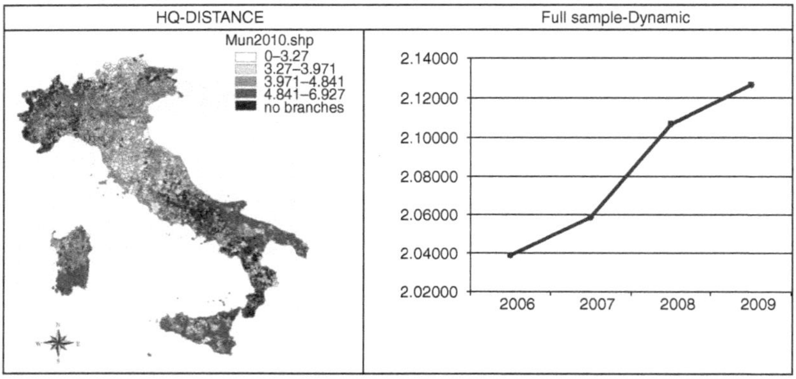

Figure 6.2 Functional distance (HQ-DISTANCE) distribution and dynamics over the period 2006 to 2009

Note: Kruskal–Wallis tests reject the null hypothesis of equality of the median efficiencies over time.

banks could be suffering from the so-called soft-budget constraint: when firms face an economic downturn, the borrower is forced to renew the relative credit line and if the loan is as large as to create bankruptcy risk for the bank this one is forced to renew the credit line. This intertemporal risk smoothing provides a sort of liquidity insurance that is especially valuable for opaque (small, young and innovative) firms, encountering difficulties in signalling their own creditworthiness (Boot and Thakor, 2000).

The current economic distress (causing credit quality depreciation) suggests including in the inefficiency model variables able to control for the credit risk. The standard financial ratios used in the literature on bank efficiency to estimate credit risk are the loan loss provisions over total net loans (*LLP*) and the non-performing loans over total net loans (*NPL*).

The *LLP* index is computed for each bank as the ratio between the flow of loan loss provisions over the stock of net loans. The loan loss provisions are determined according to the incurred loss approach. According to IAS 39 (p. 17), when there is evidence of impairment 'the amount of the loss measured as the difference between the asset's carrying amount and the present value of estimated future cash flows (excluding future credit losses that have not been incurred) discounted at the financial asset's original effective interest rate (i.e. the effective interest rate computed at initial recognition)' should be charged to profit or loss directly or through the use of an allowance account. A bank has to assess whether impairment exists for loans that are individually significant; then, loans that are not individually impaired must be included in a group of loans with similar credit risk characteristics and collectively assessed for impairment. Impairment of such groups of loans is estimated on the basis of historical loss experience, adjusted for changes in current conditions. However, recognizing expected losses as a result of future events is forbidden. Recently, many critics have focused on this approach, arguing that it does not reflect the true credit risk in loan portfolios and that a more accurate expected loss approach is advisable. Nevertheless, several authors suggest that some degree of income smoothing persists even after IFRS (International financial reporting standards) adoption implying that *LLP* can be used as a proxy for ex-ante credit risk.[8] Alternatively, the *NPL* (measured as the ratio between the stock of the non-performing loans over total net loans ratio) is backward-looking, and may be used as a proxy for ex-post credit risk[9] (cf. Fiordelisi et al., 2011). In this chapter, we suggest using these last two definitions of *LLP* and *NPL*.

In the previous literature on bank efficiency, the credit risk has been studied by simply considering its effect on the inefficiency equation (among others, Akhigbe and McNulty, 2003, 2005; Girardone et al., 2004). However, recent studies focusing on credit risk and its effects over efficiency examine the causality of the relationship between efficiency and credit risk via capital, by using simultaneous equation models (Altunbas et al., 2007) and the Granger causality approach (Fiordelisi et al., 2011). In our study, we deviate from these approaches because our aim is to evaluate the direct effect of credit risk over bank inefficiency without considering possible causality with capital. Then, we omit from our inefficiency models the capital and the loan growth rate, being highly correlated with the risk.

Finally, we suggest using as macro-indicators the annual growth rate of GDP (*GDP_RT*) and the ratio between default firms and registered firms (*DEF_RT*). The two macro-indicators are calculated in respect to the *i*-bank, weighting the indicator at the province level with the ratio of branches in the province in respect to the total amount of branches of the *i*-bank. The procedure allows to account for the different impact that each macro-indicator has on the bank, in respect to the presence of that bank in that province.

Among the group of environmental variables, we also include the ratio between non-performing loans and total net loans (*NPL*) that, using a threshold value of macro risk of 6 per cent, is defined as follows:[10]

$$\mathrm{NPL\_INDEX_i} = \frac{\sum_j \frac{\mathrm{branches}_{ij}}{\mathrm{branches_i}} * \left(\frac{\mathrm{npl}}{\mathrm{loans}}\right)_j}{\sum_j \mathrm{p_{ij}}} \tag{6.12}$$

where $p_{ij} = \begin{cases} 1 \text{ if bank}_\mathrm{i} \text{ is present in province j} \\ 0 \text{ otherwise} \end{cases}$ and

$$\left(\frac{\mathrm{npl}}{\mathrm{loans}}\right)_j = \begin{cases} \left(\frac{\mathrm{npl}}{\mathrm{loans}}\right)_j \text{ if } \left(\frac{\mathrm{npl}}{\mathrm{loans}}\right)_j > 6\% \\ 0 \text{ otherwise} \end{cases}.$$

The rationale is that the provincial macro-risk conditions may impact differently on banks' efficiency. We expect that macro-risk influences local banks more severely, as these do not have the opportunity to diversify their risk across the national territory. Conversely, large banks, supported by their branch network, can benefit from greater diversification benefits.

6.4 Results

6.4.1 Dynamics and spatial distribution of cost efficiency scores

To perform straightforward comparisons, we compute the cost efficiency scores (CE) from a translog stochastic frontier model without the (in)efficiency specification, enabling the comparison of cost efficiency over time, among groups and across the national territory. The average CE value over the analysed period and across the whole sample is 0.72, indicating that if banks are able to eliminate these inefficiencies, total costs could be reduced by 28 per cent. The most efficient banks over the entire period appear to be the minor and the mutual ones; large banks and the other commercial banks show the lowest CE values.

The average efficiency per year, calculated for the full sample of banks, increases until 2008, moving from 0.76 in 2006 to 0.80 in 2008; and then it decreases to 0.79 in 2009 (Figure 6.3). As expected, the recent financial crisis determines a generalized CE reduction for all the Italian bank groups in 2008 and 2009. However, some differences emerge with respect to the different groups considered. The large and other commercial banks decrease their CE of 3.16 per cent and 3.06 per cent respectively. The small savings and cooperative groups drop on average by 3.11 per cent and 2.9 per cent respectively. Lower reductions are detected for minor and mutual banks.

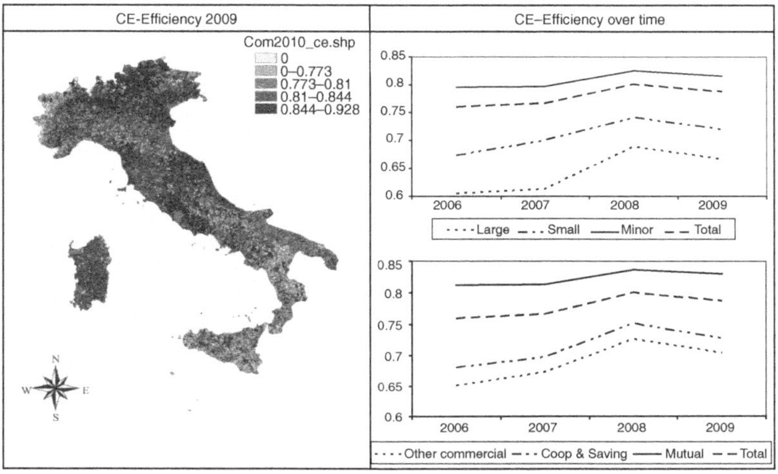

Figure 6.3 Spatial distribution and dynamics (by size and type over time) of cost efficiency
Notes: Kruskal–Wallis tests reject the null hypothesis of equality of the median efficiencies either between groups or over time for each group. The same results hold if we consider sub-samples by juridical category.

CE values are also used to evaluate the geographical distribution of efficiency of the banking system. In particular, CE at the municipality level is calculated as the average efficiency of banks located in the area, weighted by the number of their branches. The analysis allows an investigation of the geographical concentration of bank efficiency across Italy and the dynamics of the territorial efficiency distribution over the observed period of time.

The map reported in Figure 6.3 suggests at least three interesting considerations: (i) as expected, the most efficient municipalities are located in the centre and north of the country; (ii) a correspondence between distance and CE is observed; banks located in the south and farthest from their HQ appear to be less efficient than banks located in the north and close to their operational units. Among banks located in the north, the most efficient are minor banks located in Trentino Alto Adige, Veneto, Emilia Romagna, Marche and Toscana; (iii) the CE (across space) changes over time. The analysis shows that the efficiency of some large banks located in the north – for example in the Milan neighbourhood area – seriously dropped in 2008 and 2009 compared to 2006 and 2007.[11] This is not the case for banks located in peripheral regions, for example Trentino Alto Adige, that because of a different business model maintain a fairly stable value of efficiency over time. These findings suggest that not just distance but also features such as size and income diversification strategies play a role in defining different banking structure organizations and the CE distribution over time and across the territory.

6.4.2 Inefficiency cost model estimates

In order to control for the inefficiency of the Italian banking system a stochastic frontier function and a inefficiency model are estimated, as proposed in Equation (8), for the full sample of banks.[12] With respect to the banking business model, we find a negative and statistically significant relationship between *HQ-DISTANCE* and efficiency. According to the literature on distance and relationship lending, as the distance between bank branches and its HQ increases, the bank borrower's evaluating process becomes more imprecise. This, in turn increases the costs of screening and monitoring, and has a potentially negative effect in terms of CE. In the literature, the effect of financial diversification on bank performance has been well investigated, but without a general consensus. As DIV_{REV} rises, a bank becomes more diversified and less concentrated; however our results suggest that the benefit of diversification does not outweigh the cost of *NII* volatility. According to Chiorazzo et al. (2008), this implies an increase in cost inefficiency. To better investigate the effects of banking business organization structure on the inefficiency, we also control for the *SIZE* effect. Our results evidence that for the Italian banking system, economies of scale and efficiency gains do not hold. Some previous results underline, in fact, that efficiency gains due to size are verified only in the case of small banks (Akhigbe and McNulty, 2003).

As regards micro-risk conditions, model estimates reveal a positive effects of *LLP* on bank efficiency. A prudential credit risk policy realized by the ex-ante provision of funds to face future risk could imply, in the long run, a CE increase, that is 'prevention is better than cure'. As a result, in the short run an increase in the *LLP* might even increase efficiency, while an increase in the *NPL* produces an efficiency decrease. Finally, the main effects of environmental macro-conditions on efficiency are controlled for. The per capita value added growth rate (GDP) produces a positive effect on banking efficiency but it is not statistically significant. As expected, the macro-risk variables negatively affect bank efficiency.

6.5 Conclusions

In this chapter we investigate the CE of the Italian banking system and, in particular, to what extent the bank business model affects cost efficiency.

Table 6.4 Estimate results for the inefficiency model

Variable	Full sample
Banking business model	
HQ-DISTANCE	0.088*
DIV_{REV}	0.168**
SIZE	0.051*
Micro risk conditions	
LLP	−0.078*
NPL	0.078*
Environmental macro conditions	
GDP	−0.239
DEF_RT	0.319*
NPL_INDEX	0.024*
CE_pool	0.720
LL	−904.700

p-value:* 0.05;** 0.10.

The analysis of the CE evidences that the bank groups characterized by an organizational local structure (minor, mutual, small and cooperative and savings banks) are more efficient than larger and more distant banks. The average efficiency per year, calculated for the whole sample, shows a positive dynamic until 2008, and then it decreases. As expected, the recent crisis has determined a generalized CE reduction for all the Italian bank groups. However, some differences emerge; the large and small banks evidence the highest reduction of CE, and minor and mutual banks appear to react better to the financial crisis. The geographical distribution of the CE reveals other interesting features of the banking system. The most efficient municipalities are located in the centre and the north of the country. The presence of a correspondence between distance and CE is also observed: banks located in the south and farthest from their HQ appear to be less efficient than banks located in the north and close to their operational units. Moreover, regions characterized by the presence of large banks closed to their branch network suffer more than areas where a local bank model prevails. This suggests that, in addition to distance, other features, such as size and income diversification strategies, influence the different banking structure organization and affect the territorial CE distribution.

To better investigate these aspects, we consider as inefficiency determinants bank branch distance distribution, income diversification and size. The results confirm the importance of distance in determining bank efficiency; as distance increases efficiency decreases. According to the information asymmetry theory, an organizational structure with close interaction between the HQ and the peripheral operational units are more effective in disentangling asymmetric information problems between lender and borrower, thus increasing bank efficiency. Similarly, an increase in the bank size and income diversification strategies negatively affect efficiency.

The influence of some credit risk factors on CE are also investigated. We distinguish between micro- and macro-risk conditions. An increase in credit risk implies a generalized decrease in efficiency. In addition, an increase in the loan loss provision entails a better prudential credit risk policy with positive effects in terms of increased efficiency.

The empirical findings presented in this chapter also evidence that heterogeneity among banks exists in terms of either organizational models or technological sets, suggesting that the effects of distance and income diversification on efficiency may be different in respect to bank groups. Therefore different bank groups, constructed by size and category, should be studied in the future to reveal a more complete picture of the effects of distance and business models on the efficiency of the Italian banking system. Furthermore, the availability of a longer period of investigation may allow a more thorough investigation into the influence that the recent financial shocks have had on bank production processes and efficiency.

Notes

We would like to thank U. Albertazzi, E. Coletti, R. Corigliano, R. Gencay, P. Molyneux and other seminar participants to the II Rimini Workshop on Banking and Finance, the III Rimini Finance Workshop, the EWEPA, the IFABS and the Wolpertinger conferences for their helpful comments. The usual disclaimer applies.

1. According to the principal-agent theory, delegation may aggravate agency problems.
2. See, among others, Stiroh (2004a, 2004b), Stiroh and Rumble (2006), DeYoung and Rice (2004), Acharya et al. (2006), Mercieca et al. (2007), Lepetit et al. (2008), Chiorazzo et al. (2008), Berger et al. (2010).
3. The authors define small banks as credit institutions with an asset size of less than €450m and no multi-bank affiliation. 'Other' banks are by eliminating all remaining institutions. Among small banks, cooperative and savings banks account for 87 per cent of the number of institutions in the dataset, with the remainder classified as commercial, mortgage or credit banks.
4. Bank of Italy (2009), *Annual Report* – Methodological notes: tables a17.6 and a17.7.
5. The other two approaches used to define inputs and outputs in banking are: (i) the intermediation approach that assumes that banks collect deposits to

transform them, using labour and capital, into loans and other assets; (ii) the production approach that considers banks as producers of deposit and loans in terms of the number of accounts, using labour and capital.

6. The total number of municipalities in Italy is 8,094, but in 2009 only 5,929 municipalities hosted at least one branch (5,926 in 2008, 5924 in 2007 and 5,926 in 2006).
7. This is coherent with the intensive acquisition process of the southern banking system carried out by the northern banks during the nineties.
8. For an institutional comparison between the incurred and expected loss approach, see IASB (2009a, 2009b, 2009c). For an economic perspective, see among others Burroni et al. (2009) and Gebhardt and Novotny-Farkas (2011).
9. According to the Bank of Italy (see Methodological Notes to the Provincial Credit Statistics) an alternative measure of credit risk could be defined as the ratio between the flow of new non-performing loans to the stock of performing loans at the end of the previous period. Such a ratio has been used as a control variable without any substantial change in our results. Computations are available upon request to the authors.
10. We use a threshold value of 6 per cent, following the definition suggested by the Interbank Deposit Protection Fund. The choice is also supported by some empirical evidence. Over the period 2006 to 2009, the median value of NPL over total net loans has been 4.91 per cent, evidencing a substantial stability over time.
11. Data disaggregated, in respect to municipalities and over time, and maps are available on request from the authors.
12. Various null hypothesis tests associated with the cost and inefficiency models, by using log-likelihood ratio (LR) tests, are conducted. The null hypothesis that the Cobb–Douglas frontier is an adequate representation for banks is strongly rejected by the data, as well as the null hypothesis of no technical change in the inputs. As regards the model efficiency, the LR test of the one-sided error for the null hypothesis of no cost efficiency is strongly rejected, as is the null hypothesis that the explanatory variables in the model for the cost inefficiency effects have zero coefficients. The value of the estimates of the γ parameter is 0.48, which implies that a significant proportion of the total variability is associated with cost inefficiency. Test results are available on request from the authors.

References

V.V. Acharya, I. Hasan and A. Saunders (2006) Should banks be diversified? Evidence from individual bank loan portfolios. *Journal of Business*, 79 (3): 1355–412.

A. Akhigbe and J.E. McNulty (2003) The profit efficiency of small US commercial banks. *Journal of Banking & Finance*, 27 (2): 307–25.

—— (2005) Profit efficiency sources and differences among small and large U.S. commercial banks. *Journal of Economics and Finance*, 29: 289–99.

A. Akhigbe and B.A. Stevenson (2010) Profit efficiency in U.S. BHCs: Effects of increasing non-traditional revenue sources. *The Quarterly Review of Economics and Finance*, 50 (2): 132–40.

P. Alessandrini, M. Fratianni and A. Zazzaro (2009c) *The Changing Geography of Banking and Finance*, Springer US.
P. Alessandrini, A.F. Presbitero and A. Zazzaro (2009a) Banks, distances and firms' financing constraints. *Review of Finance*, 13: 261–307.
—— (2009b) Bank size or distance: What hampers innovation adoption by SMEs? *Journal of Economic Geography*, 10 (6): 845–81.
Y. Altunbas, S. Carbo, E.P.M. Gardener and P. Molyneux (2007) Examining the relationships between capital, risk and efficiency in European banking. *European Financial Management* 13: 49–70.
Bank of Italy (2009) 116th Financial Year Annual Report, available at www.bancaditalia.it
G.E. Battese and T.J. Coelli (1995) A model for the technical inefficiency effects in a stochastic frontier production function for panel data. *Empirical Economics*, 20: 325–32.
—— (1993) A stochastic frontier production function incorporating a model for technical inefficiency effects. *Working Papers in Econometrics and Applied Statistics*, 69. Department of Econometrics, University of New England.
G.E. Battese and G.S. Corra (1977) Estimation of a production frontier model: With application to the pastoral zone of Eastern Australia. *Australian Journal of Agricultural Economics*, 21: 169–79.
A.N. Berger and L.K. Black (2011) Bank size, lending technologies, and small business finance. *Journal of Banking & Finance*, 35 (3): 724–35.
A.N. Berger, A.M. Cowan and W.S. Frame (2011) The surprising use of credit scoring in small business lending by community banks and the attendant effects on credit availability, risk, and profitability. *Journal of Financial Services Research*, 39 (1): 1–17.
A.N. Berger and W.S. Frame (2007) Small business credit scoring and credit availability. *Journal of Small Business Management*, 45: 5–22.
A.N. Berger, I. Hasan and M. Zhou (2010) The effects of focus versus diversification on bank performance: Evidence from Chinese banks. *Journal of Banking & Finance*, 34 (7): 1417–35.
A.N. Berger and D.B. Humphrey (1992) Measurement and efficiency issues in commercial banking. In Z. Griliches (ed.), *Output Measurement in the Service Sectors*. Chicago: The University of Chicago Press, pp. 245–79.
A.N. Berger, N. Miller, M. Petersen, R. Rajan and J. Stein (2005) Does function follow organizational form? Evidence from the lending practices of large and small banks. *Journal of Financial Economics*, 76: 237–69.
A.N. Berger, R.J. Rosen and G.F. Udell (2007) Does market size structure affect competition? The case of small business lending. *Journal of Banking and Finance*, 31: 11–33.
A. Boot and A. Thakor (2000) Can relationship banking survive competition? *The Journal of Finance*, 55 (2): 679–713.
J.W.B. Bos, M. Koetter, J.W. Kolari and C.J.M. Kool (2009) Effects of heterogeneity on bank efficiency scores. *European Journal of Operational Research*, 195 (1): 251–61.
M. Burroni, M. Quagliariello, E. Sabatini and V. Tola (2009) Dynamic provisioning: rationale, functioning, and prudential treatment. *Bank of Italy Occasional Papers*, 57.

K. Carling and S. Lundberg (2005) Asymmetric information and distance: An empirical assessment of geographical credit rationing. *Journal of Economics and Business*, 57: 39–59.

V. Chiorazzo, C. Milani and F. Salvini (2008) Income diversification and bank performance: Evidence from Italian banks. *Journal of Financial Services Research*, 33: 181–203.

T.J. Coelli (1996) A guide to FRONTIER Version 4.1: A computer program for stochastic frontier production and cost function estimation. *CEPA Working Papers*, No. 7/96. Department of Econometrics, University of New England, Armidale.

—— (1995) Estimators and hypothesis tests for a stochastic: A Montecarlo analysis. *Journal of Productivity Analysis*, 6: 247–68.

H. Degryse and S. Ongena (2005) Distance, lending relationships, and competition. *Journal of Finance*, 60 (1): 231–66.

—— (2004) The impact of technology and regulation on the geographical scope of banking. *Oxford Review of Economic Policy*, 20: 571–90.

R. DeYoung, W.C. Hunter and G.F. Udell (2004) The past, present and probable future for community banks. *Journal of Financial Services Research*, 25 (2/3): 85–133.

R. DeYoung and T. Rice (2004) Non-interest income and financial performance at U.S. commercial banks. *The Financial Review*, 39: 101–27.

R. Felici and M. Pagnini (2008) Distance, bank heterogeneity and entry in local banking markets. *The Journal of Industrial Economics*, 56 (3): 500–34.

F. Fiordelisi, D. Marques-Ibanez and P. Molyneux (2011) Efficiency and risk in European banking. *Journal of Banking & Finance*, 35: 1315–26.

G. Gebhardt and Z. Novotny-Farkas (2011)The effects of IFRS adoption on the financial reporting quality of European banks. *Journal of Business Finance & Accounting*, 38 (3–4): 289–333.

C. Girardone, P. Molyneux and E.P.M. Gardener (2004) Analysing the determinants of bank efficiency: The case of Italian banks. *Applied Economics*, 36 (3): 215–27.

R. Hauswald and R. Marquez (2006) Competition and strategic information acquisition in credit markets. *Review of Financial Studies*, 19 (3): 967–1000.

IASB (2009a) *Loan loss accounting. Information for observers*, Agenda paper 7, March.

—— (2009b) *Loan loss provisioning. Information for observers*, Agenda paper 7a, March.

—— (2009c) *Impairment. Information for observers*, Agenda paper 7b, March 2009.

M. Kano, H. Uchida, G.F. Udell and W. Watanabe (2011) Information verifiability, bank organization, bank competition and bank-borrower relationships. *Journal of Banking & Finance*, 35 (4): 935–54.

L. Lepetit, N. Emmanuelle, P. Rous and A. Tarazi (2008) Bank income structure and risk: An empirical analysis of European banks. *Journal of Banking & Finance*, 32: 1452–67.

A. Lozano-Vivas and F. Pasiouras (2010) The impact of non-traditional activities on the estimation of bank efficiency: International evidence. *Journal of Banking & Finance*, 34, 1436–49.

S. Mercieca, K. Schaeck and S. Wolfe (2007) Small European banks: Benefits from diversification? *Journal of Banking & Finance*, 31: 1975–98.

L. Mester (1996) A study of bank efficiency taking into account risk-preferences. *Journal of Banking & Finance*, 20: 1025–45.

A. Mian (2006) Distance constraints: The limits of foreign lending in poor economies. *Journal of Finance*, 61 (3): 1465–505.

M.A. Petersen and R.G. Rajan (2002) Does distance still matter? The information revolution in small business lending. *Journal of Finance*, 57 (6): 2533–70.

—— (1994) The Benefits of Lending Relationships: Evidence from Small Business Data *The Journal of Finance*, Vol. 49, No. 1, pp. 3–37.

—— (1995), The **effect** of **credit marketcompetition** on lending relationships. *Quart. J. Econ.* 110, pp. 406—443.

J. Stein (2002) Information production and capital allocation: Decentralized versus hierarchical firms. *Journal of Finance*, 57 (5): 1891–922.

K.J. Stiroh (2004a) Do community banks benefit from diversification? *Journal of Financial Services Research*, 25(2–3): 135–60.

—— (2004b) Diversification in banking: Is non-interest income the answer? *Journal of Money, Credit and Banking*, 36 (5): 853–82.

K.J. Stiroh and A. Rumble (2006) The dark side of diversification: The case of US financial holding companies. *Journal of Banking & Finance*, 30: 2131–61.

G. Udell (2009) Financial innovation, organizations, and small business lending. In P. Alessandrini, A.F. Presbitero and A. Zazzaro (eds), *The Changing Geography of Banking and Finance*, Springer US.

7
Total and Financial Cost Efficiency in Spanish Savings Banks

Concepción Pérez-Cárceles, Juan Cándido Gómez-Gallego and Juan Gómez-García

7.1 Introduction

Efficiency can be measured by applying different methodologies from two principal groups: parametric[1] and nonparametric.[2] There is no consensus on the best method of determining the production frontier or on the unit of best practice to measure relative efficiencies; the approaches used most often to evaluate the efficiency of financial institutions differ in the assumptions made about the shape of the frontier, the treatment of random error and the distributions assumed for inefficiency and random error.

Parametric approaches impose a particular functional form on the frontier. So if the functional form is not specified correctly errors can be made in the estimates of efficiency.

Nonparametric studies impose less structure on the frontier; however random errors due to luck, problems with data or measurement errors are not taken into account. If random errors exist, efficiency measurements could be confused with random deviations from the efficiency frontier.

The conflict between parametric and nonparametric approaches becomes relevant because different rankings are obtained with the same financial institutions. Berger and Humphrey (1997) established comparisons of parametric and nonparametric rankings and between different parametric and nonparametric approaches. This study suggests adding more flexibility to parametric approaches and introducing randomness into nonparametric approaches.

An additional difference distinguished in Bauer et al. (1998) is whether the underlying efficiency is technical or economic, the nonparametric studies usually measuring technical efficiency and the parametric studies usually measuring economic efficiency.

Technical efficiency is calculated as level of inputs over level of outputs. A firm is considered technologically efficient if it minimizes its inputs with a given level of outputs or maximizes its outputs with a given level of inputs. Economic efficiency is broader than technological efficiency in that economic efficiency also involves the choice of mixes of inputs and/or outputs according to fluctuations in market prices. To be economically efficient, a firm needs to choose its input and/or output levels and mixes in order to optimize an economic goal, usually cost minimization or profit maximization. Economic efficiency requires both technical and allocative efficiency, and the use of the two different efficiency concepts may give significantly different rankings of firms, even for a given frontier approach.

Technical efficiency requires only input and output data, but economic efficiency also requires price data. Most of the early nonparametric frontier models (Charnes et al., 1978), as well as some of the early parametric frontier models (Aigner et al., 1977), are focused on technical efficiency. In recent efficiency analyses there has usually been a difference in the efficiency concepts employed in the nonparametric and parametric approaches. A majority of data envelopment analysis (DEA) studies have applied technical efficiency to inputs and outputs. However, almost all recent parametric stochastic frontier analysis (SFA), disposal frontier analysis (DFA) and thick frontier approach (TFA) studies have employed prices and examined economic efficiency.

The appropriateness of economic efficiency in the regulatory analysis of financial institutions, the availability of price data and the relevance of cost minimization in their objectives are the main reasons to select a parametric approach in this study, SFA specifically.

Aigner et al. (1997) and Meeusen and van den Broeck (1977) introduced a stochastic production function in a parametric approach. Subsequently, Pitt and Lee (1981) and Schmidt and Sickles (1984) extended this model to panel data, on the supposition that the technical efficiency of each individual unit is constant along the period studied. Cornwell et al. (1990) and Battese and Coelli (1992, 1995) proposed an advanced model that allows variable efficiency results to be estimated and covariables that explain differences among the results achieved by each unit to be included.

There is no consensus in the literature on the cost function to use in the stochastic frontier approach. In fact, if the purpose is to investigate operative efficiency, it is only operative costs that will be taken into account. Therefore, if the financial cost is added to the research into total cost efficiency, the interest rates paid by some savings banks for riskier assets will be taken into account. The majority of contributions are focused on the estimation of total cost efficiency; however the main objective of this research, following Carbó et al. (2004), relies on the analysis of financial cost efficiency in order to specify the influence of the variables included in the function. To this effect, an SFA is applied to a sample of Spanish savings banks during the period 2002 to 2007.

To understand the evolution of the Spanish banking system it is essential to consider the key role played by savings banks. In Spain, banks and savings banks account for around 90 per cent of branches (December 2009) in the financial sector. Savings banks are wholly credit banks, with full operational freedom, and equality with the rest of the entities forming the Spanish financial system. These entities, which are legally established as private foundations, specialize in channelling people's savings (40% of banking sector assets) and financing households and SMEs (just over 40% of the national banking business). They also have a strong local following, with a dense network of predominantly regional implementation branches (54% of bank branches in December 2009). This fact becomes more important given the contribution of the banking industry to the development of the Spanish economy in recent years; compared to other EU members, Germany and Spain are the countries in which savings banks have greatest weight in the system.

A second objective consists of analysing the influence that the beginning of the present financial crisis has exerted on the efficiency results in the sector. Following Bos et al. (2009), some indicators, at least partially exogenous of the state of the variables to be considered, are selected. In the case of the present study, some accounting and financial ratios of the savings banks have been calculated to be inserted as covariables in the financial cost model.

The rest of the chapter is organized as follows. In the next section the methodology is explained in detail. Section 3 collects data and variables used in the study. Section 4 shows the results. Finally, in Section 5, the conclusions are summarized.

7.2 Methodology

7.2.1 Stochastic frontier approach

This study considers the stochastic production frontier model proposed by Aigner et al. (1977) and Meeusen and van den Broeck (1977). In this model, an additional random error, v_i, is added to the non-negative random variable, u_i:

$$\ln y_i = \alpha + \sum_{j}^{n} \beta_j \ln x_{ij} + v_i - u_i, \quad i = 1,2,\ldots,I \tag{7.1}$$

where $\ln y_i$ is the production logarithm of DMU_i,[3] $\ln x_i$ is the input quantities logarithm of DMU_i and β is an unknown parameters vector to be estimated. Random error v_i takes into account measure errors and other random factors that exert influence on the output, such as the effects of time and luck ...and is assumed to be distributed as a $N(0,\sigma_v^2)$. The component u_i represents inefficiency, and is assumed to be distributed as a $N^+(0,\sigma_u^2)$. Both components are assumed to be identically distributed and statistically independent between themselves and of the regressors.

Battese and Coelli (1992) expanded the stochastic frontier model allowing effects of inefficiency to vary over time:

$$u_{it} = \{\exp[-\eta(t-T)]\} u_i \quad i = 1,2,\ldots,N \quad t = 1,2,\ldots,T \tag{7.2}$$

where u_{it} is assumed to be an exponential function of time, η is the only unknown parameter, and u_i is assumed to be independently and identically distributed generalized truncated normal random variables. Inefficiency effects can decrease, remain constant or increase with the passage of time, depending on the η sign.

Subsequently, Battese and Coelli (1995) proposed a model in which the parameters of the stochastic function and the inefficiency model are estimated simultaneously. To do this, u_{it} is the non-negative inefficiency effects, which are assumed to be independently (but not identically) distributed as a truncation at zero of $N(m_{it},\sigma_u^2)$. The mean is defined as $m_{it} = z_{it}\omega$, with z_{it} being a vector of covariables, and ω a parameters vector to be estimated.

7.2.2 Maximum likelihood estimation method

The parameters of proposed frontier functions can be estimated with maximum likelihood (ML) or with a variant of the corrected ordinary least squares (COLS), suggested by Richmond (1974). Greene (1980) analyses the properties of the ML estimator in stochastic frontier models and concludes that if the assumptions and conditions of regularity enumerated in his study are accepted the ML estimation is consistent and asymptotically efficient and normal. However, this method presented a disadvantage because of the computationally demanding numerical maximization of the likelihood function – until the appearance of software such as Limdep (Greene, 1992) and Frontier (Coelli 1992, 1996).

Coelli (1995) investigated the properties of the half-normal frontier model with finite samples through a Monte Carlo experiment, and concluded that the ML estimator is significantly better than the COLS estimator when the contribution of the technical inefficiency effects to the total variance term is large. Specifically, the ML estimator is asymptotically more efficient than the COLS estimator. On the basis of this, Coelli et al. (1998) assert that the ML estimator should be used in preference to the COLS estimator whenever possible.

The estimation method MV obtains the joint density of the error components with constant mean, 0 and μ, and variances σ_v^2 and σ_u^2, respectively, to form the density of $\ln y_i$:

$$f_{v,u}(v_i, u_i) = f_v(v_i) f_u(u_i) \tag{7.3}$$

Given that in the stochastic production frontier $\varepsilon_i = v_i - u_i$:

$$f_{\varepsilon,u}(\varepsilon_i, u_i) = f_u(u_i) f_v(\varepsilon_i + u_i) \tag{7.4}$$

[The Jacobian of the transformation of (v, u) in (ε, u) is $\det\begin{bmatrix} 1 & 1 \\ 0 & 1 \end{bmatrix}^{-1} = 1$.]

Finally, to obtain the marginal density of ε_i, the joint density function is integrated into u_i:

$$f_\varepsilon(\varepsilon_i) = \int_0^\infty f_u(u_i) f_v(\varepsilon_i + u_i)\, du_i \tag{7.5}$$

The last stage provides the contribution of observation i to the log-likelihood:

$$\ln L_i\left(\alpha, \beta, \sigma_u^2, \sigma_v^2 \,|\ln y_i, x_i\right) = \ln f_\varepsilon\left(y_i - \alpha - x_i\beta \,\middle|\, \sigma_u^2, \sigma_v^2\right) \tag{7.6}$$

This development uses a trivial modification to adjust a cost frontier. Then $\varepsilon_i = v_i + u_i$ and $f_{\varepsilon,u}(\varepsilon_i, u_i) = f_u(u_i) f_v(\varepsilon_i - u_i)$. As v_i is symmetrically distributed, the second term can be written as $f_v(\varepsilon_i - u_i) = f_v(u_i - \varepsilon_i)$. With this subtle change, it can be proved that the density of the cost logarithm can be calculated simply by changing the sign of ε_i in the functional form.

Log-likelihood estimations are consistent and asymptotically efficient (Aigner et al., 1977).

7.2.3 Efficiency estimation

This section considers the stochastic production frontier model given in Equation 7.1 and the distributional assumptions established. The half-normal distribution of inefficiency is based on the proposition that the modal value of technical inefficiency is zero, with increasing values of technical inefficiency becoming increasingly less likely.

The density function of $u \geq 0$ is given in the following equation:

$$f(u) = \frac{2}{\sigma_u \sqrt{2\pi}} \exp\left\{ -\frac{u^2}{2\sigma_u^2} \right\}, \tag{7.7}$$

with the moments

$$E(u) = \frac{\sqrt{2}}{\sqrt{\pi}} \sigma_u \tag{7.8}$$

and

$$V(u) = \left(\frac{\pi - 2}{\pi} \right) \sigma_u^2 \tag{7.9}$$

The density function of v is

$$f(v) = \frac{2}{\sigma_v \sqrt{2\pi}} \exp\left\{ -\frac{v^2}{2\sigma_v^2} \right\}. \tag{7.10}$$

Given the independence assumption, the joint density function of u and v is the product of their individual density functions, so:

$$f(u, v) = \frac{2}{2\pi \sigma_u \sigma_v} \cdot \exp\left\{ -\frac{u^2}{2\sigma_u^2} - \frac{v^2}{2\sigma_v^2} \right\}. \tag{7.11}$$

The joint density function for u and ε is:

$$f(u, \varepsilon) = \frac{2}{2\pi \sigma_u \sigma_v} \cdot \exp\left\{ -\frac{u^2}{2\sigma_u^2} - \frac{(\varepsilon + u)^2}{2\sigma_v^2} \right\}. \tag{7.12}$$

The marginal density function of ε is obtained by integrating u out of $f(u, \varepsilon)$, Weinstein (1964):

$$\begin{aligned} f(\varepsilon) &= \int_0^\infty f(u, \varepsilon) du \\ &= \frac{2}{\sqrt{2\pi}\sigma} \cdot \left[1 - \Phi\left(\frac{\varepsilon\lambda}{\sigma} \right) \right] \cdot \exp\left\{ -\frac{\varepsilon^2}{2\sigma^2} \right\} \\ &= \frac{2}{\sigma} \phi\left(\frac{\varepsilon}{\sigma} \right) \Phi\left(-\frac{\varepsilon\lambda}{\sigma} \right), \end{aligned} \tag{7.13}$$

where $\sigma = (\sigma_u^2 + \sigma_v^2)^{1/2}$, $\lambda = \sigma_u / \sigma_v$, and $\phi(\cdot)$ and $\Phi(\cdot)$ are the standard normal cumulative distribution and density functions. The reparameterization from σ_u^2 and σ_v^2 to σ and λ is appropriate, since λ provides an indicator of the contributions of u and v to ε as $\lambda \to 0$ either $\sigma_v^2 \to +\infty$ or

$\sigma_u^2 \to 0$, and the symmetric error component dominates the one-sided error component in the determination of ε. As $\lambda \to \infty$, either $\sigma_u^2 \to +\infty$ or $\sigma_v^2 \to 0$, and the one-sided error component dominates the symmetric error component in the determination of ε. The former case is an ordinary least squares production function model with no technical inefficiency, whereas the latter case is a deterministic production frontier model without noise.

A common error is to assume σ_u^2 as a variant of u_i. In fact, the variance is overestimated by the factor 3!, approximately. Given that σ_u is not the standard deviation of u_i, the design of the quantity of inefficiency suggested by the estimation is wrong. It can seem that the variance ratio σ_u^2/σ^2 is a useful indicator of the influence of the component of inefficiency over the total variance. However, the variance of the variable u_i is $\text{var}\left[U_i \middle| U_i > 0\right] = [(\pi-2)/\pi]\sigma_u^2$, so σ_u^2 is not right. In the factorization of the total variance in two components, the contribution of u_i is:

$$\frac{\text{var}[u]}{\text{var}[\varepsilon]} = \frac{[(\pi-2)/\pi]\,\sigma_u^2}{[(\pi-2/\pi)]\,\sigma_u^2 + \sigma_v^2} \tag{7.14}$$

The marginal density function $f(\varepsilon)$ is asymmetrically distributed with mean, and: variance

$$E(\varepsilon) = E(v-u) = E(-u) = -\frac{\sqrt{2}}{\sqrt{\pi}}\sigma_u \tag{7.15}$$

and

$$V(\varepsilon) = \sigma_\varepsilon^2 = V(u) + V(u) = \left(\frac{\pi-2}{\pi}\right)\sigma_u^2 + \sigma_v^2. \tag{7.16}$$

Using Equation 7.13, the log-likelihood function for a sample of N producers is:

$$\ln L = cte - N\ln\sigma^{-1} + \sum_i \ln\Phi\left(-\frac{\varepsilon_i\lambda}{\sigma}\right) - \frac{1}{2\sigma^2}\sum_i \varepsilon_i^2. \tag{7.17}$$

The log-likelihood function in Equation 17 must be maximized to obtain maximum-likelihood estimates for all parameters. These estimates are consistent as $N \to \infty$.

The log-likelihood function is integrated in softwares like Frontier 4.1 (Coelli, 1996), Limdep (Greene, 2000), Stata (Stata, Inc., 2005) and TSP (TSP International, 2005).[4]

Taking derivatives:

$$\frac{\partial \ln L}{\partial \sigma^2} = -\frac{I}{2\sigma^2} + \frac{1}{2\sigma^4}\sum_i (y_i - \beta' x_i)^2 + \frac{\lambda}{2\sigma^3}\sum_i \frac{\phi_i^*}{\left(1-\Phi_i^*\right)}(y_i - \beta' x_i)$$

$$\frac{\partial \ln L}{\partial \lambda} = -\frac{1}{\sigma}\sum_i \frac{\phi_i^*}{\left(1-\Phi_i^*\right)}(y_i - \beta' x_i)$$

$$\frac{\partial \ln L}{\partial \beta} = \frac{1}{\sigma^2}\sum_i (y_i - \beta' x_i)x_i + \frac{\lambda}{\sigma}\sum_i \frac{\phi_i^*}{\left(1-\Phi_i^*\right)}x_i \tag{7.18}$$

where x_i is a $(k \times 1)$ vector, and ϕ_i^* and Φ_i^* are the normal density and distribution functions evaluated in $(y_i - \beta' x_i)\lambda\sigma^{-1}$ respectively. It is demonstrated that at the optimum $\sum_i \frac{\phi_i^*}{(1-\Phi_i^*)}(y_i - \beta' x_i) = 0$. If we substitute this result in the first derivative, the log-likelihood estimate of σ^2 is:[5]

$$-\frac{I}{2\sigma^2} + \frac{1}{2\sigma^4}\sum_i (y_i - \beta' x_i) = 0, \tag{7.19}$$

so

$$\hat{\sigma}^2 = \frac{1}{N}\sum_i (y_i - \beta' x_i)^2. \tag{7.20}$$

The method obtains estimates of the technical efficiency of each DMU_i. We have estimates of $\varepsilon_i = v_i - u_i$, which contain information on u_i. The most likely outcome is that $\varepsilon_i > 0$, in which case u_i is not large, suggesting that this producer is relatively efficient, whereas if $\varepsilon_i < 0$, the most probable outcome is that u_i is large. A solution is obtained from the conditional distribution of u_i given ε_i which contains certain information concerning u_i. Jondrow et al. (1982) showed that if $u_i \approx N^+(0, \sigma_u^2)$, the conditional distribution of u given ε is:

$$f(u|\varepsilon) = \frac{1}{(2\pi)^{1/2}\sigma_*\left[1 - \Phi(-\mu_*/\sigma_*)\right]} \cdot \exp\left\{-\frac{(u-\mu_*)^2}{2\sigma_*^2}\right\}, \tag{7.21}$$

where $\mu_* = -\varepsilon\sigma_u^2/\sigma^2$ and $\sigma_*^2 = \sigma_u^2\sigma_v^2/\sigma^2$. Since $f(u|\varepsilon)$ is distributed as $N^+(\mu_*, \sigma_*^2)$ either the mean or the mode of this distribution are point estimators of u_i. They are given by:

$$E(u_i/\varepsilon_i) = \mu_{*i} + \sigma_*\left[\frac{\phi(-\mu_{*i}/\sigma_*)}{1 - \Phi(-\mu_{*i}/\sigma_*)}\right], \tag{7.22}$$

$$M(u_i|\varepsilon_i) = \begin{cases} -\varepsilon_i\left(\frac{\sigma_u^2}{\sigma^2}\right) & \text{if } \varepsilon_i \geq 0 \\ 0 & \text{otherwise} \end{cases} \tag{7.23}$$

Once point estimates of u_i are obtained, estimates of the technical efficiency of each producer can be obtained from:

$$TE_i = \exp(-\hat{u}_i) \tag{7.24}$$

where $\hat{u}_i$ is either $E(u_i/\varepsilon_i)$ or $M(u_i|\varepsilon_i)$.

Battese and Coelli (1988) proposed an alternative point estimator of TE_i

$$TE_i = E(\exp\{-u_i/\varepsilon_i\}) = \frac{1-\Phi[\sigma_* - (\mu_{*i}/\sigma_*)]}{1-\Phi(-\mu_{*i}/\sigma_*)} \cdot \exp\left\{-\mu_{*i} + \frac{1}{2}\sigma_*^2\right\}. \tag{7.25}$$

7.2.4 Cost frontier models

A cost frontier can be expressed as:

$$E_i \geq c(y_i, w_i; \beta), \quad i = 1, \ldots, I \tag{7.26}$$

Since EC_i is the CE of DMU_i, from Equation 7.26 is obtained:

$$CE_i = \frac{c(y_i, w_i; \beta)}{E_i}, \tag{7.27}$$

which defines CE as the ratio of minimum feasible cost to observed expenditure.

Kumbhakar and Lovell (2000) advised that in Equation 7.26 the cost frontier is deterministic, and so in Equation 7.27 the entire excess of observed expenditure over minimum feasible cost is attributed to cost inefficiency. Such a formulation ignores the fact that expenditure may be affected by random shocks not under the control of producers.

A stochastic cost frontier can be written as:

$$E_i \geq c(y_i, w_i; \beta) \cdot \exp\{v_i\}, \quad i = 1, \ldots, I \tag{7.28}$$

where $c(y_i, w_i; \beta) \cdot \exp\{v_i\}$ is the stochastic cost frontier. This consists of two parts: a deterministic part $c(y_i, w_i; \beta)$ common to all producers, and a producer-specific random part $\exp\{v_i\}$, which captures the effects of random shocks on each producer. If the cost frontier is specified as being stochastic, the appropriate measure of CE becomes:

$$CE_i = \frac{c(y_i, w_i; \beta) \cdot \exp\{v_i\}}{E_i}, \tag{7.29}$$

which defines CE as the ratio of minimum cost attainable in an environment characterized by $\exp\{v_i\}$ to observed expenditure. $CE_i \leq 1$, with $CE_i = 1$ if, and only if, $E_i = c(y_i, w_i; \beta) \cdot \exp\{v_i\}$. Otherwise, $CE_i < 1$ provides a measure of the ratio of minimum feasible cost to observed expenditure.

7.2.5 Panel data models

As explained in Kumbhakar and Lovell (2000), panel data contains more information than does a single cross-section. Consequently, it is to be expected that access to panel data will either enable some of the strong distributional assumptions used with cross-sectional data to be relaxed or result in estimates of technical efficiency with more desirable statistical properties. Schmidt and Sickles (1984) noted three difficulties with cross-sectional stochastic production frontier models. First, maximum-likelihood estimation of the stochastic production frontier model, and the subsequent separation of technical inefficiency and statistical noise, both require strong distributional assumptions on each error component. The robustness of inferences to these assumptions is not well documented, although we made some observations on robustness in the preceding section. Second, maximum-likelihood estimation also requires an assumption that the technical inefficiency error component is independent of the regressors, although it is easy to imagine that technical inefficiency might be correlated with the input vectors producers selected. Third, while the technical efficiency of producers can be estimated using the technique by Jondrow et al. (1982), it cannot be estimated consistently, since the variance of the conditional mean or the conditional mode for each individual producer does not tend to zero as the size of the cross-section increases.

Each of these limitations is avoidable if we have access to panel data. First, this enables us to adapt conventional panel data estimation techniques to the technical efficiency measurement problem, and not all of these techniques rest on strong distributional assumptions; repeated observations on a sample of producers can serve as a substitute for such assumptions. Second, not all panel data estimation techniques require the assumption of independence of the technical inefficiency error component from the regressors. Repeated observations on a sample of producers can also serve as a substitute for the independence assumption. Finally, since adding more observations on each producer generates information not provided by adding more producers to a cross-section, the technical efficiency of each producer in the sample can be estimated consistently as $T \to \infty$, T being the number of observations on each producer. Repeated observations on a sample of producers resolve the inconsistency problem with the technique of Jondrow et al. (1982). This final benefit of access to panel data can be overstated, however, since many panels are relatively short.

7.2.6 Time-invariant cost efficiency

The stochastic cost frontier is assumed to have a Cobb–Douglas form with only one output, and a panel data of N DMUs along T periods of time is available. The variability of efficiency along the period is supposed to be time-invariant. Taking into account these assumptions, the cost frontier model is expressed as:

$$\ln C_{it} = \alpha + \beta \ln y_{it} + \sum_{k}^{n} \beta_k \ln w_{ikt} + v_{it} + u_i, \tag{7.30}$$

where v_{it} represents random error, $u_i \geq 0$ represents time-invariant cost inefficiency and $\sum_k^n \beta_k$ assures homogeneity of grade +1 of the cost frontier in input prices.

The distributional assumptions on the error components in the stochastic cost frontier model are the same as in Equation (7.1). Maximum-likelihood estimation of a stochastic cost frontier panel data model with time-invariant CE is structurally similar to the procedure applied to cross-sectional data. This technique is widely used in empirical analysis.

The marginal density function $f(\varepsilon) = f(v+u)$ is the same as the marginal density function $f(\varepsilon) = f(v-u)$ of the error in a production frontier, except for the change of sign in the definition of u.

The log-likelihood function for a sample of N DMUs, each one observed along T periods, is:

$$\begin{aligned} \ln L = cte - \frac{N(t-1)}{2} \ln \sigma_v^2 - \frac{N}{2} \ln\left(\sigma_v^2 + t\sigma_u^2\right) \\ + \sum_i \ln\left[1 - \Phi\left(-\frac{\mu_{*i}}{\sigma_*}\right)\right] - \left(\frac{\varepsilon'\varepsilon}{2\sigma_v^2}\right) + \frac{1}{2}\sum_i \left(\frac{\mu_{*i}}{\sigma_*}\right)^2, \end{aligned} \tag{7.31}$$

where $\mu_{*i} = t\sigma_u^2 \bar{\varepsilon}_i \Big/ \left(\sigma_v^2 + t\sigma_u^2\right)$ and $\sigma_*^2 = \sigma_u^2 \sigma_v^2 \Big/ \left(\sigma_v^2 + t\sigma_u^2\right)$.

The conditional distribution of $(u|\varepsilon)$ is

$$f(u|\varepsilon) = \frac{1}{(2\pi)^{1/2} \sigma_* \left[1 - \Phi(-\mu_*/\sigma_*)\right]} \cdot \exp\left\{-\frac{(u-\mu_*)^2}{2\sigma_*^2}\right\}, \tag{7.32}$$

and fits into the density function of a variable distributed as a $N^{+}(\mu_{*},\sigma_{*}^{2})$. In line with Jondrow et al. (1982), either the mean or the mode of this distribution are point estimators of CE:

$$E(u_i/\varepsilon_i) = \mu_{*i} + \sigma_{*}\left[\frac{\phi(-\mu_{*i}/\sigma_{*})}{1-\Phi(-\mu_{*i}/\sigma_{*})}\right], \tag{7.33}$$

$$M(u_i|\varepsilon_i) = \begin{cases}\mu_{*i} & \text{if } \varepsilon_i \geq 0 \\ 0 & \text{otherwise}\end{cases}. \tag{7.34}$$

An alternative estimator is:

$$E(\exp\{-u_i|\varepsilon_i\}) = \frac{1-\Phi[\sigma_{*}-(\mu_{*i}/\sigma_{*})]}{1-\Phi(-\mu_{*i}/\sigma_{*})} \cdot \exp\left\{-\mu_{*i}+\frac{1}{2}\sigma_{*}^{2}\right\}. \tag{7.35}$$

7.2.7 Time variant cost efficiency

The assumption of CE being constant through time is a strong one. Particularly if the operating environment is competitive, it is hard to accept the notion that technical inefficiency remains constant throughout many time periods. The longer the panel, the more desirable it is to relax this assumption. It is possible to do so, although at the cost of additional parameters to be estimated. The following cost frontier allows variations of efficiency along the time:

$$\begin{aligned}\ln C_{it} &= \alpha_t + \beta \ln y_{it} + \sum_{k}^{n} \beta_k \ln w_{ikt} + v_{it} + u_{it} \\ &= \alpha_{it} + \beta \ln y_{it} + \sum_{k}^{n} \beta_k \ln w_{ikt} + v_{it},\end{aligned} \tag{7.36}$$

where α_t is the independent term of the cost frontier shared by all the DMUs in the period t, $\alpha_{it} = \alpha_t + u_{it}$ is the independent term of the DMU_i in the period t, and the rest of the variables have been defined previously.

Battese and Coelli (1992) proposed a time-varying technical efficiency model where:

$$u_{it} = \beta(t) \cdot u_i, \tag{7.37}$$

with $\beta(t) = \exp\{-\gamma(t-T)\}$,

which has only one additional parameter, γ, to be estimated. The function $\beta(t)$ satisfies two properties: (i) $\beta(t) \geq 0$ and (ii) $\beta(t)$ decreases at an increasing rate if $\gamma > 0$, increases at an increasing rate if $\gamma < 0$, or remains constant if $\gamma = 0$. Battese and Coelli then proceeded to make distributional assumptions (normal for v_{it} and truncated normal for u_i) and used maximum likelihood to obtain estimates of all parameters in the model. The log-likelihood function and its partial derivatives are provided in their chapter. Based on these distributional assumptions, Battese and Coelli showed that $u_i|\varepsilon_i \approx$ iid $N^+\left(\mu_{**i}, \sigma_*^2\right)$ where $\varepsilon_i = v_i + \beta \cdot u_i$ and:

$$\mu_{**i} = \frac{\mu\sigma_v^2 + \beta'\varepsilon_i\sigma_u^2}{\sigma_v^2 + \beta'\beta\sigma_u^2},$$
$$\sigma_*^2 = \frac{\sigma_u^2\sigma_v^2}{\sigma_v^2 + \beta'\beta\sigma_u^2},$$
$$\beta' = (\beta(1), \ldots, \beta(T)). \tag{7.38}$$

Notice that if CE is time invariant, $\gamma = 0 \Rightarrow \beta(t) = 1$ and $\beta'\beta = T$, and the expressions for μ_{**i} and σ_*^2 collapse to their time-invariant version.

The minimum mean squared error predictor of CE is:

$$E\left(\exp\{-u_{it}|\varepsilon_i\}\right) = E\left(\exp\{\beta(t)\cdot u_i\}|\varepsilon_i\right)$$
$$= \frac{1 - \Phi\left(\beta(t)\sigma_* - \mu_{*i}/\sigma_*\right)}{1 - \Phi\left(-\mu_{*i}/\sigma_*\right)} \cdot \exp\left\{-\beta(t)\mu_{*i} + \frac{1}{2}\beta(t)^2\sigma_*^2\right\} \tag{7.39}$$

7.3 Testing hypothesis

The validation of the model requires testing the assumptions of the functional form of the frontier, the distribution of the inefficiency term and the temporal variability of the inefficiency effects. Previously, the existence of inefficiency effects had to be tested in order for the model to make sense.

7.3.1 Testing for the existence of inefficiency effects

As has been argued in Coelli (1995), if a frontier model is considered with the assumption of a half-normal distribution for inefficiency, a test on the existence of inefficiency can be made testing the null hypothesis $\sigma_u^2 = 0$ versus the alternative one $\sigma_u^2 > 0$. This hypothesis could be proved using several statistics. One of them is the Wald test, $W = \hat{\lambda}_{MV}/S_{\hat{\lambda}_{MV}}$, that has usually been used in applications of stochastic frontier models. This statistic is asymptotically distributed as a standard normal, and tests $\lambda = 0$ versus $\lambda > 0$, where $\lambda = \frac{\sigma_u^2}{\sigma_u^2 + \sigma_v^2}$, and the critical region is defined by $\left|\frac{\hat{\lambda}_{MV}}{S_{\hat{\lambda}_{MV}}}\right| > z_{\alpha/2}$.

7.3.2 Testing the stochastic frontier model

Hereafter, different tests of hypothesis are enumerated, with the one-sided generalized likelihood ratio (LR) test to check several aspects in the specification of the stochastic frontier model (Zajc, 2006). This statistic is asymptotically distributed as a chi-square random variable with the number of degrees of freedom equal to the number of restrictions, and is calculated as:

$$LR = -2\left\{\ln\left[L\left(H_0\right)\right] - \ln\left[L\left(H_1\right)\right]\right\} \tag{7.40}$$

where $L(H_0)$ and $L(H_1)$ are the values of the log-likelihood function under the null and alternative hypotheses, respectively.

The critical region of the test with size α is defined by $LR_{\text{exp}} > \chi^2_{restrictions;\alpha}$.

Testing for temporal variability of inefficiency effects According to Lee and Schmidt (1993), $u_{it} = \beta(t) \cdot u_i$, where $\beta(t) = \exp\{-\eta(t-T)\}$; so it is distributed as an exponential function of time where u_i represents random variables i.i.d. (independent and identically distributed) as a truncated normal, and η is an unknown parameter, to be estimated. In this way, the null hypothesis of inefficiency effects with non-significant variation along the time $H_0 : \eta = 0$ is tested against the alternative hypothesis, $H_1 : \eta \neq 0$; where the critical region is defined from Expression 7.40 by $LR_{\text{exp}} > \chi^2_{1;\alpha}$.

Testing the functional form of the frontier Most of the functional forms referred to production functions have been used to specify cost functions in empirical analysis. One of most used is the Cobb–Douglas functional form. The Cobb–Douglas function is easy to estimate and to manipulate mathematically, but is restrictive because of the conditions imposed on the cost structure (as a fixed value of the technical rate of substitution and a constant elasticity of substitution equal to one).

The flexible functional form more often used in empirical studies is the translogarithmic one proposed by Christensen, Jorgenson and Lau (1973). It is a generalization of a Cobb–Douglas cost function through a second-order Taylor extension of the cost logarithm function (in terms of input prices logarithm and output logarithm). Burgess (1974) used a translog functional form to represent the multiproduct cost function.

In order to prove if the most appropriate functional form to impose on the costs frontier is the Cobb–Douglas or the translogarithmic one, the null hypothesis H_0: Cobb-Douglas is tested versus the alternative hypothesis H_1: trans log through the whole significance of the parameters of the translog that do not appear in the Cobb–Douglas, with a critical region defined as $LR_{\text{exp}} > \chi^2_{10;\alpha}$.

Testing the inefficiency distribution As the program used[6] assumes $u_i \approx N^+(\mu, \sigma_u^2)$, it is interesting to check if $H_1 : \mu \neq 0$, the distribution is a half normal, versus $H_1 : \mu \neq 0$, a truncated normal; with a critical region determined by $LR_{\text{exp}} > \chi^2_{1;\alpha}$.

7.4 Data and variables

The method proposed is applied to a sample of 46 Spanish savings banks for the period 2002 to 2007.[7] A panel dataset is used so a time-series observations on a sample of individual units is available in order to improve studying and modelling efficiency (see Baltagi and Griffin, 1988; Cornwell et al., 1990 and Kumbhakar, 1993). All necessary data was obtained from data published by the Spanish Confederation of Savings Banks (CECA).

According to the banking output, two possible approaches must be considered, due to the dual types of activity that banks may perform (Thanassoulis, 1999). It depends on whether deposits are viewed as an output or an input by the savings banks (Clark, 1988). The 'production' approach views loans and deposits as outputs. On the other hand, the 'intermediation' approach views deposits as input, or as input and output at the same time, thus savings banks are considered producers of services related directly to their role as an intermediary in financial markets. The present chapter adopts the last approach, suggested by Sealey and Lindley (1977), and followed in several studies such as Altunbas et al. (2001), Maudos and Pastor (2003), Carbó et al. (2004), Weill (2004, 2009), Bonin et al. (2005), Bos and Schmiedel (2006), Pasiouras (2008) and Lozano-Vivas and Pasiouras (2010). Table 7.1 lists the variables selected in the study and their definitions.

The model proposed by Battese and Coelli (1995) adds some factors that are at least partially exogenous and may explain some of the differences between the predictions of efficiency. Table 7.2 shows a set of indicators measuring various aspects of the activity carried out by the savings banks, their trend in the banking process and the diversification of their activity.

Table 7.1 Variable definitions

Variable	Name	Definition
y_1	Credit to clients	Sum of outstanding balance of credits of clients
y_2	Securities portfolio	Fixed and variable interest investments property of the entity
x_1	Loanable funds	Sum of the balance of deposits of clients in the entity
x_2	Physical capital	Value of tangible fixed assets of the entity
x_3	Employees	Number of employees of the entity
w_1	Price of L. Funds	Interests/total liability
w_2	Price of P. Capital	Recovery and maintenance/physical capital
w_3	Price of labour	Personal expenses/Employees
FC	Financial cost	Interests
TC	Total cost	FC+OC

7.5 Results

First, the results of the average for each year from 2002 to 2007 are reported, along with the average and standard deviation in the whole period 2002 to 2007 of the variables used in the cost function.

Table 7.3 analyses the average in the period and in each year of the variables in the cost function. In the outputs, the growth rates of the Credits and Securities portfolio are positive, more than 300 percentage points in the last case. In the inputs, only the price of physical capital shows a negative trend due to the increase in Employees. Finally, Total costs have increased more than 100 percentage points, and Financial costs more than 200 points.

The Wald test is applied to test the null hypothesis of inexistence of inefficiency effects. The null hypothesis is rejected and the parameter λ is accepted as significant at the level of 5 per cent (see Tables 7.5 and 7.7).

On checking if the effects of inefficiency vary over time, the hypothesis of nullity of the parameter η is rejected with a p-value of 0.000 for the two cases (see Table 7.4). So, total and financial CE is variable over time.

The null hypothesis that establishes a Cobb–Douglas functional form is rejected with a *p*-value of 0.000 (see Table 7.4). Therefore, it is concluded that the most appropriate functional form is the translogarithmic one.

In the test for the average value of the distribution of inefficiency, the hypothesis of nullity of the parameter μ for total and financial cost is rejected with a *p*-value of 0.000 (see Table 7.4). So, it is accepted that the distributions of their inefficiency terms are truncated normals.

Table 7.2 Ratio definitions

Liquidity (L)	Solvency (S)	Tendency (T)	Quality (Q)	Profitability (P)	Management (M)
$\frac{\text{Current liability}}{\text{Current asset}}$	$\frac{\text{Equity}}{\text{Requirable liability}}$	$\frac{\text{Credits}}{\text{Total asset}}$	$\frac{\text{Provision}}{\text{Net margin}}$	$\frac{\text{Net profit}}{\text{Equity}}$	$\frac{\text{Net margin}}{\text{Total asset}}$
	$\frac{\text{Equity}}{\text{Total asset}}$	$\frac{\text{Deposits + Credits}}{\text{Total assets}}$	$\frac{\text{Provision}}{\text{Total asset}}$		

Table 7.3 Averages of the variables in the cost function

Variable	Min.	Max.	Mean	Std dev.	2002	2003	2004	2005	2006	2007
y_1^*	150.0	162214.8	12211.7	20654.6	7021.2	8182.5	9889.0	12711.8	16369.6	19142.7
y_2^*	0.4	22160.5	1553.5	2902.2	647.4	690.6	670.7	2151.0	2159.1	3002.3
w_1	0.01	0.06	0.02	0.01	0.03	0.02	0.02	0.02	0.02	0.04
w_2	0.02	0.40	0.07	0.03	0.09	0.08	0.08	0.05	0.05	0.06
w_3	38.73	76.94	53.44	7.72	49.61	51.09	52.34	54.38	55.89	57.29
TC*	7.5	8310.8	506.3	923.4	376.1	354.2	355.9	426.5	601.0	924.1
FC*	3.9	6240.3	334.6	654.8	230.0	200.4	195.9	250.7	413.2	717.4

Notes: *Variables expressed in millions of euros;
46 savings banks, period 2002–2007, 276 observations.

Table 7.4 Results of tests on the stochastic frontier model

	Total Cost		Financial Cost	
Test	LR	d.f.	LR	d.f.
a	54.8454	1	–	–
b	182.9662	10	62.8866	6
c	12.0346	1	160.7516	1

$\chi^2_{1;0,001} = 10,8274; \chi^2_{6;0,001} = 22,4575; \chi^2_{10;0,001} = 29,5879$

The expressions of the cost functions used for the frontier are, in each case:[8]

$$\ln\left(\frac{TC}{w_3}\right) = \alpha_0 + \sum_{p=1}^{2} \beta_p \ln y_p + \sum_{m=1}^{2} \delta_m \ln\left(\frac{w_m}{w_3}\right) + \frac{1}{2}\sum_{p=1}^{2}\sum_{q=1}^{2} \beta_{pq} \ln y_p \ln y_q + \frac{1}{2}\sum_{m=1}^{2}\sum_{n=1}^{2} \delta_{mn} \ln\frac{w_m}{w_3} \ln\frac{w_n}{w_3} + \sum_{p=1}^{2}\sum_{m=1}^{2} \gamma_{pm} \ln y_p \ln\frac{w_m}{w_3} + u + v \tag{7.41}$$

$$\ln\left(\frac{FC}{w_3}\right) = \alpha_0 + \sum_{p=1}^{2} \beta_p \ln y_p + \delta_1 \ln\left(\frac{w_2}{w_3}\right) + \frac{1}{2}\sum_{p=1}^{2}\sum_{q=1}^{2} \beta_{pq} \ln y_p \ln y_q + \frac{1}{2}\delta_{11} \ln^2\left(\frac{w_2}{w_3}\right) + \sum_{p=1}^{2} \gamma_{p1} \ln y_p \ln\frac{w_2}{w_3} + \sum_{r=1}^{9} \tau_r ratio_r + u + v \tag{7.42}$$

Because of symmetry, it must be fulfilled:

$$\begin{aligned} \beta_{pq} &= \beta_{qp} \quad if \quad p \neq q \\ \delta_{mn} &= \delta_{nm} \quad if \quad n \neq m \end{aligned} \tag{7.43}$$

Following Berger and Mester (1997), a normalization has to be imposed to guarantee lineal homogeneity of cost function in input prices. Observed costs and input prices must be normalized by any input price before taking the logarithm. These specifications guarantee that a proportional increase of input prices increases costs in the same proportion. This study uses the price of the physical capital to normalize the variables mentioned previously. Therefore, two coefficients of input prices have to be estimated.

Regarding the estimation of the parameters of the cost functions presented in Tables 7.5 and 7.7,[9] the highly significant negative sign in the parameter of the first output indicates the existence of percentage decreases in the costs due to improvements in Credits (*ceteris paribus*). Furthermore, the increase of Total cost due to the improvement of the ratio price of physical capital over price of Employees increases at a growing rate. In the Financial cost function, there is a significantly decreasing rate due to increases of the ratio price of Loanable funds over the price of Employees.

In Table 7.6, the results of the average for each year from 2002 to 2007 are reported, along with the average and standard deviation in the whole period of accounting ratios used as explanatory variables in the financial cost function.

The explanatory variables considered describe a behaviour which has a negative influence, in some cases significant, on the evolution of the efficiency of financial costs since 2005.

Table 7.5 Estimation results: total costs

	Total Cost		
	Coef.	S.D.	t-ratio
α_0	3.3134E+00***	7.9686E−01	4.1581E+00
β_1	−7.2300E−10***	4.4722E−11	−1.6167E+01
β_2	4.0355E−02	7.1302E−02	5.6597E−01
δ_1	6.2155E−10	6.4643E−10	9.6151E−01
δ_2	6.9888E−02	4.9627E−02	1.7083E+00
β_{11}	−2.2587E−10	1.7073E−10	−1.7230E+00
β_{22}	1.8966E−02	6.8627E−02	2.7636E−01
δ_{11}	−1.1890E−11	6.4693E−11	−1.8379E−01
δ_{22}	8.6469E−02**	3.7982E−02	2.2766E+00
β_{12}	−6.0487E−11	6.1636E−11	−9.8137E−01
δ_{12}	2.5279E−02***	2.3163E−03	1.0914E+01
γ_{11}	−1.9332E−10	5.1845E−09	−3.7288E−02
γ_{12}	−2.1510E−03	2.0320E−03	−1.0586E+00
γ_{21}	6.8456E−11	1.2944E−09	5.2887E−02
γ_{22}	−3.4499E−02***	5.2680E−03	−6.5488E+00
σ^2	4.4349E−02***	6.5787E−03	6.7412E+00
λ	3.3271E−01***	7.8501E−02	4.2382E+00
μ	2.4294E−01***	6.5739E−02	3.6955E+00
η	1.2435E−01***	3.1107E−02	3.9975E+00

Table 7.6 Ratio averages

Ratio	Min.	Max.	Mean	Std dev.	2002	2003	2004	2005	2006	2007
L	0.000	2.960	0.422	0.353	0.404	0.403	0.421	0.393	0.433	0.482
S1	0.040	0.230	0.083	0.031	0.085	0.085	0.078	0.089	0.082	0.078
S2	0.030	0.160	0.0672	0.024	0.069	0.069	0.064	0.072	0.067	0.063
T1	0.410	0.930	0.760	0.090	0.678	0.705	0.730	0.803	0.828	0.815
T2	0.950	1.760	1.498	0.139	1.469	1.496	1.517	1.502	1.508	1.493
Q1	−0.220	0.620	0.165	0.156	0.302	0.272	0.281	0.048	0.062	0.027
Q2	−0.002	0.010	0.001	0.002	0.003	0.004	0.001	0.000	0.001	0.000
P	0.040	0.320	0.110	0.031	0.115	0.112	0.113	0.096	0.105	0.117
M	0.000	0.040	0.012	0.004	0.011	0.013	0.011	0.011	0.011	0.012

Notes: 46 savings banks, period 2002–2007, 276 observations.

Table 7.7 Estimation results: financial costs

	Financial Cost						
	Coef.	Std dev.	t-ratio		Coef.	Std dev.	t-ratio
α_0	5.4499E−01	1.0930E+00	4.9864E−01	τ_0	−9.7217E−01	6.5412E−01	−1.4862E+00
β_1	−8.1992E−10***	7.8091E−11	−1.0500E+01	τ_1(L)	−1.6389E−02	1.5836E−02	−1.0349E+00
β_2	1.9005E−01	1.2007E−01	1.5828E+00	τ_2(S1)	−1.1091E−09	4.5692E−09	−2.4273E−01
δ_1	2.2587E−09*	1.1683E−09	1.9334E+00	τ_3(S2)	1.3269E−01***	3.7050E−02	−3.5815E+00
δ_2	–	–	–	τ_4(T1)	−9.6913E−10	8.0447E−10	−1.2047E+00
β_{11}	6.7182E−02	6.0051E−02	1.1187E+00	τ_5(T2)	−1.3074E−02	1.9500E−02	−6.7043E−01
β_{22}	−8.5350E−11	2.4974E−10	−3.4175E−01	τ_6(Q1)	1.4039E−08**	5.7114E−09	−2.4581E+00
δ_{11}	2.6251E−01***	8.7682E−02	2.9939E+00	τ_7(Q2)	−4.4718E−02	3.7179E−02	−1.2028E+00
δ_{22}	–	–	–	τ_8(P)	2.7939E−11	1.2640E−09	2.2104E−02
β_{12}	−1.8076E−10*	1.0057E−10	−1.7974E+00	τ_9(M)	−9.5691E−02***	2.9312E−02	−3.2645E+00
δ_{12}	–	–	–	σ^2	1.1528E−01***	1.1085E−02	1.0399E+01
γ_{11}	1.8874E−02***	5.2577E−03	3.5898E+00	λ	3.5181E−01***	1.2906E−01	2.7259E+00
γ_{12}	–	–	–				
γ_{21}	−4.7816E−09	7.2943E−09	−6.5553E−01				
γ_{22}	–	–	–				

Table 7.7 shows the estimation results of the Financial cost frontier, including explanatory variables. Below, the development and influence of relevant covariables is explained.

The ratio *L* suffers an increase in the amount of interest on debt by increasing the departure of liquid liabilities, which is reflected in lower efficiency of financial costs (see Table 7.7).

A decrease of total assets implies better management of surplus towards more productive investments, and if this change presents an increase in resources, it will show higher levels of S2, which increases efficiency. However this ratio has presented a decreasing trend since 2005, so its influence on financial costs efficiency has been negative since then. Grigorian and Manole (2002) explain that well capitalized banks are better positioned to attract deposits. In this sense, Mester (1993) argues that executives of banks close to bankruptcy (with low capital ratios) tend to focus on the benefits and extras. The positive relationship between share of capital and cost efficiency is a conclusion that has been reached in other studies on bank efficiency, such as Hasan and Marton (2003), Nikiel and Opiela (2002), Yildirim et al. (2007), Carvallo and Kasman (2005), Casu and Girardone (2004), Chang and Chiu (2006) and Zajc (2006) – but in studies such as Freixas and Rochet (1997) and Altunbas et al. (2001) the relationship is negative.

The ratio T1, for which growing values have been obtained in the period, reflects the increase in the work of financial intermediation carried out by these institutions, thus obtaining a decrease in the levels of efficiency (negative coefficient in Table 7.7) achieved due to concentration in the traditional activity. This is in line with studies on developed countries; higher risk (higher share of loans over total assets) is often negatively correlated with costs efficiency, that is, banks with higher risk are under less pressure to control costs (Maudos et al., 2002). Berger and Mester (1997) found a statistically significant negative relationship between costs efficiency and the share of loans for US banks. Mester (1996) and Hasan and Marton (2003) found similar results. However, the literature also presents an opposing view: for example Allen and Rai (1996), which suggested that higher ratios of loans over banking assets indicate more aggressive behaviour (more lending activity), which tends to result in higher efficiency. Nikiel and Opiela (2002) found a positive and statistically significant relationship between the share of loans and costs efficiency for banks in Poland; Yildirim et al. (2007) confirm this result for 12 central and eastern European countries (CEECs). Also, Zajc (2006) found the same relationship for banks in six CEECs. The negative coefficient shown by the ratio T2 in Table 7.7 implies an oversized traditional collection of depository institutions, and indicates the need for greater diversification of sources of funding and investment for increased efficiency.

The ratio Q1 has a sharp decrease in values from 2004, the year in which the change became effective in the regulation, due to Circular 4/2004 of the Banco de España. Its positive coefficient for financial costs efficiency in Table 7.7 indicates a negative effect of the allocations to provisioning for bad debts (net) in the levels of efficiency achieved. This behaviour reflects the comparative loss of profitability compared to other more profitable investments.

Regarding profitability, an increase in income improves profitability (P) and hence the efficiency of financial costs. This result coincides with other investigations on bank efficiency, such as Berger and Mester (1997), Mester (1996, 1997), Pastor et al. (1997), Yildirim et al. (2007), Ataullah et al. (2004), Casu and Girardone (2004) and Chang and Chiu (2006). The trend during the period showed a fall in 2005 and 2006, contributing to the decrease in financial costs efficiency.

The current evolution of the ratio *M* will be a decrease because of regulatory pressure to reduce the components of the margin and the growth of total assets. However, the ratio shows a trend virtually constant along the period, so there is no advance towards efficiency in net terms.

The results of estimated efficiencies in total and financial cost are presented in Tables 7.8 and 7.9 respectively. The average financial CE shows a growing trend in the period 2002 to 2004, from 0.615 to 0.671, averaging 0.647. From 2005, the results describe an average trend, reaching 0.495 in the last year of the study, reflecting a rate decrease of 22 percentage points in just three years. This change of behaviour in efficiency of financial cost was a prediction of the complicated situation in the majority of Spanish savings banks at the time, since their ability to manoeuvre

Table 7.8 Descriptive statistics of total cost efficiency scores

Period	Median	Mean	Std dev.	C.I.Mean (95%)	Min.	Max.
2002	61.05	62.73	12.18	58.98; 66.48	42.68	92.98
2003	64.70	66.15	11.30	62.67; 69.63	47.16	93.79
2004	68.10	69.34	10.44	66.13; 72.55	51.51	94.51
2005	71.25	72.30	9.59	69.36; 75.26	55.68	95.14
2006	75.05	74.14	8.77	72.35; 77.75	59.63	95.70
2007	77.57	76.79	7.99	75.11; 80.03	63.36	96.20

Table 7.9 Descriptive statistics of financial cost efficiency scores

Period	Median	Mean	Std dev.	C.I.Mean (95%)	Min.	Max.
2002	59.22	61.49	13.33	57.39; 65.60	39.93	97.20
2003	63.66	65.45	12.12	61.72; 69.18	41.04	94.95
2004	67.62	67.14	12.59	63.27; 71.02	45.40	97.61
2005	62.27	63.70	11.70	60.10; 67.30	44.03	92.36
2006	55.47	56.56	12.59	52.69; 60.44	34.23	94.33
2007	47.05	49.53	12.23	45.76; 53.29	35.30	89.80

in order to gain advantages in the deposits market was low, given the official interest rates.

If these results are compared with those obtained in banking during 1992 to 2001 using parametric techniques by Carbó et al. (2004), a worsening in CE can be observed. This should be due to the inclusion of commercial banks in the sample of the cited work and to the worsening of the conditions in the Spanish financial system.

Total CE shows a slowdown of growth in the second half of the period. Due to the application of the proposed method, it is possible to argue for the influence that the negative trend of financial CE has exerted on this slowing down. However, the estimated efficiency annual average increased by 24 per cent, from 0.627 in 2002 to 0.776 in 2007. The total costs efficiency average for the period is 0.705, indicating that the average DMU had costs of 29.5 per cent above the potential minimum cost of the best-practice DMU producing the same output mix and operating under the same conditions. This result is very close to the 0.75–0.80 of the mean efficiency found by the 130 studies on the banking sector of 21 countries analysed by Berger and Humphrey (1997). Other authors, such as Maudos and Pastor (2003) and Lozano-Vivas and Pasiouras (2010) reported higher results: 0.90 in banks and 0.80 in savings banks in 1985 to 1996 and 0.86 in the banks of 87 countries in 1999 to 2006 respectively. In the Spanish banking system, the closest result is 0.77 in savings banks in 1989 to 1996, found by Carbó et al. (2002).

7.6 Conclusions

The present investigation has used the stochastic frontier approach to analyse total and financial costs efficiency in Spanish savings banks during the period 2002 to 2007, and to determine the contribution of this field to the final result. Several accounting and financial ratios of saving banks have also been included in the study to determine whether the beginning of the financial instability situation had influenced the results of CE.

The main conclusion is that the financial instability in the sector that began in 2005 exerted an influence on the development of financial CE, hence on the total cost efficiency of Spanish savings banks. In fact, total CE shows a slowdown of growth in the second half of the period that could have been caused by financial costs efficiency.

The levels shown by cost inefficiency reflect the characteristics of the environment in which savings banks were operating at that time. The unstable evolution of official interest rates which could affect financial cost, plus the unexpected demand for deposits of this market and therefore the cost of its exploitation, are clear examples of the uncertainty in the credit institution sector in Spain. Increased competitive pressure as a result of globalization and economic integration and the mergers that have already taken place between entities and of the continuation of this process with the consequent reduction in market power and levels of profitability, will force the Spanish savings banks to devise a strategy to reduce the levels of inefficiency.

Notes

1. Stochastic Frontier Analysis (SFA), Disposal Frontier Analysis (DFA) and Thick Frontier Approach (TFA).
2. Data Envelopment Analysis (DEA) and Free Disposal Hull (FDH).
3. Decision-making Unit
4. See Frene (2003) for discussion on the maximization of log-likelihood functions.
5. More detail of the estimation of half-normal model can be found in Aigner et al. (1977) and Greene (2003).
6. Frontier 4.1 (Coelli, 1996).
7. Some units have been excluded because of mergers or lack of data in order to maintain a constant number along the period.
8. Subscripts indicative of time and unit have been ignored in order to simplify the expressions.
9. *t*-ratio: ***critical value of 2.57 at significance level of 1 per cent, ** 1.96 of 5 per cent and * 1.64 of 10 per cent.

References

D. Aigner, C.A. Lovell and P. Schmidt (1977) Formulation and estimation of stochastic frontier production models. *Journal of Econometrics*, 6: 21–37.

L. Allen and A. Rai (1996) Operational efficiency in banking: An international comparison. *Journal of Banking and Finance*, 20(4): 655–72.

Y. Altunbas, E.P.M. Gardener, P. Molyneux and B. Moore (2001) Efficiency in European banking. *European Economic Review,* 45: 1931–55.

A. Ataullah, T. Cockerill and H. Le (2004) Financial liberalization and bank efficiency: A comparative analysis of India and Pakistan. *Applied Economics,* 36(17): 1–10.

B.H. Baltagi and J.M. Griffin (1988) A general index of technical change. *Journal of Political Economy,* 96: 20–41.

G.E. Battese and T.J. Coelli (1995) A model for technical inefficiency effects in a stochastic frontier production function for panel data. *Empirical Economics,* 20: 325–32.

G.E. Battese and T.J. Coelli (1992) Frontier production functions, technical efficiency and panel data: With application to paddy farmers in India. *Journal of Productivity Analysis,* 3: 153–69.

G.E. Battese and T.J. Coelli (1988) Prediction of firm-level technical efficiencies with a generalized frontier production function and panel data. *Journal of Econometrics,* 38: 387–99.

P. Bauer, A. Berger, G. Ferrier and D. Humphrey (1998) Consistency conditions for regulatory analysis of financial institutions: A comparison of frontier efficiency methods. *Journal of Economics and Business,* 50: 85–114.

A. Berger and D. Humphrey (1997) Efficiency of financial institutions: International survey and directions for future research. *European Journal of Operational Research,* 98: 175–212.

A. Berger and L. Mester (1997) Inside the black box: What explains differences in the efficiencies of financial institutions? *Journal of Banking and Finance,* 21: 895–947.

J. Bonin, I. Hasan and P. Wachtel (2005) Bank performance, efficiency and ownership in transition countries. *Journal of Banking and Finance,* 29: 31–53.

J.W.B. Bos, M. Koetter, J.W. Kolari and C.J.M. Kool (2009) Effects of heterogeneity on bank efficiency scores. *European Journal of Operational Research,* 195: 251–61.

J.W.B. Bos and H. Schmiedel (2006) Is there a single frontier in a single European banking market? *European Central Bank,* WP-701.

D.F. Burgess (1974) A cost minimization approach to import demand equations. *Review of Economics and Statistics,* 56: 225–34.

S. Carbó, E.P.M. Gardener and J. Williams (2002) Efficiency in banking: Empirical evidence from the savings banks sector. *The Manchester School,* 70(2): 204–28.

S. Carbó, D. Humphrey and R. López del Paso (2004) Eficiencias externa, técnica, interna y de gestión de las entidades financieras. *Papeles de Economía Española,* 101: 212–20.

O. Carvallo and A. Kasman (2005) Cost efficiency in the Latin American and Caribbean banking systems. *Journal of International Financial Markets, Institutions and Money,* 15: 55–72.

B. Casu and C. Girardone (2004) Financial conglomeration: efficiency, productivity and strategic drive. *Applied Financial Economics,* 14(10): 687–96.

T. Chang and Y. Chiu (2006) Affecting factors on risk-adjusted efficiency in Taiwan's banking industry. *Contemporary Economic Policy,* 24(4): 634–48.

A. Charnes, W.W. Cooper and E. Rhodes (1978) Measuring the inefficiency of decision making units. *European Journal of Operational Research,* 2(6): 429–44.

L.R. Christensen, D.W. Jorgenson and L.J. Lau (1973) Transcendental logarithmic production frontiers. *The Review of Economics and Statistics,* 55: 28–43.

J. Clark (1988) Economies of scale and scope at depositary financial institutions: A review of literature. Federal Reserve Bank of Kansas City. *Economic Review,* 16–33.

T.J. Coelli (1996) *A Guide to FRONTIER Version 4.1: A Computer Program for Frontier Production Function Estimation,* Department of Econometrics, University of New England, Armidale.

T.J. Coelli (1995) Estimators and hypothesis tests for a stochastic frontier function: A Monte Carlo analysis. *Journal of Productivity Analysis,* 6: 247–68.

T.J. Coelli (1992) A computer program for frontier production function estimation: FRONTIER, version 2.0. *Economics Letters,* 39: 29–32.

T. Coelli, D.S.P. Rao and G.E. Battese (1998) *An Introduction to Efficiency and Productivity Analysis.* Massachusetts: Kluwer Academic Publishers, chapter 8.

C. Cornwell, P. Schimdt and C. Sickles (1990) Production frontiers with cross-sectional and time-series variation in efficiency levels. *Journal of Econometrics,* 46: 185–200.

X. Freixas and J. Rochet (1997) *Microeconomics of Banking.* Cambridge: MIT Press.

W. H. Greene (2003) *Econometric Analysis,* 5th edn. Prentice Hall: Englewood Cliffs.

W. H. Greene (2000) *Econometric Analysis,* 4th edn. Prentice Hall: Englewood Cliffs.

W.H. Greene (1992) *LIMDEP Version 6.0: User's Manual and Reference Guide.* Econometric Software Inc.: New York.

W.H. Greene (1980) Maximum likelihood estimation of econometric frontier functions. *Journal of Econometrics,* 13: 27–56.

D. Grigorian and V. Manole (2002) Determinants of commercial bank performance in transition: An application of data envelopment analysis. *Comparative Economic Studies,* 48: 497–522.

I. Hasan and K. Marton (2003) Development and efficiency of the banking sector in a transitional economy: Hungarian experience. *Journal of Banking and Finance,* 27: 2249–71.

J. Jondrow, C.A.K. Lovell, Y.S. Materov and P. Schmidt (1982) On the estimation of technical inefficiency in the stochastic frontier production function model. *Journal of Econometrics,* 19: 233–8.

S.C. Kumbhakar (1993) Production risk, technical efficiency and panel data. *Economics Letters,* 41: 11–26.

S.C. Kumbhakar and C.A. Knox Lovell (2000) *Stochastic Frontier Analysis.* Cambridge University Press: Cambridge, England.

Y.H. Lee and P. Schmidt (1993) *A Production Frontier Model with Flexible Temporal Variation in Technical Inefficiency. The Measurement of Productive Efficiency: Techniques and Applications.* New York: Oxford University Press, pp. 237–55.

A. Lozano-Vivas and F. Pasiouras (2010) The impact of non-traditional activities on the estimation of bank efficiency: International evidence. *Journal of Banking and Finance,* 34 (7): 1436–49.

J. Maudos and J.M. Pastor (2003) Cost and profit efficiency in the Spanish banking sector (1985–96): A non-parametric approach. *Applied Financial Economics,* 13(1): 1–12.

J. Maudos, J.M. Pastor, F. Pérez and J. Quesada (2002) Cost and profit efficiency in European banks. *Journal of International Financial Markets, Institutions and Money,* 12: 33–58.

W. Meeusen and J. van Den Broeck (1977) Efficiency estimation from Cobb-Douglas production functions with composed error. *International Economic Review*, 18(2): 435–44.

L.J. Mester (1997) Measuring efficiency at U.S. banks: Accounting for heterogeneity is important. *European Journal of Operational Research*, 98(2): 230–42.

L.J. Mester (1996) A study of bank efficiency taking into account risk-preferences. *Journal of Banking and Finance*, 20: 1025–45.

L.J. Mester (1993) Efficiency in the savings and loan industry. *Journal of Banking and Finance*, 17: 267–86.

E. Nikiel and T. Opiela (2002) Customer type and bank efficiency in Poland: Implications for emerging market banking. *Contemporary Economic Policy*, 20: 244–71.

F. Pasiouras (2008) Estimating the technical and scale efficiency of greek commercial banks: The impact of credit risk, off-balance sheet activities, and international operations. *Research in International Business and Finance*, 22: 301–18.

J.T. Pastor Ciurana, A. Lozano-Vivas and J.M. Pastor (1997) Efficiency of European banking systems: A correction by environmental variables. *WP Serie EC IVIE*, 12.

M.M. Pitt and L.F. Lee (1981) The measurement and sources of technical inefficiency in the Indonesian weaving industry. *Journal of Development Economics*, 9 (1): 43–64.

J. Richmond (1974) Estimating the efficiency of production. *International Economic Review*, 15: 515–21.

P. Schmidt and R.C. Sickles (1984) Production frontiers and panel data. *Journal of Business and Economic Statistics*, 2(4): 367–74.

C.W.Jr. Sealey and J.T. Lindley (1977) Inputs, outputs, and a theory of production and cost at depository financial institutions. *Journal of Finance*, 32(4): 1251–66.

E. Thanassoulis (1999) Data envelopment analysis and its use in banking. *Interfaces*, 29(3): 1–13.

L. Weill (2009) Convergence in banking efficiency across European countries. *Journal of International Financial Markets, Institutions and Money*, 19(5): 818–33.

L. Weill (2004) Measuring cost efficiency in European Banking: A comparison of frontier techniques. *Journal of Productivity Analysis*, 21: 133–52.

M.A. Weinstein (1964) The sum of values from a normal and a truncated normal distribution. *Technometrics*, 6: 104–5.

H.S. Yildirim, C. George and G.C. Philippatos (2007) Efficiency of banks: Recent evidence from the transition economies of Europe, 1993–2000. *European Journal of Finance*, 13(2): 123–43.

P. Zajc (2006) A comparative study of bank efficiency in central and eastern Europe: The role of foreign ownership. *International Finance Review*, 6: 117–56.

8

Empirical Analysis of Intellectual Capital Disclosure Practices in Banks in Spain, Portugal and Greece

Gimede Gigante and Daniele Angelo Previati

8.1 Introduction

During the 1990s there was a rapid evolutionary shift in the established paradigm underlying the dominant model for business practices and execution. For over 200 years the success of a company was generally based on its efficient use of physical capital. However, on entering the third millennium it has become intellectual, rather than physical, capital which appears to have become the established cornerstone for a bank's future viability and success in the 'new knowledge economy'. Pulic and Bornemann (1999, p. 1), for example, wrote that in 'this new economy ...intellectual capital has become the one and only competitive advantage of a bank', as well as the pivotal component of future prosperity, growth and development. The changes in the major underlying pivotal factor of a business and national infrastructure during the 1990s raises several questions about the possible impact on related disclosures practices by banks. Two major questions can be summarized as follows:

(1) Did the intellectual capital disclosure practices of banks alter in response to the growing emphasis on the management of intellectual capital in the period leading up to the new millennium?
(2) Did a bank's level of intellectual capital performance affect the amount of intellectual capital it disclosed?

In line with the two questions outlined above, there were two major overarching objectives of this study. The first objective was to provide a longitudinal investigation of intellectual capital disclosure practices as the new millennium approached. Motivation for this objective arose from several related sources. First, based on an extensive global survey, Taylor and Associates (1998) reported that disclosure of intellectual capital issues was one of the top ten information needs of users. It is imperative, therefore, to determine if banks were reactive to the demands of users in meeting their need for information on intellectual capital matters. Research into actual intellectual capital disclosure practices, however, is virtually non-existent, particularly investigations of reporting procedures across an extended period. Second, the results from prior research into the relationship between a bank's performance and different disclosure issues have been inconclusive and mixed. Findings on the association between a bank's performance and related disclosure practices, however, have been based on measures of the bank's returns on physical capital. With the growing change from the assessment of a bank's performance based on its efficient use of physical capital to that of intellectual capital, research needs to be undertaken to determine if said change might also influence the association between performance and disclosure practices. Finally, many of the present mandatory accounting disclosure requirements issued by accounting professions are related to a bank's physical capital. In the face of a change to intellectual capital as the pivotal factor of an entity, mandatory disclosure requirements related to physical capital will become less important. It is necessary for accounting regulators to determine if firms are disclosing on intellectual capital matters; if empirical research indicates a lack of disclosure, accounting regulators may have to decide whether mandatory requirements need to be introduced to protect the interests of users.

This chapter's major contribution to the extant disclosure is fourfold. First, the analysis from this study examines an emerging area of accounting disclosures that while demanded by stakeholders has yet (at the time of writing) to be investigated to any substantial extent. Second, prior research has provided evidence of the association between the performance of a firm in terms of economic, environmental and social matters with disclosure level related to the same themes. Findings from this study assist in determining if there is also a corresponding link between the level of disclosure on intellectual capital and the actual intellectual capital performance of a firm. Also, apart from a bank's financial performance, this study assessed the relationship between other key organizational level control factors and the level of intellectual capital disclosure. Finally, there is a current lack of agreement on the measurement of economic performance. A number of intellectual capital measurement models have been proposed. Generally speaking, however, the suggested intellectual capital measurement models have been applied on only a limited basis. Findings from this study could help to define the viability of using the Value Added Intellectual Coefficient (VAIC™, developed by Pulic, 1998) across a broad spectrum of firms from a number of industry groups. Support for this measure of intellectual capital performance can assist in broadening the scope of future research into this domain.

To meet the objectives of this study, a sample of 31 Spanish, Portuguese and Greek publicly listed banks were randomly selected. The annual reports from the selected banks from 2003 to 2010 were examined. The intellectual capital performance of each bank in the years under investigation was measured using the VAIC™.

8.2 Intellectual capital

8.2.1 Definition and components of intellectual capital

Intellectual capital is a broad-based term that is considered synonymous with a bank's intangible assets. There is, however, no precise agreement on a definition of intellectual capital. Klein and Prusak (in Brooking, 1996, p. 12) provided an early definition of intellectual capital, calling it 'material that has been formalized, captured, and leveraged to produce a higher-valued asset'. Meanwhile, Stewart (1997, p. 67) defined intellectual capital as 'packaged useful knowledge'. Brooking (1996, p. 12) offered a more comprehensive definition of intellectual capital, stating that this term is 'given to the combined intangible assets which enable the company to function'. Generally speaking, definitions of intellectual capital have described this terminology as comprising:

> (a) knowledge, whether tacit or explicit; (b) knowledge transformation processes (such as research and development, knowledge networks, communities of practice and organizational learning); and (c) the end products of the knowledge transformation processes (such as patent, trademarks and other assets containing intellectual property rights).

Though a variety of definitions have utilized the concept of knowledge, Beaulieu, Williams and Wright (2002) argued that intellectual capital is 'not merely a part free-floating human brainpower, but rather assets that can be identified and used by organizations'. It is beyond the scope of this chapter to assess the respective merit of the various definitions of intellectual capital. Regardless, for the purposes of this chapter intellectual capital is defined as:

> The enhanced value of a bank attributable to assets, generally of an intangible nature, resulting from the company's organizational

function, processes and information technology networks, the competency and efficiency of its employees and its relationship with its customers. Intellectual capital assets are developed from (a) the creation of new knowledge and innovation; (b) application of present knowledge to present issues and concerns that enhance employees and customers; (c) packaging, processing and transmission of knowledge; and (d) the acquisition of present knowledge created through research and learning.

Table 8.1 provides a summary of the major classification schemes defined in previous research of the respective components of intellectual capital.

8.3 Research design

It is acknowledged that banks in Spain, Portugal and Greece has access to a variety of tools for the dissemination of information on intellectual capital. For the purposes of this study, however, it was decided that the extent of intellectual capital disclosure would be measured using annual reports as the source documentation. There is considerable support within the accounting disclosure literature for the analysis of reporting practices using annual reports. Tilt (1994) supports this view, suggesting banks can symbolically demonstrate values to the relevant public through this document. Campbell (2000) provided two further reasons to support the use of annual reports. First, this document is often the most widely distributed of all publicly produced documents of an organization. Second, management has complete editorial control of the discretionary disclosure of information in the document. Finally, Tay and Parker (1990, p. 79) state that 'actual reporting practices may be assessed more accurately from annual accounts'.

8.3.1 Measure of organizational level control variables

Prior research has suggested that organizational level factors may influence the amount of voluntary disclosure practices. There is little empirical research that may indicate which organizational level factors may be determinants of intellectual capital disclosure levels. For the purposes of this study, therefore, five organizational level control factors are included, based on the strength of previous research into voluntary disclosure practices. These five organizational level factors are: (1) organizational size; (2) industry type; (3) listing status; (4) physical capital financial performance; and (5) leverage. These factors, and the proxies used to measure them, are described below.

Table 8.1 Major classification schemes of the respective components of intellectual capital

Study	Intellectual capital component	Description of component as defined by researcher	Example of respective component
Edvinsson	Human capital	Combined knowledge, skill, innovativeness and ability of the company's individual employees to meet the task at hand.	• Company values • Company philosophy • Organizational culture
	Structural capital	The firm's infrastructure that supports an employee's productivity.	1. Software 2. Databases 3. Patents 4. Trademarks
Brinker (1997)	Structural capital	Infrastructure that supports the human capital component of intellectual capital.	• Information technology systems • Company image • Organizational concept and • Documentation
	Human capital	Capability of employees to provide solutions to customers, to innovate and to renew. This includes the dynamics of an intelligent (learning) organization in a changing competitive environment, its creativity, and innovativeness.	• Tacit knowledge • Explicit knowledge • Training programs • Recruitment
	Customer capital	Relationships with people with whom a company does business.	1. Long-term contracts 2. Customer satisfaction 3. Customer profile 4. Customer success (renewal of contracts)
Brooking (1996)	Market assets	Potential of an organization with respect to its market-related intangibles.	• Repeat business percentage • Value associated with goodwill • Dominance from marketing strategies
	Intellectual property assets	The know-how, copyright, patent, semiconductor topography rights, and various design rights of the company.	• Reputation of intellectual property • Developed • Dist. of intellectual property held • Total intellectual property investment • Intellectual property renewed/revised

	Human-centred assets	Collective expertise, creative capability, leadership, entrepreneurial and managerial skills embodied by the employees of the organization. This includes the psychometric data and indications of how individuals perform in varying situations, such as those with high stress.	Dist. employees by gender, age and Seniority Employee education investment Employee turnover
	Infrastructure assets	Technologies, methodologies and processes enabling the organization to function.	Methodologies for assessing risk Databases on markets and customers Communication systems
Draper (1998)	Structural capital	The value of what is left when the employees have gone home (human capital).	Information systems Customer lists Operational documentations
	Human capital	Accumulated value of investments in employee training, competence and future.	Employee satisfaction Employee education investment employee turnover and seniority
	Customer capital	Value of the customer base, customer relationships, and customer potential.	Customer contract renewal Customer satisfaction New customer figures
	Organizational capital	Systematized and packaged competence, combining systems for leveraging the company's innovative strength and value-creating organizational capability.	• Organizational philosophy • Company strategies and directives
	Innovation capital	Renewal strength in a company, expressed as protected commercial rights, intellectual property, and other intangible assets and values.	• Intellectual rights • Commercial rights
	Processing capital	The combined value of value-creating processes.	• Time for processing of orders • Product development time • Human resource dist. by processes

Size of organization

A number of theoretical studies have proposed a positive relationship between the size of organization and the extent of its voluntary disclosure (see, for example, Dye, 1985; Craswell and Taylor, 1992; Watts and Zimmerman, 1986). The majority of empirical studies have supported such a relationship (see, for example, Chow and Wong-Boren, 1987; Cooke, 1989a, 1991; Milgrom and Roberts, 1992). Larger banks are likely to be under greater scrutiny from the various stakeholder groups with an interest in intellectual capital, such as employees, customers, unions and the public at large. In addition, larger banks may have more stakeholder parties interested in the way they manage their intellectual capital whilst also having access to more formal channels of communication through which information related to intellectual capital can be relayed to interested parties. To control for potential organizational size effects on the quantity of intellectual capital disclosure, this control factor was measured using the natural log of the bank's average total assets.

Listing status

Recent empirical research has identified a positive relationship between a bank's foreign listing status and its extent of voluntary disclosure (see, for example, Cooke, 1991; Leftwich, Watts and Zimmerman, 1981; Malone, Fries and Jones, 1993). It has been argued that when a bank is listed on more foreign exchanges, it will be exposed to the scrutiny of a wider set of stakeholder groups. In reference to intellectual capital, therefore, as interest in this concept has expanded globally, banks listed on foreign exchanges are likely to have been made subject to demands for information made by a wider set of intellectual capital interest groups. To meet the needs of this wider set of stakeholders, such a bank is likely to disclose more details on intellectual capital than do entities that are only domestically listed. A dummy variable was used to measure this control factor; banks with multiple listings were scored with a one and those listed in only a single country with a zero.

Physical capital financial performance

Despite the growing significance of intellectual capital for shareholders and other stakeholder groups, traditional measures of a bank's performance based on its physical capital, such as ROA and ROE, still remain an important feature of a bank's profile. As a consequence, a bank will not wish to be perceived as a 'lemon' in terms of its physical capital financial performance. Prior research has suggested that banks with a sound physical capital financial performance level will have a variety of incentives compelling them to distinguish themselves from less profitable entities; one such incentive may be a desire to reduce their cost of capital. A mechanism used to distinguish themselves from less profitable companies is through voluntary disclosures (Foster, 1986). Thus, previous research suggests that physical capital financial performance will lead to an increase in voluntary disclosures, including those related to intellectual capital. To control for this factor, the bank's return on assets for each year was calculated.

Leverage

The final control factor included in this study related to the bank's leverage. Jensen and Meckling (1976) argued that there is the potential for transfers of wealth from bondholders to shareholders amongst highly leveraged banks. In an effort to protect their own self-interests, restrictive debt covenants could be constructed within the debt contracts. In an effort to reduce monitoring costs, a company's management may voluntarily disclose more information, including that related to intellectual capital. Leverage was measured as the bank's long-term debt to shareholders' equity ratio.

8.3.2 The Multiple Regression Analysis model

To analyse the possible relationship between intellectual capital performance and intellectual capital disclosure, the following multiple regression model was derived:

$$\text{QIC Disclosure in each year (2003–2010)} = a1 + \alpha 1OS + \alpha 2IT + \alpha 3LS + \alpha 4ROA + \alpha 5LEV + \alpha 6VAIC^{TM} + \varepsilon$$

where QIC Disclosure = intellectual capital disclosure score per bank.

VAIC™ measures and monitors the total value creation efficiency in the company. The subordinate concept of VAIC™, intellectual capital efficiency (ICE), describes the efficiency of IC within a company. The method is built on the premise that value creation is derived from two primary resource bases: physical capital resources and intellectual capital resources. Actually, VAIC™indicates the total efficiency of value creation from all resources employed and ICE reflects the efficiency of value created by the IC employed. The better a company's resources have been utilized, the higher the company's value creation efficiency will be. (See e.g. Pulic, 2000; Van der Zahn, Tower and Neilson, 2004, p. 13)

First, the value added (VA) of a company is calculated as outputs less inputs. Value added can be calculated with the following equation: $VA = P + C + D + A$, where P describes operating profits, C employee costs (the salaries and the social expenses of staff) and D + A the depreciation and amortization of assets. Then the human capital (HC) of the company is calculated as the sum of the total salaries for the company, and the structural capital (SC) of the company by subtracting the human capital from the value added: SC = VA – HC.

Second, the capital employed efficiency (CEE) is calculated by dividing the value added by capital employed: CEE = VA/CE. It describes how much of the company's VA is generated with the capital employed. Human capital efficiency (HCE) is calculated by dividing the value added by the human capital: HCE = VA/HC. This is an indicator of the efficiency of VA by human capital resources employed. The third efficiency component, the structural capital efficiency (SCE), is calculated by dividing the structural capital by the value added: SCE = SC/VA, and it shows how much of the company's added value is generated by means of the structural capital.

Third, the ICE is calculated by summing the human capital efficiency and the structural capital efficiency: ICE = HCE + SCE. Finally, the VAIC™is a composite sum of the intellectual capital efficiency and the capital employed efficiency: VAIC™ = ICE + CEE .

The basic proposition is that the higher the VAIC™and ICE, the better the management has utilized the existing potential of the resources employed in creating value (Van der Zahn et al., 2004). Thus, VAIC™does not present the monetary value of IC. Instead, it considers different efficiency factors related to IC, and in doing so it evaluates how effectively an organization's IC adds value to the organization.

Several advantages come with utilization of the VAIC™method. They are, among others, the following:

- The method is simple and straightforward.
- VAIC™provides a standardized basis of measurement.
- All data used in the calculation is based on audited information from financial statements.
- It can be applied on different levels (for example company, industry).
- It can be applied to large samples.
- The measure allows for broad-based comparisons, e.g. across companies (see e.g. Firer and Williams, 2003; Van der Zahn et al., 2004, p. 14).

Organizational Size (OS) = Natural log of average total assets.

Industry Type (IT) = Dichotomous variable, coded one if a bank was highly knowledge-based and coded zero otherwise.

Listing Status (LS) = Dichotomous variable, coded one if a bank is multi-listed and coded zero otherwise.
Return on Assets (ROA) = Net income + Interest Expense (1 – Tax Rate)/Total Average Assets.
Leverage (LEV) = Average debt to shareholder's equity.
Value Added Intellectual Coefficient (VAIC™) = Measure of bank's intellectual capital performance during the year.

8.4 Results

8.4.1 Descriptive statistics

Descriptive statistics of the survey sample with respect to the extent of intellectual capital disclosure, intellectual capital performance and organizational level factors for each of the year investigated are shown in Table 8.2.

After analysing the VAIC™of selected sample of banks, the following banks were chosen for the base:

Portugal – Caixa Geral de Depositos
Spain – Banco de España
Greece – Attica Bank

These banks have the highest level of VAIC™and were used as a basic variable for the given country.

The breakdown in Table 8.2 suggests that between 2003 and 2010 the average amount of voluntary disclosure on intellectual capital tended to increase annually during the survey period. Analysis of the extent of disclosure related to the four major categories of intellectual disclosure described in this chapter suggests the increase in total disclosure on this concept was due to increases in all four major categories of this concept. In relative terms, however, the largest increase in the extent of disclosure was related to intellectual capital in intellectual property. For this category, the average amount of disclosure increased 242.08% from 2003 to 2010. The next largest percentage increase was for intellectual capital in information technology and processes, at 57.46%. The percentage increases in average disclosures for intellectual capital in customer and intellectual capital in human resources were 23.61% and 16.05%, respectively.

Across the survey period there does not appear to be any distinguishable trend associated with the average amount of intellectual capital performance amongst the survey sample. In absolute terms, there

Table 8.2 Descriptive statistics of the sample for three countries

	Countries						Comparison	
	Spain		Portugal		Greece		-	-
	Mean	*Std dev.*	*Mean*	*Std dev.*	*Mean*	*Std dev.*	*Mean*	*Std dev.*
Intellectual capital disclosure practices								
Overall total disclosure	0.2363	0.0067	0.2744	0.0087	0.3187	0.0094	0.3537	0.0097
Human resource capital	0.2423	0.0078	0.2398	0.0900	0.2630	0.1010	0.2795	0.1082
Customer capital	0.3414	0.1175	0.3709	0.1209	0.3884	0.1593	0.4086	0.1433
Information technology capital	0.2473	0.0076	0.2855	0.1033	0.3273	0.0096	0.3787	0.1113
Intellectual property capital	0.1143	0.1374	0.2013	0.1456	0.2961	0.1492	0.3480	0.1539
Intellectual capital performance (VAIC^{TM})	7.3485	17.460	2.3263	29.904	7.4980	12.077	5.0013	12.2419
Organizational level factors								
Average total assets (in millions of Euro)	30.200	58.549	35.600	71.311	38.400	74.210	47.400	94.202
Average total income (in millions of Euro)	7.500	9.562	6.510	6.022	6.740	5.915	8.870	8.835
Physical capital financial performance, %	12.78	9.65	11.55	8.33	11.39	8.33	10.68	7.05
Leverage, %	9.12	13.23	12.92	19.5	10.17	16.57	8.07	12.92

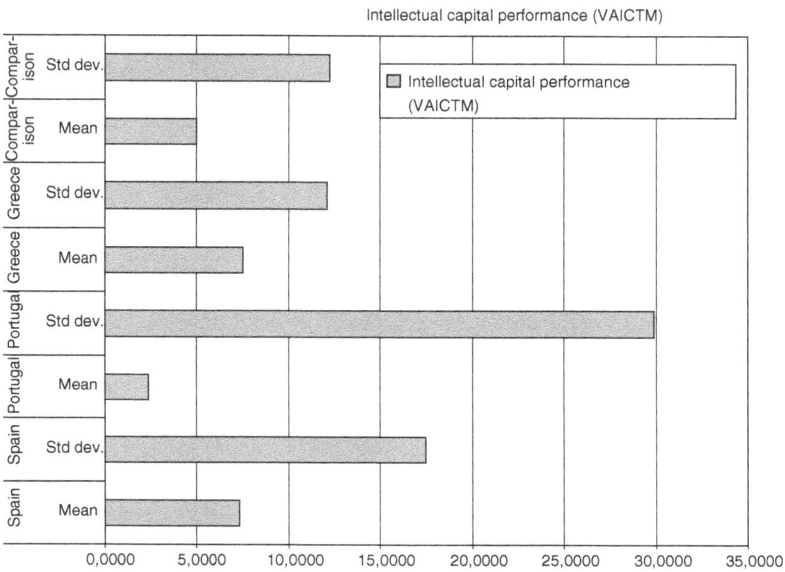

Figure 8.1 IC's performances across the three countries
Source: Our elaborations.

appears to be little difference between the average amount of intellectual capital performance in the years 2003, 2005 and 2010, respectively. In 2003 to 2005 and 2008 to 2009, however, there were declines in the average amount of intellectual capital performance before another rise. The decline in 2003 to 2005 appears more substantial than that in 2008 to 2009. Based on a comparison of the upward trend in intellectual capital disclosures and random movement in intellectual capital performance, there does not appear to be any correlation between the two.

With regard to the organizational level characteristics of the survey sample, there was a general upward trend in the average amount of total assets. The relative increase in terms of the average amount of total sales between 2003 and 2010 was more substantial than that for the average amount of total assets. Unlike the average amount of total assets, however, the average amount of total sales for the survey sample did not follow a consistent upward trend between each year. Between 2003 and 2005 there was a decline in the average amount of sales; this was followed by a slight increase between 2005 and 2006, and larger increases in the next couple of year-brackets. The physical capital financial performance of the survey sample, as measured by the return on assets, exhibited a

Table 8.3 Disclosure scores for the sample by countries and disclosure category

		Wilcoxon matched-pair signed rank tests					Paired sample t-tests	
		Decrease	Increase	Ties	Z- Score	*p*-value	t-statistic	*p*-value
Intellectual capital performance								
2003–2010 change in Spain	N =	17 (13,35) Λ	14 (19,21)	0	−0.412	0.681	0.599	0.554
2003–2010 change in Portugal	N =	18 (14,97)	12 (16.29)	1	−0.761	0.447	−0.948	0.351
2003–2010 change in Greece	N =	16 (16,56)	15 (15.40)	0	−0.333	0.739	0.852	0.401
Comparison	N =	14 (15,14)	17 (16.71)	0	−0.705	0.481	−0.413	0.683
Weighted disclosure score								
2003–2010 change in Spain	N =	12 (9,92)	18 (19.22)	0	−2.335	0.020 β	−2.920	0.007 β
2003–2010 change in Portugal	N =	3 (16,33)	27 (15.41)	0	−3.775	0.000 α	−4.373	0.000 α
2003–2010 change in Greece	N =	7 (7,64)	24 (18.44)	0	−3.812	0.000 α	−4.682	0.000α
Comparison	N =	7 (15,93)	23 (15.37)	1	−2.940	0.013 β	−2.560	0.016 β

Note: Λ = Mean Rank Change; ! = p < 0.001; $ = p < 0.050; % = p < 0.100.

gradual and steady decline between all the years covered by this survey. The average amount of leverage, however, followed a random path.

To examine if the changes in the average amount of intellectual capital disclosure and intellectual capital performance each year was significant, two tests – one non-parametric (Wilcoxon matched-pair sign rank test) and one parametric (paired sample *t*-tests) – were performed. Results relating to these tests are shown in Table 8.3.

One pragmatic reason for performing the Wilcoxon matched-pair signed rank is that it shows the number of companies that increased their intellectual capital disclosure and intellectual capital performance levels between the respective years under investigation. This test indicates that in terms of intellectual capital performance the number of companies that had an increase was generally close to the number of decreases for each year-pairing. In contrast, the raw number of banks that increased their level of intellectual capital disclosure was generally more substantial than the number recording a decrease. In terms of significant differences between the years, the results from both the Wilcoxon matched-pair signed test and the paired *t*-test indicate that the change in intellectual capital performance was not significant between any of the consecutive years during the survey period. The results relating to the average amount of intellectual capital disclosure, however, suggested that the changes between each of the paired years were in fact statistically significant.

Table 8.4 reports the results from the regression equations investigating the association between the extent of the intellectual capital disclosure, the intellectual capital performance and the organizational level control factors for each year covered by this study. The explanatory power of each model varies from a high for the year 2006 of 31.6% to a low in 2003 of 22.0%. Overall, the explanatory power of the model in each year is considered comparable to findings in other studies on disclosure practices that have included the organizational level control factors from this study. Concentrating on the results related to intellectual capital performance, the results detailed in Table 8.4 indicate the coefficient for this independent variable was only statistically significant in explaining variations in intellectual capital disclosure levels in 2003 and 2006 respectively. A result of more significance related to this independent variable, however, is that the directional sign on the coefficient was negative in each year, a finding contrary to expectations.

Contributing to the explanatory power of the model in each year was the significance of some of the organizational level control variables. In 2003, for example, the coefficient for a bank's listing status was found to be statistically significant. This factor was also significant in explaining the variation in intellectual capital disclosures in 2005, although the level of significance was only marginal. The directional sign for the coefficient related to listing status was as predicted in all annual regression models. Leverage also contributed to the explanatory power of the 2005 regression model. These two organizational level control factors were also significant explanatory variables of the variation in intellectual capital disclosures in 2006, 2007 and 2010 respectively. Directional signs on the coefficients related to leverage were as predicted in all annual regression models. It is interesting to note that in the case of leverage

Table 8.4 Multiple regression results of impact of same-year intellectual capital performance

	Countries						Comparison	
	Spain		Portugal		Greece		-	-
	t	*p-value*	*t*	*p-value*	*t*	*p-value*	*t*	*p-value*
Intellectual capital disclosure								
VAIC™	−1.975	0.062**	1.015	0.321	2.283	0.033**	−0.424	0.676
Control variables								
Organizational size	1.577	0.130	0.873	0.392	0.812	0.426	0.310	0.760
Listing status	3.142	0.005*	1.777	0.090**	1.504	0.147	1.318	0.202
Physical capital financial performance	−0.926	0.365	0.458	0.644	1.226	0.234	−0.530	0.601
Leverage	1.554	0.135	1.730	0.090**	1.874	0.075**	2.246	0.036**
Constant	1.903	0.071	1.809	0.085	2.135	0.045**	1.460	0.159
Model summary								
R-squared	45.4%		47.9%		52.1%		45.5%	
Adjusted R-squared	22.0%		25.5%		31.6%		22.1%	
F-statistic	1.942		2.144		2.540		1.945	
Significance of F-statistic	0.101		0.072**		0.038**		0.101	

Note: * = significant at p<0.0.05; ** = significant at p<0.10.

the statistical significance of this factor appears to become greater with each year. Contrary to expectations and to findings from prior literature, none of the coefficients related to organizational size and physical capital financial performance were statistically significant in any of the years under investigation. Also contrary to expectations, the directional sign on the coefficient for physical capital financial performance in 2003 and 2007 was negative rather than positive.

Prior research has suggested that a bank's performance may have a lagged affect on its disclosure practices. Both in line with this prior research and in an effort to further extend the application of this study, the relationship between a bank's lagged intellectual capital performance and intellectual capital disclosure practices is examined. Results from the respective annual regressions are shown in Table 8.5.

Table 8.5 Multiple regression results of impact of lagged-year intellectual capital performance

	Countries						Comparison	
	Spain		Portugal		Greece		-	-
	t	*p-value*	*t*	*p-value*	*t*	*p-value*	*t*	*p-value*
Intellectual capital disclosure								
VAIC™	1.571	0.131–	1.728	0.091**	0.233	0.818–	1.673	0.109
Control variables								
Organizational size	1.586	0.128	0.775	0.447	1.025	0.317	0.229	0.821
Listing status	2.908	0.008*	1.730	0.098**	1.386	0.180	1.501	0.148
Physical capital financial performance	−0.548	0.589	0.597	0.557	1.286	0.212–	0.758	0.457
Leverage	1.295*	0.209	1.669	0.099**	2.063	0.043*	2.234	0.037
Constant	1.841	0.080**	1.849	0.079**	2.185	0.040*	1.377	0.183
Model summary								
R-squared		42.1%		48.9%		48.8%		45.3%
Adjusted R-squared		17.3%		27.1%		26.9%		21.9%
F-statistic		1.696		2.237		2.226		1.936
Significance of F-statistic		0.153		0.062**		0.063**		0.102

The explanatory power of the models including a lagged term for intellectual capital performance was less than that of tests conducted without this independent variable being lagged. The range of the adjusted R- squared value for the lagged intellectual capital performance models extended from a high of 27.5% to a low of 17.3%. This compared to a range of 31.6% (high) to 22.0% (low) when the independent variable was not lagged. The coefficients on the lagged intellectual capital performance variable are found to only be statistically significant, and only marginal at best, in explaining variations in intellectual capital disclosures in 2005. Again, the directional sign on the coefficient related to lagged intellectual capital performance was contrary to expectations. Patterns of significance and directional signs for coefficients related to the organizational level control variables followed patterns similar to

Table 8.6 List of banks

Banks of Portugal
Caixa Geral De Depositos
UBS AG In Lissabon
Banco Nacional Ultrmarino
Banco BPI
Clariden Leu Escritorio de Representacao Amoreiras
Banco Popular Portugal
Barclays Bank Portugal
Millenium BPC
Finibanco
Banco de Portugal – Bank of Portugal
Banks of Spain
Banco de Espagna
Argentaria
Banco Central Hispano
Banco Gallego
Banco Multisectorial de Inversiones
Banesto
Banco Bilbao Vizcaya
Banco Sabadell
Bankinternet
Bankpyme
Banks of Greece
Attica Bank
Bank of Cyprus
EFG Eurobank Ergasias
Emporiki Bank
Geniki Bank
Hellenic Bank
National Bank of Greece
Panellinia Bank
Piraeus Bank
Proton Bank

those described above for models that did not have intellectual capital performance lagged.

8.5 Conclusions

Results from this study indicated that organizational size and physical capital financial performance were not associated with the amount of intellectual capital information disclosed by publicly listed companies. The lack of an association between organizational size and the amount of disclosure is somewhat contrary to previous research into accounting disclosure practices. There are no clear reasons for the lack of an association reported in this chapter concerning organization size and the extent of intellectual capital disclosure. It is proposed, however, that lack of an association could be due to several factors. First, the total sample included in this chapter is quite small, meaning that the variation in organization size may not be substantial enough to derive any significant effects. Second, the publicly listed companies in this study were from the FTSE-100. Collectively, companies comprising the FTSE-100 generally include the larger publicly listed banks from Spain, Portugal and Greece. As a consequence, the sample surveyed may have included banks of a similar size that did not fully enable the potential impact of organizational size to be exhibited. Finally, contrary to some previous empirical results, physical capital financial performance was found not to be associated with greater disclosure. Again, there is no clear explanation from prior literature for the lack of an association between the extent of intellectual capital disclosure and physical capital financial performance. The literature on intellectual capital has, however, indicated that intellectual capital and physical capital are two separate concepts. Due to the separation between these two concepts, management may not feel that the amount of intellectual capital disclosure is dependent upon the bank's physical capital financial performance.

As with previous research, this study has certain limitations. Empirical tests were performed on a relatively small sample of a greater magnitude of publicly listed banks in Spain, Portugal and Greece. This small sample may limit the generalizability of the findings to some extent. Furthermore, while an extensive effort was made to develop an accurate proxy for intellectual capital performance, the measurement of intellectual capital is still in its infancy. As such, there is room for potential debate as to whether or not the proxy selected was representative of a bank's intellectual capital performance. Data constraints, however, limit the application of other potential measures. Thus, despite possible questions about construct validity, VAIC™is considered an appropriate proxy for intellectual capital performance, given the available data. Finally, given the complex nature of the banking environment and the concept of intellectual capital, there are various inherent limits on the ability of empirical research to capture all of the potential dimensions that could have an impact on intellectual capital decision-making and reporting strategies.

Despite the limitations of this study, it has brought a number of valuable insights and contributions to the current literature and debate on intellectual capital. These insights also provide a number of ideas for future research. First, as noted above, this study used a relatively small sample; future research should expand on this study by examining the intellectual capital disclosure practices of a larger number of publicly listed, and potentially private, banks in Spain, Portugal and Greece. Second, this study has examined the intellectual capital disclosure practices in only a single nation. Intellectual capital is, however, a global phenomenon. Hence, future research should attempt to investigate the intellectual capital disclosure practices of banks in other nations and factors affecting practices in other nations. Finally, as acknowledged above, proxies included in this study did not capture all of the variations in intellectual capital disclosure practices; further research may be undertaken to determine the influence of other possible determinants, such as varying levels of exposure to information technology or varying standards of education in a global context.

References

P. Beaulieu, S.L.M. Williams and M. Wright M. (2002) Intellectual capital disclosure practices in Sweden. In N. Bontis (Ed.), *Organizational Intelligence: The Cutting Edge of Intellectual Capital and Knowledge Management*. Butterworth-Heinemann: Toronto, Canada.

A. Brooking (1996) *Intellectual Capital: Core Assets for the Third Millennium Enterprise*. Thomson Business Press, London, United Kingdom.

D.J. Campbell (2000) Legitimacy theory or managerial reality construction? Corporate social disclosure in Marks and Spencer Plc corporate reports, 1969–1997. *Accounting Forum*, 24 (1): 80–100.

C.W. Chow and A. Wong-Boren (1987) Voluntary financial disclosure by Mexican corporations. *The Accounting Review*, 62 (3): 533–41.

T.E. Cooke (1989a) Voluntary corporate disclosure by Swedish companies. *Journal of International Financial Management and Accounting*, 1 (2): 171– 95.

T.E. Cooke (1989b) Disclosure in the corporate annual reports of Swedish companies. *Accounting and Business Research*, 19 (74): 113–24.

T.E. Cooke (1991) An assessment of voluntary disclosure in the annual reports of Japanese corporations. *The International Journal of Accounting*, 26 (2): 174–89.

T.E. Cooke (1992) The effect of size, stock market listing and industry type on disclosure in the annual reports of Japanese listed corporations. *Accounting and Business Research*, 22 (87): 229–37.

A.T. Craswell and S.L.Taylor (1992) Discretionary disclosure of reserve by oil and gas companies: An economic analysis. *Journal of Business Finance and Accounting*, 19 (January): 295–308.

R. Dye (1985) Disclosure of nonproprietary information. *Journal of Accounting Research*, 23 (Spring): 123–45.

S. Firer and S.M. Williams (2003) Intellectual capital and traditional measures of corporate performance. *Journal of Intellectual Capital*, 4 (3): 348–60.

M.C. Jensen and W.H. Meckling (1976) Theory of the firm: Managerial behavior, agency costs and ownership structure. *Journal of Financial Economics*, 3 (4): 305–60.

D.A. Klein and L. Prusak (1994) Characterising intellectual capital. Working paper, Centre for Business Innovation. Ernst & Young: Cambridge, MA, United States of America.

R.W. Leftwich, R.L. Watts and J.L. Zimmerman (1981) Voluntary corporate disclosure: The case of interim reporting. *Journal of Accounting Research*, 19: 50–77.

D. Malone, C. Fries and T. Jones (1993) An empirical investigation of the extent of corporate financial disclosure in the oil and gas industry. *Journal of Accounting, Auditing and Finance*, 8 (30): 249–75.

Milgrom, P. and J. Roberts (1992) *Economics, Organization and Management*. Prentice-Hall: Englewood Cliffs, NJ, United States of America.

A. Pulic (1998) Measuring the performance of intellectual potential in knowledge economy. Available at: www.measuring-ip.at/Opapers/Pulic/Vaictxt.vaictxt.html.

Pulic, A. (2000) VAIC™ -- an accounting tool for IC management. *International Journal of Technology Management*, 20 (5–8): 702–14.

A. Pulic and M. Bornemann (1999) The physical and intellectual capital of Austrian banks.

T.A. Stewart (1997) *Intellectual Capital: The New Wealth of Organizations*. Doubleday/Currency, New York, New York, United States of America.

H.Y. Tay and R.H. Parker (1990) Measuring international harmonization and standardization. *Abacus*, 26 (1): 71–88.

S. Taylor and Associates (1999) Full Disclosure 1998, Shelley Taylor, London, United Kingdom.

R.M.Tennyson, R.W. Ingram and M.T. Dugan (1990) Assessing the information content of narrative disclosures in explaining bankruptcy. *Journal of Business Finance and Accounting*, 17 (4): 391–410.

C.A. Tilt (1994) The influence of external pressure groups on corporate social disclosure: Some empirical evidence. *Accounting, Auditing and Accountability Journal*, 7 (4): 47–72.

J-L.W.M. Van der Zahn, G. Tower and J. Neilson (2004) Intellectual capital and the efficiency of value added: Trends in the Singapore capital market 2000–2002. Poseidon Books: Burleigh, Queensland, Australia.

W.D. Walden and B.N. Schwartz (1997) Environmental disclosures and public policy pressure. *Journal of Accounting and Public Policy*, 16 (2): 125–54.

R.S.O. Wallace, K. Naser and A. Mora (1994) The relationship between comprehensiveness of corporate annual reports and firm characteristics in Spain. *Accounting and Business Research*, 25 (97): 41–53.

R.L. Watts and J.L. Zimmerman (1986) *Positive Accounting Theory*. Prentice Hall: Englewood Cliffs, NJ, United States of America.

8.6 Sources of Statistical Data

1. Bankinter, Annual Report 2010.
2. 2003–2010 Investment Climate Statement – Spain, Bureau of Economic, Energy and Business Affairs, March 2011.
3. BBVA, Annual Report 2009.
4. BSCH, Annual Report 2010.
5. 2003–2010 Investment Climate Statement – Portugal (2003–2010), Bureau of Economic, Energy and Business Affairs, April 2011.
6. J. Guthrie and R. Petty (2010) Intellectual capital: Annual reporting practices. *Journal of Intellectual Capital*, 1 (3).
7. 2003–2010 Investment Climate Statement – Greece, Bureau of Economic, Energy and Business Affairs, June 2011.
8. Archive annual reports (2003–2010). Banks of Portugal. Access mode: on request.
9. Archive annual reports (2003–2010). Caixa Geral De Depositos. Access mode: on request.
10. Archive annual reports (2003–2010). UBS AG In Lissabon. Access mode: on request.
11. Archive annual reports (2003–2010). Banco Nacional Ultrmarino. Access mode: on request.
12. Archive annual reports (2003–2010). Banco BPI. Access mode: on request.
13. Archive annual reports (2003–2010). Clariden Leu Escritorio de Representacao Amoreiras. Access mode: on request.
14. Archive annual reports (2003–2010). Banco Popular Portugal. Access mode: on request.
15. Archive annual reports (2003–2010). Barclays Bank Portugal. Access mode: on request.
16. Archive annual reports (2003–2010). Millenium BPC. Access mode: on request.
17. Archive annual reports (2003–2010). Finibanco. Access mode: on request
18. Archive annual reports (2003–2010). Banco de Portugal – Bank of Portugal. Access mode: on request.
19. Archive annual reports (2003–2010). Banco de Espagna. Access mode: on request.
20. Archive annual reports (2003–2010). Argentaria. Access mode: on request.
21. Archive annual reports (2003–2010). Banco Central Hispano. Access mode: on request.

22. Archive annual reports (2003–2010). Banco Gallego. Access mode: on request.
23. Archive annual reports (2003–2010). Banco Multisectorial de Inversiones. Access mode: on request.
24. Archive annual reports (2003–2010). Banesto. Access mode: on request
25. Archive annual reports (2003–2010). Banco Bilbao Vizcaya. Access mode: on request.
26. Archive annual reports (2003–2010). Banco Sabadell. Access mode: on request.
27. Archive annual reports (2003–2010). Bankinternet. Access mode: on request.
28. Archive annual reports (2003–2010). Bankpyme. Access mode: on request.
29. Archive annual reports (2003–2010). Attica Bank. Access mode: on request.
30. Archive annual reports (2003–2010). Bank of Cyprus. Access mode: on request.
31. Archive annual reports (2003–2010). EFG Eurobank Ergasias. Access mode: on request.
32. Archive annual reports (2003–2010). Emporiki Bank. Access mode: on request.
33. Archive annual reports (2003–2010). Geniki Bank. Access mode: on request.
34. Archive annual reports (2003–2010). Hellenic Bank. Access mode: on request.
35. Archive annual reports (2003–2010). National Bank of Greece. Access mode: on request.
36. Archive annual reports (2003–2010). Panellinia Bank. Access mode: on request.
37. Archive annual reports (2003–2010). Piraeus Bank. Access mode: on request.
38. Archive annual reports (2003–2010). Proton Bank. Access mode: on request.

9

Too Small or Too Low? New Evidence on the Four-Factor Model

Paola Brighi, Stefano d'Addona and Antonio Carlo Francesco Della Bina

9.1 Introduction

In 1992, Fama and French published a landmark paper in which they provided, by means of a cross-sectional analysis, strong evidence of explanatory power by size and book-to-market factors, compared with little or no ability by the market factor to explain differences in equity returns. After this, a large body of literature came out evidencing the beta model's weakness in explaining asset returns. Empirical works have mostly used US data, and most of them reject the beta Capital Asset Pricing model (CAPM – see, for example, Grinold, 1993). In another paper, Fama and French (1993), using a time-series approach, found basically the same evidence. However, further evidence for their model (Lakonishok et al., 1994; Haugen, 1995), highlighted the role of investor overreaction (De Bondt and Thaler, 1985) in explaining the value anomaly. Based on the overreaction/under-reaction argument to information, Jegadeesh and Titman (1993) and Rouwenhorst (1998) document the existence of a momentum anomaly: over a medium time horizon, firms with high returns over the previous three months to one year continue to outperform firms with low past returns over the same period.

Building upon Fama and French (1993), we investigate the factor structure of the Italian stock market, through a Generalized Method of Moments (GMM) test of their three-factor model augmented by a momentum effect, using stock market data from 1986 to 2010.[1] With respect to the previous literature, we provide an up-to-date empirical analysis to shed further light on the relevance of factors in addition to the beta, with particular emphasis on the momentum effect, to explain equity returns over a medium time horizon. Our empirical evidence shows that the expected returns anomalies persist over the time horizon analysed, and are mainly connected to size and value characteristics while the momentum anomaly plays only a marginal role. Which means, in a nutshell, that by estimating a four-factor model using a GMM procedure on 25 years of data, we find that the size and the value factor in addition to the beta contributes to the explanation of stock returns in Italy. However, our asset pricing tests support the momentum factor as an additional explanatory variable only partially.

The rest of the chapter is organized as follows: in Section 2 we provide a review of the main related literature, while in Section 3 we describe the data used for the empirical analysis and we explain the procedure adopted to construct the portfolios and the mimicking portfolios for the explanatory factors. Section 4 presents the results, while Section 5 concludes.

9.2 Related literature

9.2.1 CAPM, Fama and French thesis and multifactor models

Even if the CAPM by Sharpe (1964), Lintner (1965) and Black (1972) has been extensively studied and accepted, there is strong evidence in the literature rejecting its validity (see, for example, Grinold, 1993, and Fama and French, 1996). Many attempts have been made to extend the CAPM model to multifactor models in order to explain in greater depth the cross-section of stock returns. This approach is based on the empirical evidence that the intercept of the linear function of the CAPM is statistically different from zero: that is,. the beta alone does not explain the average stock returns.

In their seminal work, Fama and French try to explain how the stock returns depend not only on market factors measured by the beta in the classic CAPM theory, but also on other factors. Mainly, they find that the strongest consistency in explaining the average returns is represented by size and book-to market value, or similarly the earnings–price ratio, the cash–price ratio or the dividend–price ratio.[2]

The first critics to the standard CAPM emerged in the 1980s, highlighting a positive relation between the firm size and the average stock return (Banz, 1981). Similarly a positive relation holds between the firm leverage and the average stock return (Bhandari, 1988).

At the same time some other authors find that the US average stock returns are positively linked to the book-to-market value ratio (Stattman, 1980 and Rosenberg et al., 1985). Basu (1983) shows that the earnings–price ratio improves the estimation of the average cross-sectional US stock returns when in the statistical test firm size and market are considered at the same time. What Fama and French (1992) add to the previous literature is the joint role of market beta, size, price–earnings ratio, leverage and book-to-market ratio with reference to NYSE, AMEX and NASDAQ stock returns. They find that the CAPM model does not hold in the US market for the period between 1941 and 1990. In addition, they show that the univariate relations between average return and size, leverage, E/P, and book-to-market value are strong. Their main conclusion is that stock risks are multidimensional: one dimension of risk is proxied by size, and the other is proxied by the ratio of book value to its market value. In this way Fama and French (1992) confute the role of beta in the explanation of the stock returns; in other terms if there is a role for beta in average returns, it has to be found in a multifactor model.[3]

9.2.2 The Fama and French model and the critics

Even if the Fama and French insights have given birth to a new and rich stream of the literature, their results are vulnerable to criticisms based mainly on the observation that the violations of the CAPM model are not simply linked to missing risk factors but to the existence of market imperfections, to the presence of irrational investors and to the inclusion of biases in the empirical methodology (see, for example, De Bondt and Thaler, 1985; Lakonishok et al., 1994; Haugen, 1995; MacKinlay, 1995 and Knez and Ready, 1997).

De Bondt and Thaler (1985), Lakonishok et al. (1994) and Haugen (1995) point out that the so-called 'value' strategies – small market capitalization and high book-to-market equity stocks – yield higher returns than 'glamour' strategies – large market capitalization and low book-to-market equity stock – because of investor overreaction rather than compensation for risk bearing. They argue that investors systematically overreact to recent corporate news, unrealistically extrapolating high or low growth into the future. This, in turn, leads to the underpricing of value and the overpricing of glamour stocks. The value strategies produce higher returns, because these strategies exploit the suboptimal behaviour of the typical investor but not because these strategies are fundamentally riskier. The explanation for this difference has been the subject of numerous studies using different methods of investigation to find out whether there is a risk premium for value stocks. Some of the results are controversial.

Lakonishok et al. (1994), with reference to the US stock market (NYSE and AMEX) from April 1968 to April 1990, find little support for the view that value strategies are fundamentally riskier than glamour strategies: they report that value betas are higher than growth betas in good times but are lower in bad times.

More recently, Petkova and Zhang (2005) and Chen, Petkova and Zhang (2008) further investigate this aspect, finding that value betas tend to covary positively, and growth betas tend to covary negatively, with the expected market risk premium. This result holds for most sample periods and for various value and growth strategies. However, although the time-varying risk goes in the right direction, the magnitude of the value premium remains positive and mostly significant after controlling for time-varying risk. Therefore, it is necessary to consider other possible drivers of the value anomaly that could be found in a momentum factor (cf. Section 2.3 below).

Other investigations base their arguments on the empirical methodology. MacKinlay (1995) evaluates the plausibility of multifactor models *à la* Fama and French using ex-ante analysis instead of ex-post. The author shows that ex ante it will be very difficult to empirically detect CAPM deviations due to missing risk factors, whereas deviations resulting from non-risk-based sources are easily detectable. He concludes that multifactor pricing models alone do not entirely resolve CAPM deviations. The empirical test of the Fama and French multifactor model conducted by Knez and Ready (1997) suggests that the size effect is completely driven by sample extreme observations that represent less than 1 per cent of each month's data. The least trimmed squares (LTS) regression used instead of Fama and French's ordinary least squares (OLS) implies that most small firms actually do worse than larger firms. In fact, the LTS regression implies a positive relation between firm size and average return that is exactly the opposite of what Fama and French obtained in their study. The result obtained by Knez and Ready (1997) could be particularly relevant for the Italian stock market, made up mostly by small firms. However, further empirical analysis would be useful to accept such a result as an economic regularity rather than a sampling error. Concerning this point, many authors (see, for example, Ferson et al., 1999) caution against using empirical regularities as explanatory risk factors. According to this line of criticism, Black (1993) argues that Fama and French results are strongly biased by a sort of data mining – a certain way of doing a study, including various combinations of explanatory factors, various periods and various models. For example, with reference to the size effect, Black (1993, p. 9) criticizes the fact that Fama and French results hold for the entire period analysed (1963–1990) but not for the eighties (1981–1990). In this sense, their results cannot be considered robust, and suffer from data mining. On the other hand, Fama and French find that the value premium holds for both halves of the period, and that gives a correct prediction of the firm's subsequent accounting performance; a low book-to-market value predicts a high subsequent accounting performance. Both these reasons do not seem, however, to Black (1993) to be enough to eliminate data mining from the Fama and French analysis. Black (1993, p. 10) suggests that these results can be better connected to market inefficiencies than to 'priced factors'. For these reasons, Black (1993) asserts that the analysis conducted by Fama and French is not enough to say that the CAPM is dead. However, there also emerges from Black's studies a misalignment between the theoretical CAPM prediction and the empirical estimates that in Black's analysis can be attributed mainly to two reasons: (i) the existence of borrowing restrictions; and (ii) the mis-measurement of the market portfolio due to the neglect of foreign stocks. 'World capital markets are becoming more integrated all the time. In a fully integrated capital market, what counts is a stock's beta with the world market portfolio, not its beta with the issuer country market portfolio. This may cause low beta stocks to seem consistently underpriced. If investors can buy foreign stocks without penalty, they should do so; if they cannot, stocks with low betas on their domestic market may partly substitute for foreign stocks. If this is the reason the line is flat, they may also want to emphasize stocks that have high betas with the world market portfolio' (Black, 1993, p. 11). According to this observation, one way to test the empirical validity of both the CAPM and the Fama and French three-factor model could be to use international factors (cf. Section 2.4).[4]

9.2.3 The momentum effect

Since the relevant period to evaluate the performance is medium term, not long term as in Lakonishok et al. (1994), some authors – see, for example, Jegadeesh and Titman (1993) and Rouwenhorst (1998) – suggest that a momentum anomaly can exist. They document that over a medium time horizon, performance persists: firms with high returns over the past 3–12 months continue to outperform firms with low past returns over the same period. In other words, the momentum effect holds. The momentum anomaly originates from the propensity of investors to extrapolate the market value of future stock prices from previous prices. With reference to the US market, Jegadeesh and Titman (1993,

2001) show that strategies that involve taking a long (short) position in well (poorly) performing stocks on the basis of past performance over the previous 3–12 months tend to produce significantly positive abnormal returns of about 1 per cent per month for the following year. These return-continuation strategies – momentum return in individual stocks – should not be justified if markets were efficient. For these time horizons, what goes up tends to keep rising, and vice versa. Two reasons can account for these results. One reason can be found in the variability of firms' fundamentals; when earnings growth exceeds expectations or consensus, forecasts of future earnings are revised upwards, and an 'earnings momentum' is observed (Chan et al., 1999). The second reason can be reconnected to the fact that strategies based on price momentum and earnings momentum may be profitable because they exploit market under-reaction to different information. For instance, earnings momentum strategies may exploit under-reaction to information about the short-term prospects of companies that will ultimately be manifested in near-term earnings; price momentum strategies may exploit slow reactions to a broader set of value-relevant information, including long-term information that have not been fully captured by near-term earnings forecasts or past earnings growth. If both these explanations were to hold, then a strategy based on past returns in combination with a strategy based on earnings momentum should lead to higher profits than should either strategy individually.

The evidence is mixed. In the recent past, a large and growing body of research supported the presence of a momentum anomaly with reference not only to European markets (Rouwenhorst, 1998), but also to Asian markets (Chui et al., 2000), Canadian market (L'Her et al., 2004) and minor markets like Italy (Mengoli, 2004). Recently some authors have further investigated this aspect, finding opposite results. Hwang and Rubesam (2008), for example, find that the risk-adjusted momentum premium is significantly positive only during certain periods and that is going to disappear from the late 1990s in a process which was delayed by the occurrence of the high-technology stock bubble of the 1990s.

Moreover, Bulkley and Nawosah (2009) point out a general problem in testing asset pricing models, because the residual pricing errors from the model specified may be interpreted erroneously as momentum. Removing the effect of unconditional expected returns from the raw returns and then testing for momentum in the resulting series over the whole sample period implies the complete disappearance of the momentum effect.

9.2.4 International and local factors

An extension of the multifactor model to an international framework was originally advanced by Fama and French (1998). They argue that an international CAPM cannot explain the difference between value and glamour stock returns. Having observed evidence of an existing value premium in 12 markets outside the USA during the 1975–1995 period, Fama and French (1998) show that an international two-factor model that includes a risk factor for relative distress seems to capture the value premium in the returns for major markets. This result also holds for emerging markets. However, they do not compare the world factor model to country-specific models. In an effort to understand if the explanatory power of world factors are driven by the country-specific components, Griffin (2002) proceeds to this comparison, examining whether country-specific or aggregate versions of a three-factor model better explain returns on portfolios and individual stocks in four countries – the USA, the UK, Canada and Japan. The main results show that the domestic models explain more time-series variation and generally provide more accurate pricing than does the world model. Moreover, no benefits are found from the extension of the Fama and French three-factor model to a global context. Even if from a statistical point of view the world model seems more significant than a country model, from an economic point of view it implies a small increase in explanatory power. In fact, a country-specific three-factor model has lower in-sample and out-of-sample pricing errors than have models that include foreign factors.

More recently Fama and French (2011) extended the analysis to 23 countries. The aim of the paper is twofold. First, an analysis of international return determinants by group: the sample covers all sizes of group, from large to tiny stocks. Second, they examine 'local versions of the models in which the explanatory returns (factors) and the returns to be explained are from the same region' (p. 2). To better disentangle whether asset pricing is integrated across regions, they also investigate models that use global factors to explain global and regional returns. The main results suggest that value premiums hold in average returns in all four areas examined (North America, Europe, Japan and Asia Pacific), and there are strong momentum returns in all regions except Japan. As for size of groups, Fama and French (2011) find that value premiums are larger for small stocks except in Japan. The same results holds for the momentum factor that decreases from smaller to bigger stocks for all countries except Japan. Moreover, the analysis shows that global models and integrated asset pricing could be used successfully to capture the performance of a mutual fund that holds a global portfolio of stocks – as long as the portfolio does not have a strong tilt towards microcaps or the stocks of a particular region. However, as suggested by the authors, 'the global models do not do well when asked to explain average returns on regional size-B/M or size momentum portfolios. ...It suggests shortcomings of integrated pricing across the four regions – or other bad model problems. We would not use the global models in applications to explain regional portfolio returns' (p. 22), suggesting that to explain regional returns it could be better to use local models. In other terms, there are no benefits to extending the four-factor model to an international or global model to evaluate regional performance.[5]

9.3 Data and methodology

9.3.1 Data

The data used to test the multifactor models are derived from the closing price of the domestic Italian firms listed on the Milan stock exchange for the period between 1 January 1986 and 1 February 2010. Our dataset, based on a monthly frequency, includes survivor stocks for the entire period considered, and delisted stocks for just the period during which the firms were traded.[6] For a firm to be included in the sample we require that it has complete market and accounting/financial data for price, market capitalization, dividend per share, earnings per share, and book value of equity provided by the Thomson Reuters Datastream and Worldscope databases. Additionally a firm must have a minimum of 12 consecutive and discrete monthly returns. Finally, we considered firms with voting shares, thus excluding limited-voting shares when a company listed both, while we included limited-voting shares if these were the unique class of securities traded for a particular company. The total number of stocks is 489. All data are expressed in euros, converted from Italian lire when a firm was delisted prior to January 1999. The risk-free rate used in our empirical tests is the three-month Italian treasury bill rate from the Bank of Italy, converted to the equivalent monthly rate.[7]

9.3.2 Methodology

The aim of this section is to explain the methodology adopted to test the Fama and French three-factor model (Fama and French, 1992, 1993, 1996) on the Italian stock market. The theoretical ex-ante Fama and French model can be expressed as follows:

$$E(\widetilde{R}_i) - R_f = \beta_i \left[E(\widetilde{R}_m) - R_f \right] + \gamma_i E(\widetilde{R}_{SmB}) + \delta_i E(\widetilde{R}_{HmL}) \tag{9.1}$$

where $E(\widetilde{R}_i) - R_f$ is the expected excess return on asset i, $E(\widetilde{R}_m) - R_f$ is the expected excess return on market portfolio, $E(\widetilde{R}_{SmB})$ is the expected return on the mimicking portfolio for the Small minus Big size factor, $E(\widetilde{R}_{HmL})$ is the expected return on the mimicking portfolio for the High minus Low value-growth factor, and R_f is the return on a risk-free asset.

If the market determines the asset i price at the beginning of each period according to Equation 9.1, and given the hypothesis of rational expectations for the CAPM, the asset i return observed ex-post for every period will respect the following empirical expression of the model:

$$R_{it} - R_{ft} = \alpha_i + \beta_i(R_{mt} - R_{ft}) + \gamma_i(R_{SmBt}) + \delta_i(R_{HmLt}) + \varepsilon_{it} \tag{9.2}$$

where ε_{it} is an i.i.d. (independent and identically distributed) error term normally distributed with 0 mean and constant variance.

We test the restricted Fama and French model ($\alpha = 0$) using a GMM procedure. The basic idea of the GMM is to choose the parameters to be estimated to match the moments of the model itself with the empirical ones. The restricted model to be estimated is obtained by converting Equation 9.1 into the following empirical counterpart:

$$R_{it} - R_{ft} = \beta_i(R_{mt} - R_{ft}) + \gamma_i(R_{SmBt}) + \delta_i(R_{HmLt}) + \varepsilon_{it} \tag{9.3}$$

with $i = 1,\ldots,$ N and $t = 1,\ldots,$T

where $R_{it} - R_{ft}$ is the realized excess return on asset i, $R_{mt} - R_{ft}$ is the realized excess return on market portfolio, R_{SmBt} is the realized return on the mimicking portfolio for the Small minus Big size factor, and R_{HmLt} is the realized return on the mimicking portfolio for the High minus Low value-growth factor with four sample moment conditions for each portfolio:

$$\left[1/T\sum_{t=1}^{T}\varepsilon_{it}(R_{mt} - R_f),\ 1/T\sum_{t=1}^{T}\varepsilon_{it}(R_{SmBt}),\ 1/T\sum_{t=1}^{T}\varepsilon_{it}(R_{HmLt}),\ 1/T\sum_{t=1}^{T}\varepsilon_{it}\right]$$

and three parameters ($\theta = \beta_i, \gamma_i, \delta_i$) to be estimated.

We can test the over-identifying restrictions using the Hansen's (1982) J statistic, which is appropriate with the GMM estimator. We compute the GMM estimator (see MacKinlay and Richardson, 1991; Campell, Lo and MacKinlay, 1996) as:

$$\hat{\theta} \equiv \arg\min_{\theta} G(\theta) \tag{9.4}$$

where $G(\theta) = g_T(\theta)'\ W\ g_T(\theta)$ is the quadratic function of the moment conditions, $g_T(\theta) = \frac{1}{T}\sum_{t=1}^{T} f_T(\theta)$ is the empirical moment conditions vector and $\boldsymbol{W}$ is the weighted matrix used for estimating the parameters. For the test to be valid, $\boldsymbol{W}$ must be the inverse of the covariance matrix of the moment condition ($\boldsymbol{S}^{-1}$).

Under the null hypothesis that the over-identifying restrictions are satisfied, the GMM estimator times the number of regression observations is asymptotically χ^2, with degrees of freedom equal to the number of over-identifying restrictions (# of moment conditions – # of parameters):

$$T \cdot J = T \cdot \left[\arg\min_{\theta} g_T(\theta)' S^{-1} g_T(\theta) \right] \tilde{}\, \chi^2\,(\#of\ mom - \#of\ par)$$

Finally, for calculating the standard errors of our estimated parameters, we use the Newey and West (1987) variance–covariance estimator.

9.3.3 Construction of the risk factors

In order to obtain the mimicking portfolios for the risk factors, we construct three groups of assets based on size tertiles and three groups of assets based on the price–earnings ratio (P/E) tertiles. By the intersection of these groups we obtain nine portfolios, named R1V, R2V, R3V, R1M, R2M, R3M, R1G, R2G, R3G; where 1, 2, 3 indicate respectively small, medium and large firms, while V, M and G indicate respectively value, medium and growth firms. This means that for example R3G is the portfolio containing the firms with a high market value (large firms) and a high P/E ratio (growth firms). On those portfolios we calculate the value-weighted returns. Each portfolio is rebalanced yearly.

The next step is to construct the mimicking portfolios for each risk factor. The market factor (MKT) is constructed by calculating the monthly value-weighted return of the stocks included in the sample.[8] The risk factor is calculated by subtracting the relevant monthly risk-free rate. The size factor (SMB) is obtained as the average return on the three 'small firms' portfolios minus the average return on the three 'big firms' portfolios:

$$SmB_t = \sum_{i=V,M,G} \frac{1}{3} Ri1_t - \sum_{i=V,M,G} \frac{1}{3} Ri3_t \tag{9.5}$$

The value factor (HML) is obtained as the average return on the three 'value firm' portfolios minus the average return on the three 'growth firm' portfolios:

$$HmL_t = \sum_{i=1}^{3} \frac{1}{3} RiV_t - \sum_{i=1}^{3} \frac{1}{3} RiG_t \tag{9.6}$$

To obtain the momentum factor, a different sorting procedure is needed. In practice, we construct the momentum factor from a three-by-three tertiles sort on size and firm's past return, calculated according to the Carhart (1997) procedure as the compound 11-month returns lagged one month. By the intersection of these groups we obtain nine portfolios, named R1W, R2W, R3W, R1WL, R2WL, R3WL, R1LS, R2LS, R3LS; where, as above, 1, 2 and 3 indicate small, medium and big firms, while W, WL and LS indicate, respectively, winner, winner–loser and loser firms so that, for example, R3W is the portfolio containing the winners, with a high market value. The momentum factor (WML) is obtained as is the average return on the three winner firms' portfolios minus the average return on the three loser firms' portfolios:

$$WmL_t = \sum_{i=1}^{3} \frac{1}{3} RiW_t - \sum_{i=1}^{3} \frac{1}{3} RiLS_t \tag{9.7}$$

The new unrestricted and restricted models to be estimated are obtained by augmenting the initial three-factor model (see Equations 9.2 and 9.3) with the momentum factor. Thus, we obtain five sample moment conditions for each portfolio and an extra parameter to be estimated:

$$R_{it} - R_{ft} = \alpha_i + \beta_i(R_{mt} - R_{ft}) + \gamma_i(R_{SmBt}) + \delta_i(R_{HmLt}) + \eta_i(R_{WmLt}) + \varepsilon_{it} \tag{9.8}$$

$$R_{it} - R_{ft} = \beta_i(R_{mt} - R_{ft}) + \gamma_i(R_{SmBt}) + \delta_i(R_{HmLt}) + \eta_t(R_{WmLt}) + \varepsilon_{it} \tag{9.9}$$

$$\left[1/T\sum_{t=1}^{T} \varepsilon_{it}(R_{mt} - R_f),\ 1/T\sum_{t=1}^{T} \varepsilon_{it}(R_{SmBt}),\ 1/T\sum_{t=1}^{T} \varepsilon_{it} (R_{HmLt}),\ 1/T\sum_{t=1}^{T} \varepsilon_{it}(R_{WmLt}),\ 1/T\sum_{t=1}^{T} \varepsilon_{it} \right]$$

To obtain the dependent variables of our time-series regression (that is, the portfolios to be tested with the factor models), we calculate the value-weighted returns for the 16 portfolios obtained from the four-by-four quartiles sort of market capitalization size rankings and trailing P/E value-growth rankings of the firms.[9] In this case P is the actual price at the end of month t and E is the fully diluted earnings per shares with fiscal year in year (*t-1*). Negative trailing P/E are excluded according to the procedure reported in Thomson Reuters Worldscope.

Table 9.1 Correlations between Fama–French–Carhart Factors

Correlation	MKT[a]	SMB[b]	HML[c]	WML[d]
MKT	1			
SMB	−0.3931	1		
HML	0.0836	−0.0533	1	
WML	−0.0517	0.0214	0.0634	1
p-value				
MKT-SMB	0.0000	***		
MKT-HML	0.1561			
MKT-WML	0.1484			
SMB-HML	0.3664			
SMB-WML	0.9434			
HML-WML	0.1085			

Notes: (a) MKT is the Market Factor = averaged value-weighted returns of all the assets included in the sample minus the risk free rate. (b) SMB = Small Minus Big is the return on the mimicking portfolio for the size factor. (c) HML = High Minus Low is the return on the mimicking portfolio for the value-growth factor. (d) WML = Winners Minus Losers is the return on the mimicking portfolio for the momentum factor. Monthly data from 1-Jan-86 to 1-Feb-2010.

9.4 Results

9.4.1 Summary statistics

In this subsection we report some preliminary results. Table 9.1 shows that the correlations between the four factors are low, and in only one case (market factor and size factor) statistically different from zero. This result provides some support for using the factors as explanatory variables in our test.

As shown in Table 9.2, all the mimicking portfolios series exhibit in line with the existing literature (see, for example, Fama, 1965 or Blattberg and Gonedes, 1974) a consistent evidence of absence of normality in the monthly returns. For this reason it could be advisable to move from the OLS test to a GMM procedure. Generally speaking, the annualized return on the size-mimicking portfolio (SMB) is about 4.6 per cent, with a 19 per cent volatility. This is consistent with the theory of a risk premium for the smaller firms. On the other hand, the annualized return of the value-growth-mimicking portfolio (HML) is about 0.7 per cent with a volatility of 13 per cent. The annual excess return of the market index (MKT) is about 2 per cent with a volatility of about 22 per cent, hence consistent with the assumption of risk aversion. Finally, the annual excess return on the momentum-mimicking portfolio (WML) is about −0.6 per cent with

Table 9.2 Basic descriptive statistics

	MKT[a]	SMB[b]	HML[c]	WML[d]
Mean	0.0016	0.0037	0.0006	−0.0006
Median	−0.0029	0.0042	0.0008	0.0059
Maximum	0.2728	0.1791	0.1951	0.2176
Minimum	−0.1771	−0.1621	−0.1942	−0.6792
Std. dev.	0.0646	0.0429	0.0373	0.0675
Skewness	0.5324	0.213	0.4549	−4.2573
Kurtosis	4.7585	5.2593	11.523	38.8088
Annualized	0.0191	0.0458	0.0073	−0.0073
Annualized	0.2239	0.1485	0.1291	0.234

Notes: (a) MKT is the Market Factor = averaged value-weighted returns of all the assets included in the sample minus the risk free rate. (b) SMB = Small Minus Big is the return on the mimicking portfolio for the size factor. (c) HML = High Minus Low is the return on the mimicking portfolio for the value-growth factor. (d) WML = Winners Minus Losers is the return on the mimicking portfolio for the momentum factor. Monthly data from 1-Jan-86 to 1-Feb-2010.

a volatility of about 22 per cent. This preliminary descriptive analysis seems to suggest the absence of a momentum effect in the Italian stock market.

The above intuitions on the economic significance of the risk factors are confirmed also in Figures 9.1–9.4. For the time horizon analysed, we report the average return on the various factor portfolios, namely market, size, value and momentum. The first observation, for February 1986, is the average between January 1986 and February 1986. Subsequently, the mean is computed by adding one observation at a time until February 2010. Each point can be interpreted as the average (monthly percentage) return of an investment starting in January 1986 and ending in the relevant month. The graphs can also be interpreted as a description of estimates of the time-varying risk premium on each portfolio. Given the length of the sample period, we have decided to split it into three sub-periods to better encapsulate how the external macroeconomic and financial conditions could have influenced the average returns of our four factors. We named these three periods as: (i) the eighties (1986–1991), characterized by a strong international financial market liberalization with high stock market performance across several markets and an unprecedented crash event on 19 October 1987 (see Shiller, 1989); (ii) the nineties (1991–2000), characterized by the European convergence process that under the Maastricht Treaty led to the European Monetary Union; (iii) the new millennium decade (2001–2010) characterized by

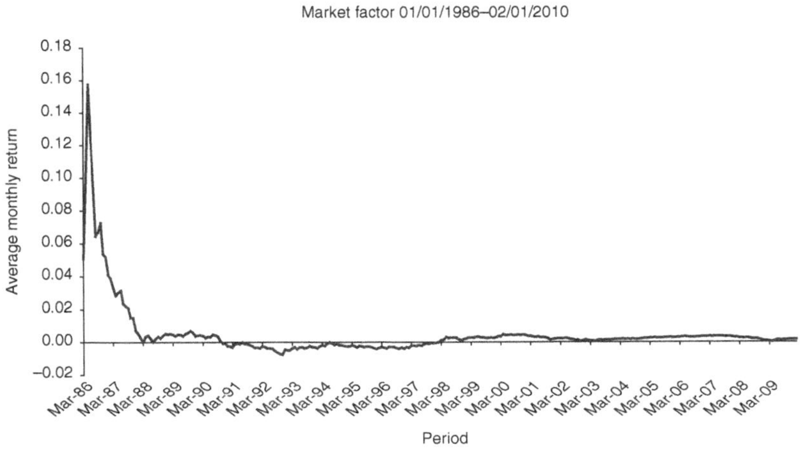

Figure 9.1 Market factor
Notes: The first observation, for February 1986, is the average between January 1986 and February 1986. The mean is computed by adding one observation at a time until February 2010. Each point can be interpreted as the average (monthly percentage) market return of an investment starting in January 1986 and ending in the relevant month.

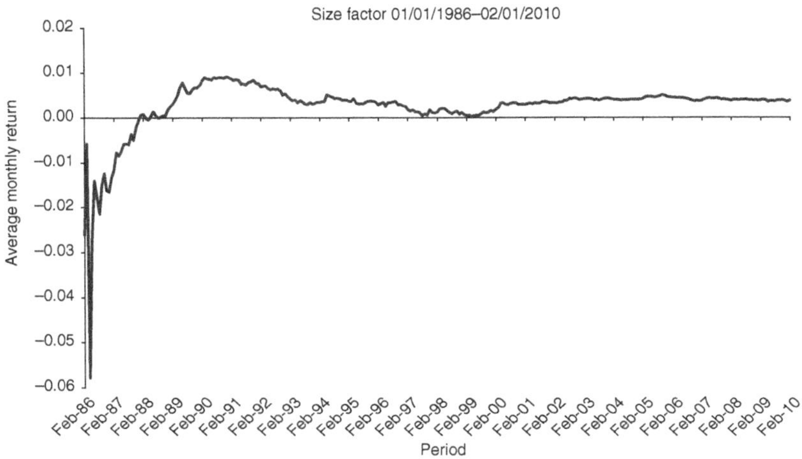

Figure 9.2 Size factor
Notes: The first observation, for February 1986, is the average between January 1986 and February 1986. The mean is computed by adding one observation at a time until February 2010. Each point can be interpreted as the average (monthly percentage) market return of an investment starting in January 1986 and ending in the relevant month.

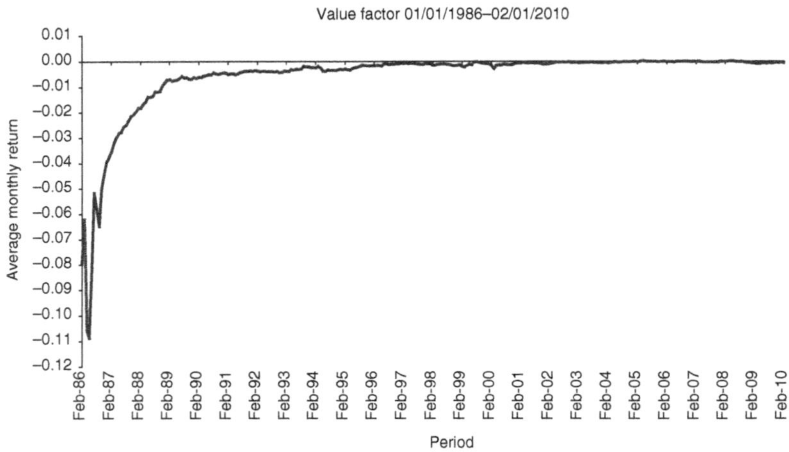

Figure 9.3 Value factor
Notes: The first observation, for February 1986, is the average between January 1986 and February 1986. The mean is computed by adding one observation at a time until February 2010. Each point can be interpreted as the average (monthly percentage) market return of an investment starting in January 1986 and ending in the relevant month.

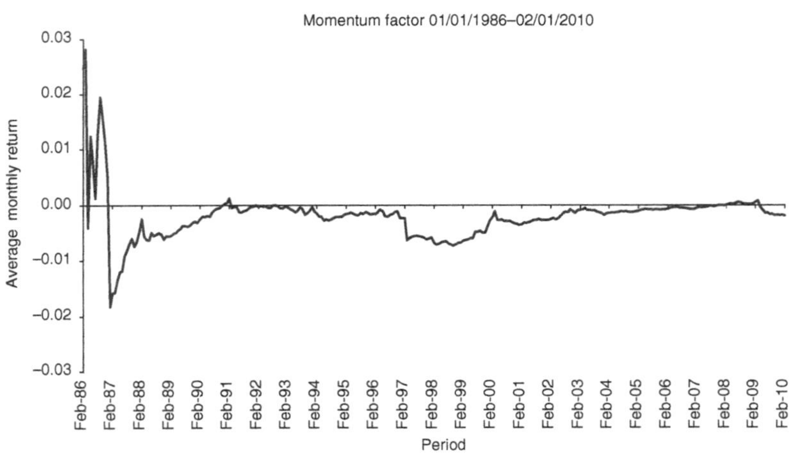

Figure 9.4 Momentum factor
Notes: The first observation, for February 1986, is the average between January 1986 and February 1986. The mean is computed by adding one observation at a time until February 2010. Each point can be interpreted as the average (monthly percentage) market return of an investment starting in January 1986 and ending in the relevant month.

the new economy bubble at the beginning, and by the subprime crisis towards the end of the period.

Starting from the analysis of the market return (see Figure 9.1) the macroeconomic conditions that characterized Italy along our sample period imply: (i) in the eighties a high public debt with a decreasing importance of the market return factor that becomes negative during the speculative attacks that forced Italy outside the European Monetary System in 1992; (ii) entry into the European Union implies an increased credibility, and the market premium becomes positive; (iii) finally we observe a decrease in both 2001 and 2008, corresponding to the technology bubble in the first case and to the Lehman default in the second case.

Except for the first part of the period analysed, the size factor contributes (see Figure 9.2) positively to the average Italian equity return. It is strongly positive during the early nineties; then decreases during the technology boom, and after that is once again positive. Its positive persistence could appear as a structural characteristic of the Italian market.

The HML factor (see Figure 9.3) is negative in the first part of the sample, but becomes and remains substantially positive from the mid-nineties till the end of our sample period, even if after the technology bubble it reduces to almost zero. Our results are coherent with a previous study by Beltratti and Di Tria (2002).

Finally the momentum effect shows an irregular trend (see Figure 9.4) with a negative effect over the entire period analysed, being strongly negative before the technology bubble, but close to zero during the subprime crisis.

9.4.2 OLS and GMM results

As a preliminary analysis, Table 9.3 displays the OLS results to test if the pricing errors (α) are different from zero. In nine portfolios the intercept term is not statistically significant; that is, looking at the classical OLS statistics, we can reject the null hypothesis at a 1 per cent confidence level of $\alpha = 0$, for seven portfolios out of sixteen. In these seven cases, because of the thinness of the market, the composition of the portfolios is based on one or only a very few stocks at the beginning of the sample period. This characteristic can lead to rejection of the null hypothesis, because in practice we are testing with the same regression two totally different assets: a single stock at the beginning of the sample and a diversified portfolio in the remaining period.

Table 9.4 reports the results for the GMM analysis to test the restricted three-factor model developed by Fama and French applied to the Italian stock market. The results seem to support the model in nine out of sixteen

Table 9.3 OLS preliminary estimation of unrestricted Fama–French Model

Dependent variable[a]	α_i^{b}	βi [b]	$\gamma i^{b,d}$	$\delta_i^{b,e}$	F(3,285)[f]	R^2	Adj-R2
R11	0.0060*	0.9268***	1.1065***	0.5662***	105.52	0.5262	0.5212
	−0.080	*0.000*	*0.000*	*0.000*	*0.000*		
R12	0.003	0.8696***	0.7633***	0.3067***	129.44	0.5767	0.5723
	−0.913	*0.000*	*0.000*	*0.000*	*0.000*		
R13	−0.002	0.8735***	−0.5970***	0.0284	90.59	0.4881	0.4827
	−0.937	*0.000*	*0.000*	*−0.802*	*0.000*		
R14	0.0074**	0.9907***	1.1122***	−0.2551***	133.15	0.5836	0.5792
	−0.020	*0.000*	*0.000*	*−0.005*	*0.000*		
R21	0.0098***	1.1534***	0.5826***	0.6553***	158.25	0.6249	0.6209
	−0.002	*0.000*	*0.000*	*0.000*	*0.000*		
R22	0.0064***	0.9182***	0.4307***	0.0925	216.69	0.6952	0.692
	−0.003	*0.000*	*0.000*	*−0.115*	*0.000*		
R23	0.0033	0.8640***	0.4725***	0.2612***	173.87	0.6467	0.6429
	−0.881	*0.000*	*0.000*	*0.000*	*0.000*		
R24	0.0037	0.7988*	0.6252***	−0.1319*	78.37	0.4521	0.4463
	−0.252	*0.000*	*0.000*	*−0.137*	*0.000*		
R31	0.0093***	1.0222***	0.3520***	0.5140***	115.76	0.6683	0.6648
	0.000	*0.000*	*0.000*	*0.000*	*0.000*		
R32	0.0039	0.9440***	0.3137***	−0.923*	137.77	0.6563	0.6527
	−0.121	*0.000*	*0.000*	*−0.178*	*0.000*		
R33	0.0046**	0.8388***	0.2407***	0.1931***	159.63	0.6454	0.6416
	−0.036	*0.000*	*0.000*	*−0.002*	*0.000*		
R34	0.0032	0.9765***	0.3566***	−0.2631***	116.63	0.6928	0.6895
	−0.180	*0.000*	*0.000*	*0.000*	*0.000*		
R41	0.0006	0.9182***	−0.063	0.5505***	176.99	0.7259	0.722
	−0.788	*0.000*	*−0.252*	*0.000*	*0.000*		
R42	0.0028	0.9118***	−0.6833	0.4899***	257.98	0.7931	0.791
	−0.122	*0.000*	*−0.132*	*0.000*	*0.000*		
R43	0.0014	0.9197***	−0.1173***	0.1083***	253.59	0.8622	0.8607
	−0.344	*0.000*	*−0.001*	*−0.007*	*0.000*		
R44	0.0047***	1.0813***	−0.1123***	−0.335***	693.02	0.8758	0.8748
	−0.006	*−0.009*	*−0.009*	*0.000*	*0.000*		

Notes: (***) = statistically significant at the 1% level; (**) = statistically significant at the 5% level; (*) = statistically significant at the 10% level. (a) The dependent variables are represented by sixteen portfolios. They have been constructed by subdividing the sample in four groups of assets based on value-growth ranking and on size ranking of firms. We identify two distinct set of assets as Growth-Value (four groups of assets based on P/E ratio quartiles) and Size (four groups of assets based on Market Value quartiles). From the intersection of the eight groups of assets we obtain the above sixteen portfolios. (b) the associated *p*-value is contained in parentheses below the coefficient estimate. (c) β_i is the Market-factor beta (d) γ_i is the Size-factor beta (e) δ_i is the Value Growth-factor beta. (f) The *p*-value is contained in parentheses below the F-stat. Monthly data from 1-Jan-86 to 1-Feb-2010.

Table 9.4 GMM tests of restricted Fama–French–Carhart factors

Dependent variable[a]	$\beta i^{b,c}$	$\gamma_i^{b,d}$	$\delta_i^{b,e}$	GMM-stat[f]
R11	0.8047***	0.7970***	0.3001	4.7571*
	0.000	*0.000*	*−0.404*	*−0.029*
R12	0.8668***	0.7592***	0.3062**	0.0145
	0.000	*0.000*	−0.009	*−0.904*
R13	0.8769***	0.6007***	0.0212	0.0077
	0.000	*0.000*	*−0.888*	−0.93
R14	0.8858***	0.9952***	−0.1283	6.7780**
	0.000	*0.000*	−0.450	*−0.009*
R21	1.0460***	0.5598***	0.1333	9.7917**
	0.000	*0.000*	*−0.511*	−0.002
R22	0.8659***	0.4891***	0.2226*	8.8042**
	0.000	*0.000*	−0.058	*−0.003*
R23	0.8621***	0.4732***	0.2627***	0.0236
	0.000	*0.000*	*−0.001*	*−0.878*
R24	0.8090***	0.6383***	−0.048	1.3458
	0.000	*0.000*	*−0.643*	−0.246
R31	0.9585***	0.3571***	0.4232***	13.3407***
	0.000	*−0.001*	*0.000*	0.000
R32	0.9240***	0.3115***	−0.044	2.6528
	0.000	*−0.002*	*−0.768*	*−0.103*
R33	0.8084***	0.2837***	0.2278**	4.3689*
	0.000	*0.000*	*−0.022*	−0.037
R34	0.9504***	0.3419***	−0.2285	2.059
	0.000	*−0.001*	−0.120	*−0.151*
R41	0.9163***	−0.0591	0.5574	0.074
	0.000	−0.453	*0.000*	−0.786
R42	0.8901***	−0.0438	0.5339	2.4581
	0.000	*−0.549*	*0.000*	*−0.117*
R43	0.9180***	−0.1156**	0.1221*	0.9513
	0.000	*−0.021*	*−0.100*	−0.329
R44	1.0635***	−0.088	−0.3132***	7.6710**
	0.000	*−0.109*	*0.000*	−0.006

Notes: (***) = statistically significant at the 10% level; (**) = statistically significant at the 5% level; (*) = statistically significant at the 1% level. (a) The dependent variables are represented by sixteen portfolios. They have been constructed by subdividing the sample in four groups of assets based on value-growth ranking and on size ranking of firms. We identify two distinct set of assets as Growth-Value (four groups of assets based on P/E ratio quartiles) and Size (four groups of assets based on Market Value quartiles). From the intersection of the eight groups of assets we obtain the above sixteen portfolios. (b) the associated *p*-value is contained in parentheses below the coefficient estimate. (c) β_i is the Market-factor beta. (d) γ_i is the Size-factor beta. (e) δ_i is the Value Growth-factor beta (f) The generalized method of moments (GMM) test statistic testing the three-factor model holds, is distributed as a chi-square with (# moment conditions - # of parameters) degrees of freedom. Monthly data from 1-Jan-86 to 1-Feb-2010.

Table 9.5 GMM tests of unrestricted Fama–French Model

Dependent variable[a]	α_i^{b}	βi [b,c]	γi [b,d]	$\delta_i^{b,e}$	R^2	Adj-R^2
R11	0.0060***	0.9258***	1.1060***	0.5659	0.5262	0.5212
	−0.029	*0.000*	*0.000*	*−0.111*		
R14	0.0078***	0.9837***	1.1078***	−0.2576	0.5836	0.5712
	−0.009	*0.000*	*0.000*	*−0.132*		
R21	0.0098***	1.1510***	0.5812***	0.6546**	0.6249	0.6209
	−0.002	*−0.0020*	*−0.0020*	*−0.017*		
R22	0.0064***	0.9175***	0.4302***	0.0922	0.6952	0.692
	−0.003	*0.000*	*0.000*	*−0.412*		
R31	0.0093***	1.0177***	0.3494***	0.5125***	0.6683	0.6648
	0.000	*0.000*	*−0.001*	*0.000*		
R33	0.0047**	0.8342***	0.2384***	0.1917*	0.6453	0.6416
	−0.037	*0.002-0*	*−0.002*	*−0.065*		
R44	0.0047***	1.0820***	−0.1120**	−0.3313***	0.8758	0.8744
	−0.006	*0.000*	*−0.039*	*0.000*		

Notes: (***) = statistically significant at the 10% level; (**) = statistically significant at the 5% level; (*) = statistically significant at the 1% level. (a) The dependent variables are represented by sixteen portfolios. They have been constructed by subdividing the sample in four groups of assets based on value-growth ranking and on size ranking of firms. We identify two distinct set of assets as Growth-Value (four groups of assets based on P/E ratio quartiles) and Size (four groups of assets based on Market Value quartiles). From the intersection of the eight groups of assets we obtain the above sixteen portfolios. (b) the associated *p*-value is contained in parentheses below the coefficient estimate. (c) β_i is the Market-factor beta (d) γ_i is the Size-factor beta (e) δ_i is the Value Growth-factor beta. Monthly data from 1-Jan-86 to 1-Feb-2010.

portfolios; the null hypothesis cannot be rejected, as shown by the GMM statistics, with a 1 per cent confidence level. We reject the null hypothesis that the over-identifying restrictions are satisfied in seven out of sixteen portfolios: R11, R14, R21, R22, R31, R33 and R44.

To understand the motivation behind the rejection of the null hypothesis in the above-mentioned seven portfolios, we investigate if there are other factors that can be used in the model to explain the portfolio returns. First of all, we estimate the unrestricted model (see Equation 9.2) with a GMM procedure to investigate if the model is characterized by some pricing errors. We find that in all these portfolios the constant term is significantly different from zero (see Table 9.5)

Even if the descriptive analysis provided above does not support a momentum effect for the Italian market, the lack of this risk factor could represent a possible explanation of the rejection of our model in seven

Table 9.6 GMM tests of restricted Fama–French Model

Dependent variable[a]	$\beta_i^{b,c}$	$\gamma_i^{b,d}$	$\delta_i^{b,e}$	$\eta_i^{b,f}$	GMM-stat[g]
R11	0.7842***	0.8375***	0.3731	−0.1246	4.6090*
	0.000	*0.000*	*−0.237*	*−0.401*	*−0.032*
R14	0.8892***	0.9998***	−0.1193	0.0121	6.8365**
	0.000	*0.000*	*−0.473*	*−0.885*	*−0.009*
R21	1.0734***	0.6060***	0.2218	0.0397	10.5276***
	0.000	*0.000*	*−0.334*	−0.757	*−0.001*
R22	0.8583***	0.4801***	0.1833	−0.6805*	8.694***
	0.000	*0.000*	*−0.131*	*−0.058*	−0.003
R31	0.9598***	0.3629***	0.4206***	−0.1393	13.3870***
	0.000	*0.000*	0.000	*−0.797*	*0.000*
R33	0.8188**	0.2842***	0.2493***	0.0561	4.5736*
	0.000	*0.000*	*−0.008*	*−0.343*	*−0.032*
R44	1.0753***	−0.8777	−0.2857**	0.0607	8.3298***
	0.000	*−0.104*	*0.0000*	*−0.157*	*−0.004*

Notes: (***) = statistically significant at the 10% level; (**) = statistically significant at the 5% level; (*) = statistically significant at the 1% level. (a) The dependent variables are represented by sixteen portfolios. They have been constructed by subdividing the sample in four groups of assets based on value-growth ranking and on size ranking of firms. We identify two distinct set of assets as Growth-Value (four groups of assets based on P/E ratio quartiles) and Size (four groups of assets based on Market Value quartiles). From the intersection of the eight groups of assets we obtain the above sixteen portfolios. (b) the associated p-value is contained in parentheses below the coefficient estimate. (c) βi is the Market-factor beta (d) γ_i is the Size-factor beta (e) δ_i is the Value Growth-factor beta (f) η_i is The Momentum-factor beta. The generalized method of moments (GMM) test statistic testing the four-factor model holds, is distributed as a chi-square with (# moment conditions - # of parameters) degrees of freedom. Monthly data from 1-Jan-86 to 1-Feb-2010.

out of sixteen portfolios. To analyse this possibility, we run a GMM test on the restricted Fama and French model augmented by a momentum effect. As shown in Table 9.6, for all the seven portfolios considered we reject the null hypothesis that the over-identifying restrictions are satisfied. This result confirms our preliminary intuition that there is a very weak momentum effect in the Italian stock market. In fact, only portfolio R22 shows a significant coefficient at a 10 per cent level with a negative sign.

9.5 Conclusions

This chapter empirically tests a multifactor model on the Italian stock market using 25 years of data. Our main results can be summarized as follows. Firstly, we find that the size premium is confirmed for a domestic Italian investor. The GMM test of the three-factor specification appears to support the Fama and French model applied to the Italian stock market. In nine out of sixteen portfolios the null hypothesis that the over-identifying restrictions are satisfied cannot be rejected. Finally, we found very weak evidence of a momentum effect in the Italian stock market.

Notes

1. Some studies on the Italian stock market have been produced both on the empirical relevance of the Fama and French three-factor model (Beltratti and Di Tria, 2002) and on the source of momentum and contrarian strategies (Mengoli, 2004). For a recent analysis of benchmark-factor construction for US and European OECD stocks, see Schmidt et al. (2011).
2. As suggested by Lakonishok et al. (1994, p. 1547) 'B/M is not a *clean* variable uniquely associated with economically interpretable characteristics of the firms'; however they can be successfully proxied by the market's expectations of future growth and the past growth of the firms involved. The expected growth can be proxied by various measures of profitability to price that according to Gordon's formula are: dividend-to-price ratio (D/P), cash-to-price ratio (C/P) and earning–price ratio (E/P). An alternative way to classify stocks is based on past growth rather than on expectations of future growth. In this case, past growth is measured by growth in sales since sales are less volatile than either cash flow or earnings. The above analysis, supported empirically by Lakonishok et al. (1994) and by Fama and French (1998), implies that to estimate stock values we can choose among our regressors the ratios B/M, D/P, E/P and C/P indifferently. This is the reason why – without any loss of generality – in our following econometric analysis we use the E/P ratio instead of B/M. Another way to proxy the B/M ratio is through the Tobin's Q, which is in turn a measure of future investment opportunities. For further development on this point, see also Anderson and Brooks (2006).
3. Unlike in past literature on the Arbitrage Pricing Theory, Fama and French (1992) suggest that adding more factors than two does not improve the estimates obtained by their model on stock returns. In an augmented Fama–French model augmented by macro factors – such as industrial production growth, consumer prices, both expected and unexpected, risk premiums, interest term structure, the federal funds rate, housing initiatives, the producer index and an idiosyncratic return proxy – Merville et al. (2001) find that the most significant factors for an individual common stock can be associated with: (i) the market return – beta; (ii) the market capitalization – size; and (iii) the investment opportunity set – value. Higher-order factors can be uniquely associated with macroeconomic variables that, however, add little explanatory power to the standard three-factor Fama–French model.
4. Taking into account both the momentum factor and an international dimension, Schmidt et al. (2011, p. 24) show that 'risk factors appear to be

astonishingly highly correlated with their counterpart in the U.S., with the exception of the size factor'.
5. For other development in this direction, see also Schmidt et al. (2011).
6. In this case, delisted firms are eliminated from the time of their delisting till the end of our sample period. On the survivorship bias problem see, among others, Banz and Breen (1986) and Fama and French (1998).
7. As alternative proxies for the risk-free rate, we also use the average between ask and bid rates of the Italian interbank rate quoted on the London Interbank Market published by Datastream. The choice of these variables does not produce significant differences in our results for the expected premiums and for asset pricing tests.
8. To confirm the correctness of our methodology we calculate the correlation between the Market Factor and the Morgan Stanley Capital International Index (MSCI Italy) and the Milan Stock Exchange Index (FTSE Italy All Shares). The results are more than comforting: 98 per cent and 99 per cent on the entire sample period.
9. We use the price–earnings ratio (P/E) instead of the market-to-book ratio (M/B) used by Fama and French. The P/E ratio is then used to identify a firm as a 'value' or as a 'growth' firm. We replicate our tests using the M/B, and the main results remain unchanged.

References

K.P. Anderson and C. Brooks (2006) The long-term price-earnings ratio. *Journal of Business Finance and Accounting*, 33 (7–8): 1063–86.

R.W. Banz (1981) The relationship between return and market value of common stocks. *Journal of Financial Economics*, 9: 3–18.

R.W. Banz and W. Breen (1986) Sample dependent results using accounting and market data: Some evidence. *The Journal of Finance* 41(4): 779–93.

S. Basu (1983) The relationship between earnings yield, market value, and return for NYSE common stocks: Further evidence. *Journal of Financial Economics*, 12: 129–56.

L.C. Bhandari (1988) Debt/Equity ratio and expected common stock returns: Empirical evidence. *The Journal of Finance*, 43 (2): 507–28.

A. Beltratti and M. Di Tria (2002) The cross-section of risk premia in the Italian stock market. *Economic Notes*, 31 (3): 389–416.

F. Black (1993) Beta and return. *Journal of Portfolio Management*, 20: 8–18.

F. Black (1972) Capital market equilibrium with restricted borrowing. *Journal of Business*, 45: 444–55.

L.C. R. Blattberg and N. Gonedes (1974) A comparison of the stable and Student distributions as statistical models of stock prices. *The Journal of Business*, 47 (2): 244–80.

G. Bulkley and V. Nawosah (2009) Can the cross-sectional variation in expected stock returns explain momentum? *Journal of Financial and Quantitative Analysis*, 44 (4): 777–94.

J.Y. Campbell, A.W. Lo and A.C. MacKinlay (1996) *The Econometrics of Financial Markets*. Princeton University Press: Princeton, New Jersey.

M. Carhart (1997) On persistence in mutual fund performance. *The Journal of Finance*, 52 (1): 57–82.
L.K. Chan, N. Jegadeesh and J. Lakonishok (1999) The profitability of momentum strategies. *Financial Analysts Journal*, 55 (6): 80–90.
L. Chen, R. Petkova and L. Zhang (2008) The expected value premium. *Journal of Financial Economics*, 87 (2): 269–80.
A. Chui, S. Titman and K.C. Wei (2000) Momentum, legal systems and ownership structure: an analysis of Asian stock markets. *Working paper*, The Hong Kong Polytechnic University, University of Texas at Austin, Hong Kong University of Science and Technology.
W. De Bondt and R. Thaler (1985) Does the stock market overreact? *The Journal of Finance*, 40 (3): 793–805.
E. Fama (1965) The behaviour of stock market prices. *The Journal of Business*, 38 (1): 34–105.
E. Fama and K. French (2011) Size, value, and momentum in international stock returns. *Working paper* 11/10, University of Chicago.
E. Fama and K. French (1998) Value versus growth: the international evidence. *The Journal of Finance*, 53 (6): 1975–99.
E. Fama and K. French (1996) Multifactor explanations of asset pricing anomalies. *The Journal of Finance*, 51 (1): 55–84.
E. Fama and K. French (1993) Common risk factors in the returns of stocks and bonds. *Journal of Financial Economics*, 33 (1): 3–56.
E. Fama and K. French (1992) The cross-section of expected stock returns. *The Journal of Finance*, 47 (2): 427–65.
W.E. Ferson, S. Sarkissian and T. Simin (1999) The alpha factor asset pricing model: A parable. *Journal of Financial Markets*, 2: 49–68.
J.M. Griffin (2002) Are the Fama and French factors global or country specific? *The Review of Financial Studies*, 15 (3): 783–803.
R. Grinold (1993) Is beta dead again? *Financial Analysts Journal*, 49: 28–34.
L. Hansen (1982) Large sample properties of generalized methods of moments estimators. *Econometrica*, 50 (4): 1029–54.
R. Haugen (1995) *The New Finance: The Case against Efficient Markets*. Prentice Hall: Englewood Cliffs, New Jersey.
S. Hwang and A. Rubesam (2008) The disappearance of momentum. *Working paper*, Cass Business School.
N. Jegadeesh and S. Titman (2001) Profitability of momentum strategies: an evaluation of alternative explanations. *The Journal of Finance*, 56 (2): 699–720.
N. Jegadeesh and S. Titman (1993) Returns to buying winners and selling losers: Implications for stock market efficiency. *The Journal of Finance*, 48 (1): 65–91.
P.J. Knez and M.J. Ready (1997) On the robustness of size and book-to-market in cross-sectional regressions. *The Journal of Finance*, 52 (4): 1355–82.
J. Lakonishok, A. Shleifer and R.W. Vishny (1994) Contrarian investment, extrapolation, and risk. *The Journal of Finance*, 49 (5): 1541–78.
J.F. L'Her, T. Masmoudi and J.M. Suret (2004) Evidence to support the four-factor pricing model from the Canadian stock market. *International Financial Market Institutions and Money*, 14 (4): 313–28.

J. Lintner (1965) The valuations of risk assets and the selection of risky investments in stock portfolios and capital budgets. *Review of Economics and Statistics*, 47: 13–37.

A.C. MacKinlay (1995) Multifactor models do not explain deviations from the CAPM. *Journal of Financial Economics*, 38 (1): 3–28.

A.C. MacKinlay and M. Richardson (1991) Using generalized methods of moments to test mean-variance efficiency. *The Journal of Finance*, 46 (2): 511–27.

S. Mengoli (2004) On the source of contrarian and momentum strategies in the Italian equity market. *International Review of Financial Analysis*, 13: 301–31.

L.J. Merville, S. Hayes-Yelsken and Y. Xu (2001) Identifying the factor structure of equity returns. *The Journal of Portfolio Management*, 27 (4): 51–61.

W. Newey and K. West (1987) A simple positive-definite, heteroskedasticity and autocorrelation consistent covariance matrix. *Econometrica*, 55 (3): 703–5.

R. Petkova and L. Zhang (2005) Is value riskier than growth? *Journal of Financial Economics*, 78 (1): 187–202.

B. Rosenberg, K. Reid and R. Lanstein (1985) Persuasive evidence of market inefficiency. *The Journal of Portfolio Management*, 11 (3): 9–16.

K.G. Rouwenhorst (1998) International momentum strategies. *The Journal of Finance*, 53 (1): 267–84.

P. Schmidt, V. Von Arx, A. Schrimpf, A. Wagner and A. Ziegler (2011) On the construction of common size, value and momentum factors in international stock markets. *Working Paper* 10/58, Swiss Finance Institute.

W.F. Sharpe (1964) Capital asset prices: A theory of market equilibrium under conditions of risk. *Journal of Finance*, 19: 425–42.

R. Shiller (1989) *Investor Behavior in the October 1987 Stock Market Crash: Survey Evidence*. MIT Press: Boston.

D. Stattman (1980) Book values and stock returns. *The Chicago MBA: A Journal of Selected Papers*, 4: 25–45.

10
A Business Model Map in the Wealth Management Industry

Caterina Lucarelli and Simona Maggi

10.1 Introduction[1]

Literature on strategic planning puts forward alternative choices that a company can make between standardization and customization of business processes, as suggested by the seminal works of Lampel and Mintzberg (1996) and Gilmore and Pine (1996, 1999). Recent studies reconsider mass customization (Salvador et al., 2009; Logina, 2010) and suggest that a designed mix of standardization/customization may drive alternative business models in the right direction (Sheehan and Vaidyanathan, 2007; Xia and Rajagopalan, 2009; Markides and Oyon, 2010; Berman, 2010).

A combined mix of standardization and customization of processes may also be of merit in uncovering alternative business models in banking, especially when considering the wealth management industry. A wealth manager (WM) should adapt the customization of internal processes in relation to the specific features of his/her clients, with a clear result in terms of the advisory content of the services provided. Typically, the offer of a customized financial service requires large investments (in, for example, human resources or technology) in order to reach a qualified differentiation from standardized contracts. Coherently, in the wealth management industry the amount (quantity) of wealth under management seems to be the prevailing rule in order to cluster customers (high net worth individuals, HNWIs), to organize specialized business units and to offer customized advice services.

This rule, confirmed by statistics at the international level (Capgemini and Lynch, 2010), indirectly assumes that WM business models are widely dominated by a breakeven perspective. The implicit assumption is that 'quantities' of production (that is, the size of the wealth under management) is considered to cover the (higher) total fixed costs absorbed by a (more) customized service.

The chapter starts with investigating whether the breakeven perspective is sufficient to cluster customers and to coherently address the customization of business processes. We have reason to question this perspective because a theoretical assumption of the breakeven formula is that the unit selling price is constant as quantities increase. This assumption fails to consider that if quantities (of wealth) are raised from the same customer, his/her bargaining power has a marginal unit selling price decrease, as a sort of monopsony disturbing noise. This noise is particularly strong when the concentration of large wealth owners is high, and the wealth industry tends to contend with a price rather than quality competition (Porter, 1985). By exploiting a unique dataset provided by the Italian Wealth Managers Association (Associazione Italiana Private Banking – AIPB), we statistically prove evidence of a non-linear relationship between revenues and wealth.

The core aim of the chapter is to propose a theoretical framework which sets alternative business models in the wealth management industry, and to test it with experimental data. Our map of business models arises when WMs potentially make a mix of business process standardization/customization, together with 'make or buy' choices, after an external and internal strategic analysis has been carried out. As far as the demand side is concerned, the breakeven perspective is integrated with a new criterion to cluster customers, which also considers the client's risk propensity and his/her willingness to diversify investments. In addition, internal conditions in the WM organization are covered. Demand and supply operational information, referring to a unique dataset of Italian wealth managers, allows us to test the reliability of our theoretical layout and to show the positioning of a relevant sample of Italian WMs.

10.2 The business model: traditional literature and recent developments

In recent years, the business model has been the focus of attention by both academics and practitioners. However, despite the substantial relevance of the issue, there is neither a common and broadly shared language nor a widely accepted definition of what a business model is, giving rise to multiple possible interpretations. Hence, we offer our definition of a business model and so place our chapter within a proper theoretical framework.

Firstly, the business model is often studied without explicitly defining the concept. Our approach, consistent with the representational nature that is often attributed to the business model (Morris et al., 2005), refer to it as 'a concise representation of how an interrelated set of decision variables in the areas of venture strategy, architecture and economics are addressed to create sustainable competitive advantage in defined markets'. In this sense, we converge on the more recent research on business models (Zott et al., 2010) by assuming that:

- the business model is a new concept, distinct from a firm's product-market position or strategy, representing a potential source of competitive advantage for the wealth manager;
- the business model is a system-level concept, implying a discussion on not just what businesses do (that is, what products and services they produce to serve needs in addressable market spaces), but also on how they do it (that is, how they bridge factor and product markets in serving the needs of the customers);
- the business model is a firm-centric yet boundary-spanning organizational activity system;
- the business model focuses on value creation.

For the purpose of our analysis, research into the business model can be organized around two complementary streams: the first aims to describe a generic business model, and provides a taxonomy of possible alternatives (business model archetypes); the second stream focuses on the components of a business model, and analyses these components through the lens of the main factors potentially affecting a business model configuration (business model drivers). The studies on business model archetypes have been less concerned with casual explanations or empirical testing; their contribution is mostly descriptive and aims to easily organize a set of alternatives that a firm can face in developing its own business. Accordingly, none of the papers in this literature stream has analysed the relationship between any business component and the business choice, rendering difficult the discussion of potential antecedents and consequences of the business model. This aim has been more specifically addressed by the second stream of research on business model drivers.

Business model archetypes: several scholars have attempted to classify business models by describing types. What is common to all the approaches is an attempt to pigeonhole the plethora of perceived business archetypes, but following different dimensions. The aspect that concerns our analysis is the level of customization (mass vs. customized content). In this regard, various taxonomies have been proposed; Pine (1993), for example, describes four types of customization strategies a firm might undertake: point of delivery customization; customizable product or service design; quick response (reducing lead times through the supply chain); and modular product design. Gilmore and Pine (1996) present a framework that indentifies four alternative ways of providing customization and classifies them based on product variants as well as their representations: adaptive customization, cosmetic customization, transparent customization, and collaborative customization. Lampel and Mintzberg (1996) propose a bottom-up approach for customization, where the choice of customizing is more and more upstream within the production process. Swaminathan (2001) focuses on dominant operational strategies employed by firms engaging in customization to meet the needs of their businesses. These include: part standardization, process standardization, product standardization and procurement standardization.

Recently, the traditional contraposition between customization and standardization is converging into the hybrid concept of 'mass customization'. This term was first popularized by Pine (1993) who defined it as 'developing, producing, marketing and delivering affordable goods and services with enough variety and customization that nearly everyone finds exactly what they want'. In other words, mass customization is the capability to offer individually tailored products or services on a large scale; the key is to view mass customization as a *process* for developing a set of organizational capabilities and aligning an organization with its customers' needs. Salvador et al. (2009) stress the concept by arguing that a company should 'customize even its mass customization' based on the requirements of its customers, the state of its competition and the technology available. The idea of customizing mass customization paves the way for the introduction of modularity into products and processes (Swaminathan, 2001); specifically, a modular product is one that can be made by appropriately combining the different components, while a modular process is one where each product undergoes a discrete set of operations, making it possible to store inventory in a semi-finished form where products differ from each other in terms of the subset of operations that are performed on them.

Business model drivers: in addition to providing typologies that identify and describe various generic business models, researchers have also attempted to distinguish some drivers that may influence the choice and performance of a business configuration, especially in terms of value creation. For example, Amit and Zott (2001) propose four potential sources of value creation that may influence the shape of a business model (NICE – Novelty, Lock-in, Complementarities, Efficiency). Salvador et al. (2009) identify three fundamental abilities of a company to mass customize its offering that are either industry- or product-specific: solution to space development (identification of product attributes along which customer needs mostly diverge), robust process design (recombination of existing organizational and value chain resources to fulfil a stream of differentiated customers' needs), and choice of navigation (support to the customer in identifying their own solutions). Sheehan and Vaidyanathan (2007) suggest that the best way to tweak a business model is to find a new combination of three suggested building blocks that fits market conditions better. The three fundamental value-creation building blocks are: industrial efficiency, network services and knowledge-intensive services.

Both streams of business model literature will be valuable in our analysis. Specifically, the business model archetypes will be useful for developing a specific taxonomy of different strategies a wealth manager might undertake in developing its activity; the business model drivers may give some suggestions about the internal and external constraints that a wealth manager might consider in choosing his/her own business model from the continuum of possible alternatives.

10.3 The grounds: breaking the breakeven point

The wealth management business implies that the production process is the management of money. Coherently, the breakeven point is the amount of wealth (w) in euros, over which an individual becomes an HNWI and coherently should be entitled to ask for customized services. We exploit an AIPB unique dataset containing figures of wealth (w) and revenues (r) of a random sample of almost 560 HNWIs for the years 2009 and 2010. Data refers to customers of 16 relevant Italian WMs. In Lucarelli and Maggi (2011), we run two alternative cross-sectional models to capture the marginal effect of wealth under management on unit revenue. First, we model elasticity of unit price (that is, unit revenue) to wealth under management, and we show that for each marginal euro under management the unit price/revenue decreases by 15.3 per cent. In addition, we follow an alternative pattern to demonstrate that the unit price/revenue decreases in relation to size under management. We look for non-linearity (concavity) in the function that links total revenues and wealth under management. So we build a model which allows us

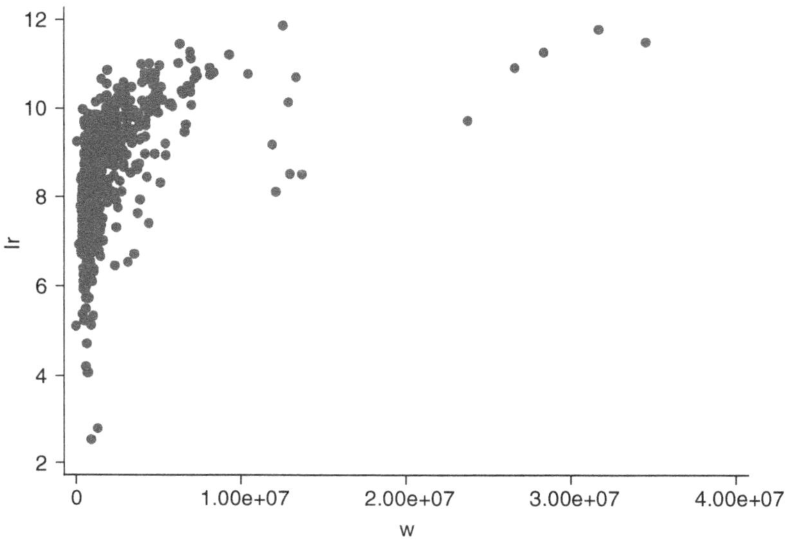

Figure 10.1 Log-revenues (lr) and wealth under management (w)
Note: Data refer to a sample of more than 1,200 customers of 16 Italian WMs for the 2009 and 2010 period.

to test if revenues and size under management, by customer, are related by a quadratic function. Results of estimations, in Lucarelli and Maggi (2011), shows that the relationship between revenues and wealth is well approximated by a function with a positive inclination and concavity, as also shown graphically in Chart 1.

Overall, we have evidence that the bargaining power of customers is relevant in the wealth management industry. As the amount of wealth increases, the marginal revenue obtained by WMs decreases; ergo, the unit selling price is not constant and the breakeven formula could not be effective to ensure that (increased) fixed costs, related to the (more customized) service, will be covered.

10.4 Alternative business models in the wealth management industry: the theoretical layout

The previous paragraph proposes the idea that the amount of wealth cannot be considered as the sole variable to drive the strategic organization of a WM. This deduction induces us to propose alternative business models for this industry, where customization is offered in a modular perspective (that is, mass customization is also included). Thus firstly we offer an overview of the most relevant activities which a WM undertakes to create value in his/her industry; secondly we consider the main strategic choices that a WM may alternatively select to organize each (or a combination of these) activity/ies. Then we combine these potential strategic choices and obtain a theoretical map of business models.

At this point, in order to understand which business model a WM may embark on, we consider a set of conditions, both external and internal. Some features of the demand side, as well as the strengths/weaknesses of the WM operational functioning, may represent either degrees of freedom or constraints for each specific business model. That is, if a WM aims at sophisticated business models, external and internal features represent conditions which should be strictly satisfied.

By exploiting the unique figures of the Italian wealth management industry, this theoretical layout has been empirically tested and offers an experimental analysis of the Italian WMs' positioning in our map. This situation may be considered as either an end point or a starting point. In the first case (end point), a WM is supposed to consider the present business model as appropriate, and coherent with its long-term vision. In the second case (starting point), a WM receives crucial information on the present positioning, and is offered a set of alternative business models which may be feasible. Nevertheless, their practicability depends on the WM's ability to transform some internal/external conditions from a degree of freedom to constraints.

10.4.1 Step 1: identification of activities creating value in the WM industry

From the seminal work of Porter (1985, 1996), concepts have been developed such as vertical architecture (Jacobides and Billinger, 2006), open innovation (Chesbrough and Appleyard, 2007), innovation value chain (Hansen and Birkinshaw, 2007), strategic networks (Gulati, 1998), co-opetition (Brandenburger and Nalebuff, 1997), and value networks (Alee, 2002; Normann and Ramirez, 1993; Parolini, 1998); they are built on a value chain, but at the same time they provide a complementary view which allows consideration of new forms of network as well as co-evolution dynamics and co-dependencies existing between the firm and its environment. However, the classical value chain suggested by Porter (1985, 1996) fits the purpose of our analysis better, since it mainly considers intra-firm activities over which a firm may exert control and make strategic choices.

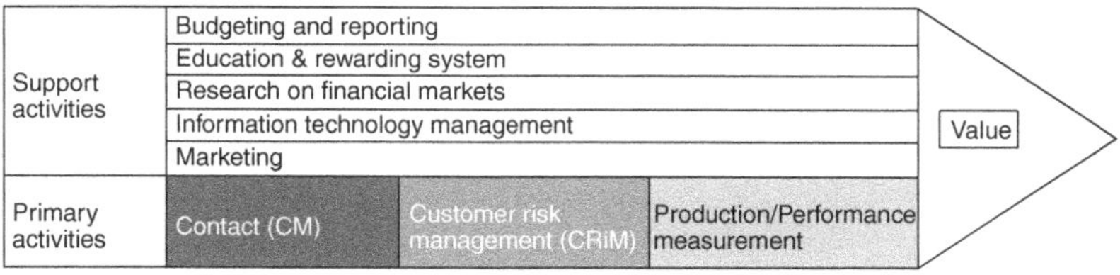

Figure 10.2 The value chain in the WM business

We present the activities that are able to create value in the WM industry by following Porter's well established value chain model (1985) and adapting it to the WM business. Figure 10.2 displays our proposal by distinguishing the primary and support activities that can drive value.

The layout of the primary activities follows a bottom-up approach, including, firstly, Contact Management (CM), the activity closest to customers; secondly, Customer Risk Management (CRiM), the activity referred to the collection, fulfilment and monitoring of a customer's financial needs; and finally, Production, the activity linked to the production of financial services.

Contact Management is specifically the client-interface function responsible for the financial triage of customers. CM engages with the customers' main general requirements and selects the most appropriate pattern to satisfy their needs within the WM organization.

CRiM consists of ex-ante, core and ex-post functions. Ex-ante CRiM embraces the understanding the customer needs *before* providing the WM service. The areas of interest for ex-ante CRiM are:

1. the emotional individual risk tolerance, investigated through alternative tools (the Contact Management feedback; an emotional-risk-tolerance questionnaire for new customers; an emotional track record of past financial choices for old customers);
2. the time-horizon expectations/needs (cash flow needs; wealth expectations in relation to the customer's standard of living; wealth vulnerability);
3. the wealth-implicit dynamicity in terms of underlying expectations resulting from wealth: financial investments; hedonistic investment; passion investments (luxury collectibles; sports investments ...); philanthropic investments (advice on financial planning and tax).

Then, core CRiM consists of an effective investment of the customer's wealth in financial/non-financial solutions, coherent with his/her

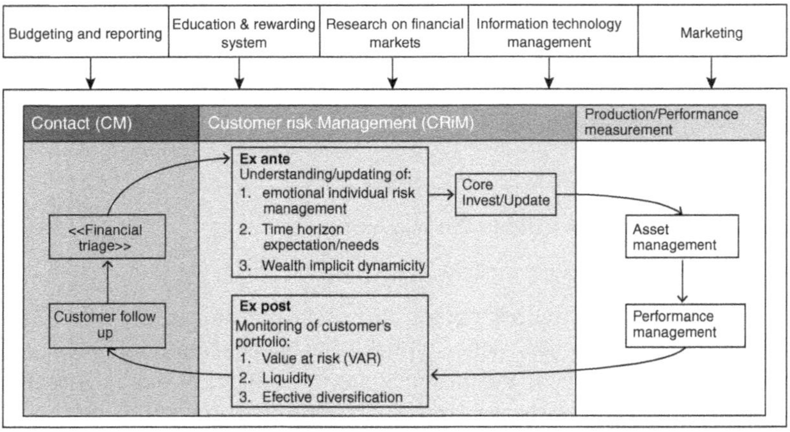

Figure 10.3 Value creation network for WM

ex-ante screening. Finally, after receiving the portfolio's performance measurements, ex-post CRiM includes the monitoring of the customer's portfolio in terms of its Value at Risk (if coherent with his/her ongoing emotional individual risk tolerance), its liquidity (if coherent with his/her time-horizon expectations/needs) and finally its diversification (if in line with his/her wealth-implicit dynamicity).

The Production activity refers to the typical asset management process: research, strategic (long-term) asset allocation, and tactical (short-term) asset allocation, and it concludes with the measurement of asset performance.

Figure 10.3 shows that a WM's primary activities are organized in a network that are mainly based on circular dependence. Each of them is affected by support activities such as budgeting and reporting, education and rewarding, research, IT and marketing. Note that in this chapter we uniquely focus on strategic choices which may affect primary value-adding activities, and we are postponing the analysis of support activities to future research developments.

10.4.2 Step 2: the main strategic choices

We consider the alternative strategic choices that a WM can potentially make for each activity (primary and support) shown in Figure 10.2 and Figure 10.3. A codified approach to set alternatives of standardization and customization is provided by the seminal methodology of Lampel and Mintzberg (1996) and Gilmore and Pine (1996, 1999) and is followed in

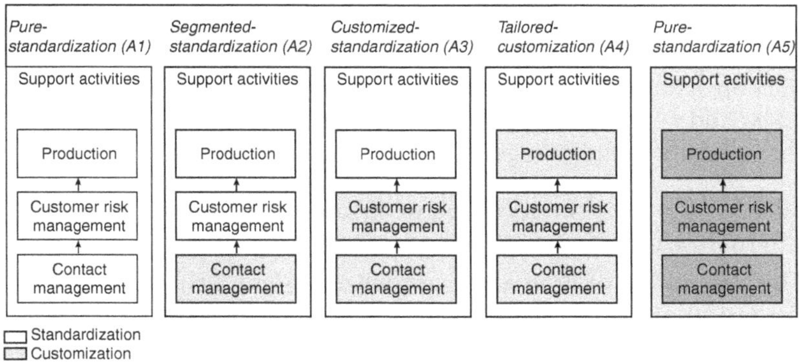

Figure 10.4a Standardization/customization alternatives in the wealth management industry
Source: Lampel and Mintzberg, 1996.

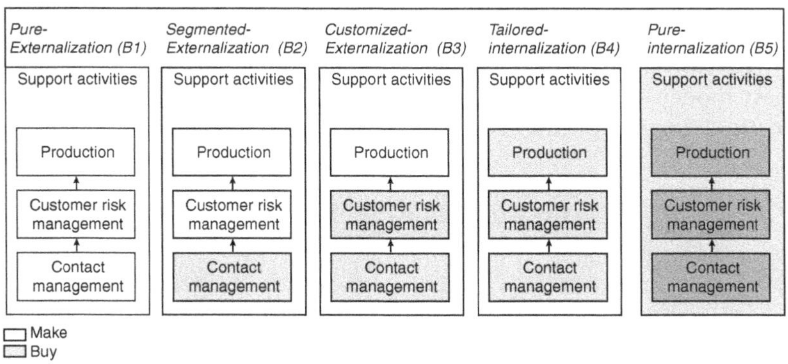

Figure 10.4b Make or buy alternatives in the wealth management industry

Figure 10.4a. We also take into account alternatives in terms of externalization (buying) or the internalization (making) of operational processes underlying the same chain of activities, as shown in Figure 10.4b.

A clear assumption of Figure 10.4 is the *incremental* process of both customization and internalization of our value-driver activities. Let us consider the organizational choice A3; when we assume that the wealth manager decides to customize CRiM, we indirectly state that he/she also customizes CM. A different strategic choice would appear to be inconsistent, because the exploitation of the customization of the clients' understanding, satisfying and monitoring caan reasonably be obtained only if the contact is also customized.

The same is true when considering the 'make or buy' choice. Let us consider alternative B4 of Figure 10.4b. When a WM internalizes the production of financial services, we indirectly assume that it also internalizes CRiM and CM. In fact, if these two activities were not internalized, the intermediary would change its nature, becoming an asset/fund manager.

10.4.3 Step 3: the interception of customization and internalization: the business model map

The assumption of *incremental* customization/internalization of activities technically allows a further step, that is the building of the *business model map*.[2] In Figure 10.5 we merge the standardization-customization choices in Figure 10.4a (Y axis) with the make/buy ones in Figure 10.4b (X axis). This is operated exclusively as far as the primary activities are concerned because support activities are to be considered in future researches. This X–Y combination in Figure 10.5 becomes the map for alternative business organization that a WM may potentially follow to provide customers with wealth services.

The variety of positions within this map represents alternative business models that a WM may potentially undertake according to our methodology. Implications of this theoretical layout are threefold.

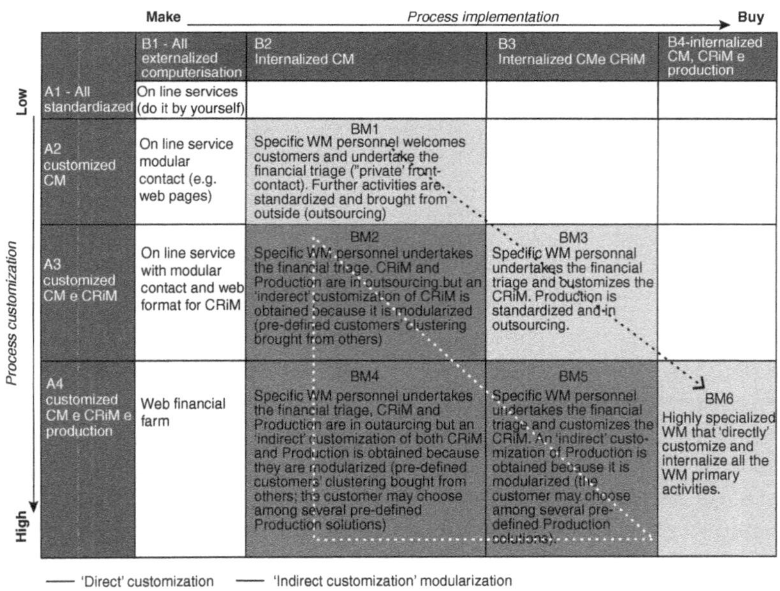

Figure 10.5 The map of business models in the WM industry

Firstly, the map is a matrix where the diagonal, lower triangle and upper triangle positions hold specific meanings: diagonal positions correspond to business models where customization/internalization choices are precisely coordinated. We refer to a direct customization, where BM1, BM3 and BM6 correspond to those business models where WMs coherently choose to customize *and* internalize CM activity (BM1), or CM *and* CRiM activities (BM3), or finally CM, CRiM *and* Production activities (BM6). The lower triangle positions refer to the combinations of strategic choices where a customization is offered even if the activities are not internalized. We technically define this condition as indirect customization, that is, a customization obtained through modularization so as to allow customers to reach the fulfilment of their specific needs by combining/customizing a predefined set of (standardized) alternatives that the WM has sourced from others. This condition also indicates a process of mass customization. On the other hand, the upper triangle positions have been discarded in the analysis because we believe them not to be particularly convenient/reasonable for a WM to internalize a level/mix of activities which are not customized.

Secondly, the B1 column refers to business models where all the primary activities of a WM have been externalized. This condition occurs when IT is used a lot, and the WM's business is mainly driven through online/web services. These kinds of business models seem to be realistic and valuable. In fact, higher levels of customization are obtained with a self-service combination of a wide variety of predefined modular offers. Nevertheless, in this chapter we mainly focus on business models that are not so strongly dominated by technology. As such, we have neglected the models arising from B1 columns and have postponed this analysis for future research.

Thirdly, the more the primary activities are customized, the higher the advisory content of the service offered by WMs. This is the way we believe that this theoretical layout may be of some help in order to differentiate the value provided to customers and to also adequately address the WM's pricing policies.

10.4.4 Step 4: the external and internal conditions: degrees of freedom and constraints for business models

A WM may potentially undertake a variety of business models according to his/her strategic positioning in our map of Figure 10.5. This positioning is technically a *conditional positioning* because certain external and internal conditions should be satisfied in order to state whether (or

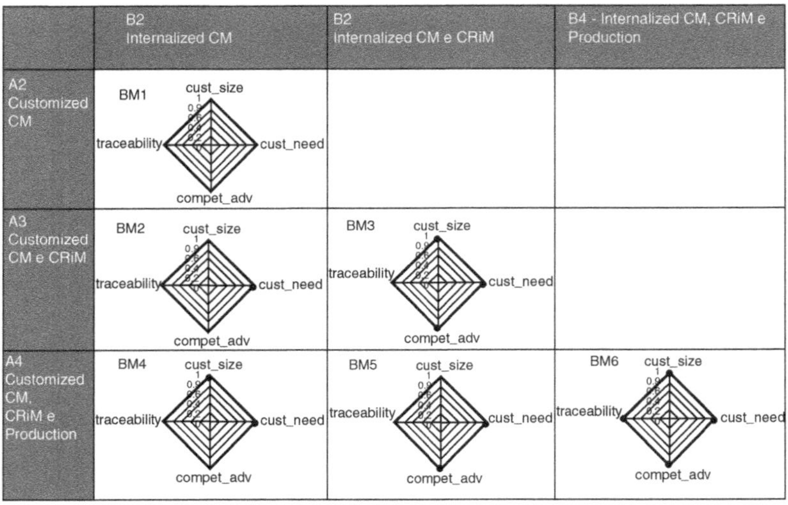

Figure 10.6 'Conditional positioning': degrees of freedom and constraints for business models

not) a business model is feasible for a WM in a modular organization perspective (Shank, 1999; Swaminathan, 2001).

External constraints mainly refer to demand features. We consider customers' wealth size (*cust_size*) but also include variables that refer to customers' needs (*cust_need*). As far as internal constraints are concerned, we consider competitive advantages (*compet_adv*) and *traceability* of information within the WM value chain. Since this inception, we set our variables to assume values in a range of zero to one, because we would like to prepare the ground to test our theoretical illustration with empirical data.

Figure 10.6 offers the selection of business models relevant for the purpose of our chapter (BM from 1 to 6). We have drawn a circle at each place where one of the four variables mentioned above represents a constraint for a WM in order to hold/reach a specific business model positioning. Precisely when a variable enjoys degrees of freedom for a given business model, its value may also be low and there is no circle; conversely, when a variable represents a constraint for that specific position, its value should be high, at best close to 1, and consequently a circle has been inserted.

For example, in order to undertake business model BM1 (*conditional positioning*), where the WM is only required to customize/internalize Contact Management, no condition seems to be necessarily satisfied as far as the demand and the supply side is concerned (no circle). On the contrary, as business models involve higher levels of customization, stricter conditions are reasonably required on the demand side: a WM should customize CM & CRiM (BM2 and BM3) only if customers show special needs (thus a circle on the *cust_need* variable). Moreover, the choice of Customizing Production (BM4, BM5 and BM6) also seems to be reasonable only if the amounts of wealth under management will be large enough to justify the undertaking of this kind of activity.

A similar approach is followed when setting internal conditions which need to be controlled in order to define the implementation of a specific process. If a WM aims to undertake a business model where the internalization of CM and CRiM is required (BM3 and BM5), it should also hold an unwavering competitive advantage on the field (*compet_adv* as a constraint with a circle). Finally, the most sophisticated business model (*conditional positioning*, BM6) implies that the WM customizes and internalizes all primary activities of the WM value chain; this means that all our four variables should be controlled as constraints. This also signifies that if a WM undertakes (or aims at undertaking) BM6, he/she should be facing a qualified demand for both financial need and size under management, and should be enjoying both a stable competitive and an accurate internal information system to control quality/costs/profitability of operational processes.

10.5 Testing the map: the AIPB experiment

We run a natural experiment by exploiting a database collected by the Associazione Italiana Private Banker (AIPB). The demand-side indicators are computed using the data provided by Italian WMs who are AIPB associates. We can rely on the data of almost 30 wealth managers covering 88 per cent of the total Italian wealth management industry.[3] Each of these WMs provided AIPB with financial information that included a sample of 60 customers for 2009 and 2010. The supply-side indicators concern the same set of WMs, but the data refers to their overall business (not a sample or a part of it).

By exploiting the features of the sample customers of AIPB WMs, we computed proxies of the external conditions that are faced when they strategically think of their demand-side: the *cust_size* and *cust_need* variables. Figures of the overall WM activity allow the computation of our proxies for their operational functioning: the *compet_adv* and *traceability* variables. In the following, a brief description of the computational criteria is offered. Further details are provided in Lucarelli and Maggi (2011).

10.5.1 The computation of variables

The *cust_size* variable derives from the wealth size distribution of customers. A WM may be dealing with wealth of different sizes from client to client. WMs may be able to attract large amounts of wealth, or he/she may be induced to accept medium or small wealth sizes. To proxy the demand feature regarding the sizes offered to a WM, we use the fifth centile (cent5) of the customers' wealth distribution. Values in euros of centiles have been normalized in order to range between 0 and 1.

The *cust_needs* variable indicates the willingness of customers to undertake a risky and diversified allocation of assets. In order to obtain a proxy of this willingness, we exploited the information of the individual asset allocation of each customer. For both 2009 and 2010, we can rely on a dataset made up of 631 HNWI individuals, each with his/her specific asset allocation. Each wealth under management has been allocated by WMs in the following six asset classes: deposits (de), bonds (bo), stocks (st), mutual funds (mf), private portfolios (pt) and insurance contracts (in). We assume that the generic asset allocation of customers could be biased by the selling strategies undertaken by WMs. Coherently, from the generic customers' asset allocation, we have to separate, on the one hand, the common component due to the WM competitive advantage and, on the other hand, the individual (idiosyncratic) propensity/aversion of customers towards specific asset classes. So we set up different models (see Lucarelli and Maggi, 2011) addressing this purpose and estimated them for our dataset of clients' asset allocations. From these estimates, we obtained the customers' idiosyncratic propensity/aversion towards specific asset classes. This idiosyncratic component is associated with an econometrical measure of residual (see Lucarelli and Maggi, 2011). When this variable is equal to zero for a specific customer of a given WM in relation to a type of asset class, this means that the customer holds a percentage of that asset class corresponding to the average sold by its WM to all the other customers. Conversely, when the residual is positive/negative, it means that the customer has over/under-invested in that asset class, compared to the average percentage bought by the other clients of that WM. The extremes of each residual are -1 (maximum idiosyncratic aversion to that asset class) and +1 (maximum idiosyncratic propensity to that asset class). This idiosyncratic behaviour, compared to the common component of the asset allocation on average sold by a given WM, represents for us the individual's willingness to hold or to refuse a specific asset class. According to this deduction, we define the positive component of the respective residual as the propensity of a customer to a given asset class for a given WM. Coherently, following a conservative approach, we define the risk propensity, shown by customers of a given WM, the average of their propensity to stock investments. Then, we define the wealth diversification of the demand side faced by each WM, the average of the (idiosyncratic) propensity shown by its customers to all the asset classes, deposits excluded. Our *cust_needs* is the normalized average of these two sub-indicators. Values of these indicators, by their computations, range from 0 to 1.

Moving from external to internal variables, the competitive advantage of a WM has been obtained after the computation of three different sub-indicators: WM diversification, WM growth and income specialization. WM diversification represents the qualitative side of the competitive advantage (how the WM wins), and it originates from the amount of asset under management that is placed in allocations different from deposits, that is direct securities investments, asset management and insurance contracts. WM growth represents the quantitative side of the competitive advantage (how much a WM is able to win) and it stems from the development of its asset under management. We follow a specific methodology in order to assign to each WM its specific (idiosyncratic) change of asset under management without any problems of time series persistence and annual seasonality (see for details Lucarelli and Maggi, 2011). WM income specialization represents the monetary side of the competitive advantage (how much money a WM wins); it is the ratio of income arising from services and total income. Our *compet_adv* variable is the average of these three indicators, and it ranges from 0 to 1.

Finally, the traceability variable should indicate the precision of the WM informative system in order to verify if the WM is able to control/update/monitor all the information inherent in his/her customer relationship and his/her costs and profitability. At this stage of the analysis, we were lacking a precise figure which could attest to this precision, so we deduced it indirectly by exploiting the missing data, that is the data which had not been provided to AIPB for reasons other than an explicit privacy strategic requirement. The indicator traceability is obtained as the ratio of regularly filled items on the overall number of figures which should be filled for AIPB. The higher the traceability, the higher the informational completeness of the dataset provided by each WM.

Table 10.1 Average values of variables for each WM cluster

	Market share	*cust_size*	*cust_need*	*compet_adv*	Traceability
Cluster 1	19.1%	0.4	0.6	0.7	0.9
Cluster 2	25.8%	0.9	0.7	0.7	0.8
Cluster 3	7.9%	0.4	0.8	0.7	0.4
Cluster 4	10.1%	0.2	0.5	0.5	0.4
Cluster 5	37.1%	0.5	0.5	0.8	0.4

10.5.2 The conditional positioning of WM clusters within the business model map

We compute the four variables (*cust_size, cust_need, compet_adv* and *traceability*) for all of our 30 WMs. However, it turns out that certain random figures for some AIPB associates are missing. So the final list of WMs who regularly sent data to AIPB and allowed the computation of all our variables is made up of 15 companies. Still, these companies cover more than the 70 per cent of the Italian wealth management industry.

We run a hierarchical cluster analysis using Ward's linkage as the method to group observations. A quite conservative dissimilarity measure of 0.30 allows us to group our 15 WMs into five clusters: cluster 1 is made up of 5 WMs; cluster 2 of 2 WMs; cluster 3 of 3 WMs; cluster 4 of 2 WMs; and cluster 5 of 3 WMs, as shown in Table 10.1. We reveal the distinctive features of our five clusters by computing average values for the four variables which originated our clustering. Table 10.1 demonstrates that, as expected from the statistical methodology used, each cluster is very different from all the others.

The aim of this section of the chapter is mainly to test the reliability of our theoretical map of business models with empirical data. Coherently, we are less interested in the specific positioning of each WM. We prefer to check if the map is feasible for the overall industry and if it allows an indicative conditional positioning for WMs. This is the reason why we must first group our sample of 15 WMs representative of the Italian wealth management industry. Then must allocate each group of WMs (cluster) in the conditional positioning of our business model map.

The coordinates for the conditional positioning of a WM in the business model map in Figure 10.6 depends on the values of our four-item variables. Low values, in the 0–1 range, mean that the variable has a degree of freedom; high values mean that the variable is controlled as

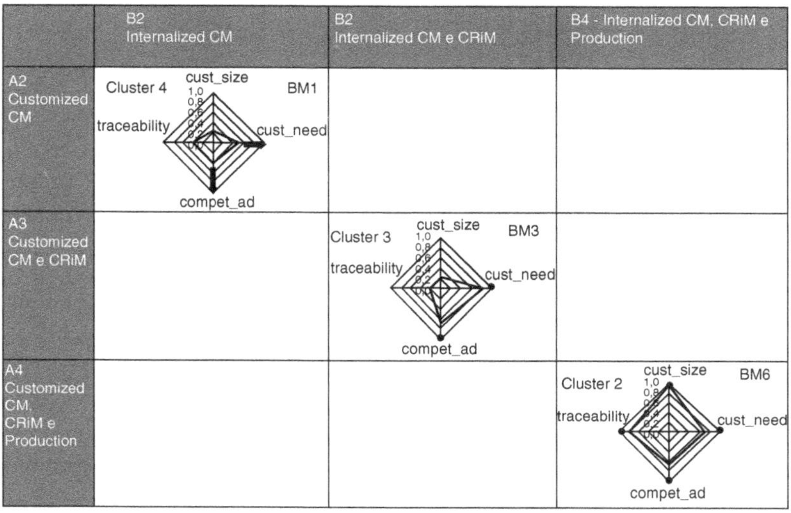

Figure 10.7 Testing of the business models map: the Italian WMs 'conditional positioning'

a constraint. The variables' average values for our clusters are shown in Table 10.1. Given our empirical data, we state that a variable reaches the level of constraint if its value is more than 0.7. This condition has been marked in Table 10.1 with bold figures.

Now, the conditional positioning of Italian WMs in our business model map appears straightforward (see Figure 10.7). For example, cluster 4 refers to WMs which show low levels for all our variables. This means that both the external and internal features of these companies are non controlled as constraints. As a consequence, the conditional positioning of these WMs is BM1. This is the business model where only CM activity (the customer's triage) is customized and internalized. All the other primary activities (CRiM and Production) are standardized and bought from others.

The value of this experimental positioning is twofold. Firstly, it allows a WM to understand if its *real* positioning is coherent with a business model which is practicable for its demand side and its operational conditions (that is, the conditional positioning). So in the case of WMs belonging to cluster 4, WMs may check if they are actually undertaking BM1 activities or different business models. If so, they may receive an alert signal because in any other case than BM1 they should have some variables as conditions to be satisfied. For example, if cluster 4

WMs engaged in real business models different from B1 (such as BM2 or BM3), they should be controlling for some external/internal feature as constraints, that is customer needs to reach BM2, and both customer needs and competitive advantages to reach BM3.

Coherently, WMs receive a second source of value from this experimental conditional positioning because they can focus their investments on specific external/internal targets in order to start from a precise present positioning in the map in order to reach a different expected positioning. So, in our example, if some WMs belonging to cluster 4 (now positioned in BM1) wanted to aim at undertaking a BM3, he/she clearly knows where to direct his/her energy: both in selecting customers more willing to risk/diversify (*cust_need*) and to foster internal competitive advantages (*compet_adv*).

As far as further clusters are concerned, Table 10.1 indicates that other two clusters are unambiguously positioned in our business model map: cluster 3 for BM3 and cluster 2 for BM6. This implies that the external/internal conditions of Italian WMs allow them to unmistakably undertake models of direct customization, that is BMs covering the diagonal of our matrix. This means that WMs belonging to cluster 3 and cluster 2 could reasonably undertake a coordinated mix of customization/internalization of primary activities, that is customize the level of activity which is also internalized.

Conversely, cluster 1 and cluster 5 refer to a more undefined strategic positioning. On the one hand, both clusters reveal that their WMs hold a good position as far as their internal condition is concerned (cluster 1, for both *traceability* and *compet_adv*, cluster 5 only for the latter). Nevertheless, these WMs reveal weaknesses in terms of the features of their demand side. It seems that they may reasonably aim at sophisticated business models (BM3, BM5 or even BM6). However, their stable strategic positioning on these business models is strongly dependent on how they can attract clients with either a broader range of sizes or more varied financial needs.

10.6 Conclusions

In this chapter we raised the question of whether the size under management is sufficient to cluster customers and to coherently address the customization of business processes. Coherently, we propose a theoretical framework which puts forward alternative business models for the wealth management industry in relation to strategic choices of a combined mix of standardization/ customization, together with 'make or buy' choices. Specific WM external and internal conditions are also considered within each theoretical business model. So we tested this layout with experimental data and ran an analysis to find a conditional positioning of WMs from their real data in our theoretical map.

Our analysis comes to the overall conclusion that the test has been passed. The three theoretical BMs corresponding to direct customization, that is, BMs covering the diagonal of our matrix (BM1, BM3 and BM6), may unambiguously be undertaken by three different clusters of Italian WMs (cluster 3, cluster 4 and cluster 2, respectively). Figures for the residual WMs' clusters (cluster 1 and cluster 5) reveal their potential positioning ,which could be developed towards both direct customization and modularization (either the diagonal or the lower triangle of the map). The decision will depend on the WM's ability to deal with a more focused client policy.

Notes

1. We would like to thank Dr. Bruno Zanaboni, Secretary-General of AIPB, for the ongoing confidence that he has shown during our analysis, and all AIPB associates for contributing their data. A special thanks goes to Nicoletta Marinelli for her scientific support in writing paragraph 2, and to all the AIPB Research Team (Federica Bertoncelli, Adalberto Pizzi and Francesco Bassi) for their substantial assistance in collecting, checking and testing figures and computations.
2. Without this assumption the map would become a three-dimensional space.
3. WMs who are associates of AIPB represent 95 per cent of the total Italian wealth manager industry; 93 per cent of them take an active part in AIPB surveys.

References

V. Alee (2002) *The Future of Knowledge: Increasing Prosperity through Value Networks.* Boston: Butterworth-Heinemann.

R. Amit and C. Zott (2001) Value creation in e-business. *Strategic Management Journal*, 22: 493–520.

B. Berman (2010)Products, products everywhere. *MIT Sloan Management Review*, 51 (4), available at http://sloanreview.mit.edu/executive-adviser/2010-3/5239/products-products-everywhere.

A. Brandenburger and B.J. Nalebuff (1997) *Co-opetition: A Revolution Mindset That Combines Competition and Cooperation: The Game Theory Strategy That's Changing the Game of Business.* New York: Doubleday.

Capgemini and M. Lynch (2010) *World Wealth Report.*

H.W. Chesbrough and M.M. Appleyard (2007) Open innovation and strategy. *California Management Review*, 50: 57–76.

J.H. Gilmore and J.B. Pine (1999) *The Experience Economy.* Harvard Business School Press: Boston, MA.

—— (1996) The four faces of mass customization. *Harvard Business Review*, 75 (1): 91–101.

R. Gulati (1998) Alliances and networks. *Strategic Management Journal*, 19: 293–317.

M.T. Hansen and J. Birkinshaw (2007) The innovation value chain. *Harvard Business Review*, 85: 121–30.

M.G. Jacobides and S. Billinger (2006) Designing the boundaries of the firm: From 'make, buy, or ally' to the dynamic benefits of vertical architecture. *Organization Science*, 17: 249–61.

J. Lampel and H. Mintzberg (1996) Customizing customization. *MIT Sloan Management Review*, 38 (1): 21–30.

O. Logina (2010) Competitive effect of mass customization. *Working Paper*.

C. Lucarelli and S. Maggi (2011) *A Business Model Map in the Wealth Management Industry* (13 September). Available at SSRN: http://ssrn.com/abstract=1926867.

C.C. Markides and D. Oyon (2010) What do against disruptive business models (When and how to play two games at once). *MIT Sloan Management Review*, 51 (4): 25–32.

M. Morris, M. Schindehutte and J. Allen (2005) The entrepreneur's business model: towards a unified perspective. *Journal of Business Research*, 58: 726–35.

R. Normann and R. Ramirez (1993) From value chain to value constellation: designing interactive strategy. *Harvard Business Review*, Jul–Aug, 71 (4): 65–77.

C. Parolini (1998) *The Value Net: A Tool for Competitive Strategy*. Chichester, England: Jhon Wiley & Sons Ltd.

J.B. Pine (1993) *Mass Customization: The New Frontier in Business Competition*. Cambridge, MA: Harvard Business School Press.

M.E. Porter (1996) What is a strategy? *Harvard Business Review*, 74: 61–78.

—— (1985) *Competitive Advantage: Creating and Sustaining Superior Performance*. New York: The Free Press.

F. Salvador, P. Martin and F. Piller (2009) Cracking the code of mass customization. *MIT Sloan Management Review*, 50 (3), available at http://sloanreview.mit.edu/executive-adviser/2010-3/5239/products-products-everywhere/.

M. Shank (1999) Creating the modular organization. In S.H. Haeckel (ed.), *Adaptive Enterprise: Creating and Leading Sense-and-Response Organizations*. Boston, Massachussets: Harvard Business School Press.

N.T. Sheehan and G. Vaidyanathan (2007) The path to growth. *The Wall Street Journal, Business Insight: The Journal Report, A Joint Venture with MIT Sloan Management Review*, published online by *MIT Sloan Management Review* (sloanreview.mit.edu/wsj/insight/strategy/2007/03/03/01/).

J.M. Swaminathan (2001) Enabling customization using standardized operations. *California Management Review*, 43 (3):125–35.

N. Xia and S. Rajagopalan (2009) Standard vs. customized products: variety, lead time, and price competition. *Marketing Science*, 28(5): 887–900.

C. Zott, R. Amit and L. Mass (2010) The business model: theoretical roots, recent developments, and future research. *Working Paper*.

Index